10 ⁰⁰   Review Copy.   LTS Rev. Spr 77

COVENANT
and
PROMISE

BOOKS BY JOHN BRIGHT

PUBLISHED BY THE WESTMINSTER PRESS

*Covenant and Promise: The Prophetic Understanding
of the Future in Pre-Exilic Israel*

A History of Israel
(SECOND EDITION)

COVENANT
and
PROMISE

THE PROPHETIC UNDERSTANDING OF
THE FUTURE IN PRE-EXILIC ISRAEL

JOHN BRIGHT

THE WESTMINSTER PRESS
PHILADELPHIA

Scripture quotations from the Revised Standard Version of the Bible are copyright, 1946 and 1952, by the Division of Christian Education of the National Council of Churches, and are used by permission.

BOOK DESIGN BY DOROTHY E. JONES

PUBLISHED BY THE WESTMINSTER PRESS®
PHILADELPHIA, PENNSYLVANIA

PRINTED IN THE UNITED STATES OF AMERICA

Library of Congress Cataloging in Publication Data

Bright, John, 1908–
　Covenant and promise.

　Includes bibliographical references and indexes.
　1. Bible. O.T. Prophets—Theology. 2. Prophets. 3. Jews—History—953-586 B.C. I. Title.
BS1505.2.B74　　224'.06　　76-13546
ISBN 0-664-20752-9

Contents

Preface

The Alumni Association and the Board of Trustees of Austin Presbyterian Theological Seminary established a lectureship in 1945 to bring to the seminary campus each year a distinguished scholar to address an annual midwinter convocation of ministers, students, faculty, and other interested people on some phase of Christian thought.

In 1950 the Thomas White Currie Bible Class of Highland Park Presbyterian Church of Dallas, Texas, undertook the support of this lectureship in memory of the late Dr. Thomas White Currie, founder of the class and president of the seminary.

In 1971 Dr. Bright delivered the Currie Lectures to our Midwinter Ministry Colloquium, and both provoked, stirred, and stimulated thinking and rethinking on the part of his hearers of the role of eschatology, particularly in terms of covenant and promise as expressed in the Old Testament prophets.

We are proud to have sponsored the lectures and now to join with him and The Westminster Press in making these important interpretations of Old Testament prophecy available.

PRESCOTT H. WILLIAMS, JR., *President*
Austin Presbyterian Theological
Seminary, Austin, Texas

Foreword

This book represents, in a somewhat expanded form, the Thomas White Currie Lectures, which were delivered at Austin Presbyterian Theological Seminary, Austin, Texas, in the winter of 1971. The idea for the lectures, and their general plan, however, took shape considerably earlier. The material had its origin in classroom lectures and informal discussions with my own students, and it had on several occasions been presented in different forms before groups of pastors, teachers, and theological students in other institutions over a period of perhaps four or five years. But, though the subject seemed on each occasion to be one that attracted the interest of the hearers, I had never thought of preparing the material for publication. When the invitation to deliver the Currie Lectures came, carrying with it as it did the obligation to publish, I accepted with pleasure, yet with some trepidation. I was not at all sure that what I had to say was of sufficient importance to merit publication. I can only hope that what has proved to be of interest—and, I trust, of help—to its hearers when delivered orally will likewise be of help to a wider circle through the medium of the printed page.

I had hoped, and had confidently expected, to complete the preparation of the manuscript long before now. Though the delay was occasioned by circumstances over which I had little or no control, I nevertheless regret it and apologize for it. Still, I believe that it has worked out for the best. The time that has elapsed has afforded the opportunity for further reading and reflection, and has allowed me to take into consideration more recent literature on the subject and the discussion that this has provoked. Moreover, I have had the opportunity to present the subject matter of the lectures in various forms before audiences of colleagues, pastors, and students in other theological institutions—most recently as the Smyth Lectures at Columbia Theological Seminary, Decatur, Georgia, in the spring of 1975, and as the Heyward Lectures at Acadia Theological College, Wolfville, Nova Scotia, and as the Nils W. Lund Lectures at North Park Theological Seminary, Chicago, Illinois, in the fall of the same year. Time and again, questions raised by my hearers have pointed out to me places where my presentation was questionable or less than clear, and have forced rethinking and revision. Though I am embarrassed by the delay, I believe that the end product is the better for it.

The lectures as originally delivered were prepared for an audience consisting chiefly of pastors and undergraduate theological students. On virtually all the other occasions when the material was presented, similar audiences were before me. To be sure, colleagues were frequently present too—and able and distinguished ones, at that—but I was not speaking primarily to them. Rather, I sought to address those hearers who were interested in, and concerned with, the message of the Scriptures but who did not necessarily have any specialized training in Old Testament studies. The lectures therefore did not seek to break new ground, or to expound any novel thesis, but represent rather the attempt to present in a manner that would be interesting, clear, and (that much-abused word!) relevant to a generally informed and intelligent public certain features in the theology of the Old Testament—specifically in that of the pre-exilic prophets—in the hope that the message of Scripture as a whole might be made more meaningful thereby.

The book has been held to the same aim, and it seeks to address a similar audience. Though the material has been considerably expanded (the Currie Lectures were but four in number), the outline of the lectures as delivered orally has been followed. Moreover, the temptation to carry the discussion forward into the exilic and post-exilic periods has been resisted. This was a real temptation, for the inclusion of the later prophets in the discussion would for many and obvious reasons have been desirable. But to have done this would have occasioned still further delay and would have resulted in a considerably larger book that would have corresponded but little to what was actually delivered as the Currie Lectures. Furthermore, although we shall be obliged to take position with regard to a number of warmly disputed issues, technical discussion has been, as far as possible, avoided, and footnotes, though of course they cannot be dispensed with, have been held to a (it is hoped) reasonable minimum. They have been employed to acknowledge indebtedness, to point to the views of other scholars perhaps of contrary opinion, and also to provide the interested reader with some guidance toward the relevant literature. There are risks involved in attempting a book of this sort, and I am fully cognizant of them. When one attempts to deal with disputed issues, and to do so in relatively brief compass and in nontechnical language, one is exposed to the dangers of superficiality and oversimplification. Though one does not run the risk of such dangers gladly, it is probable that in a book of this sort they cannot entirely be avoided. So the risk will have to be accepted. If this book should succeed in helping the reader to acquire a better understanding of the prophetic message, I shall feel justified in having taken it.

It is hoped that the reader will keep his English Bible at his elbow as he reads, and will follow through by looking up the various Scripture references that are scattered throughout the text. Only so will he hear the Bible's own words, and not just the comments of the author. In many cases the impact of the argument will not be felt, nor can its strengths or weaknesses be judged, unless this is done. Though passages of Scripture are frequently quoted *in extenso*, this could not in every case be done lest the book be expanded beyond reason. Translations of Scripture, where they do not follow the Revised Standard Version, or are not credited to a particular scholar, are my own. References to Scripture by chapter and verse follow the English versions rather than the Hebrew, where these diverge. (Occasionally both versifications are indicated, but on many occasions this is not done.)

I must now express my thanks to those who in one way or another have had a part in bringing this book into being. First and above all, I must thank the members of the faculty of Austin Presbyterian Theological Seminary, especially Dr. David L. Stitt, who was president of the seminary at the time the lectures were delivered and through whom the invitation to deliver them was extended to me, and Dr. Prescott H. Williams, Jr., his successor in that office, during whose tenure the work on the manuscript was completed. I am grateful to these friends for the honor they conferred upon me in inviting me to deliver the Currie Lectures, and for the gracious—and quite typical— hospitality that they showed me during my stay in Austin. I also owe thanks to the many friends and colleagues who heard the substance of the lectures presented on various occasions at various places, whose comments have encouraged me, and whose questions and friendly criticisms have not infrequently moved me to reshape the material and, I trust, improve it. I cannot possibly list them all here, but I have them in my mind. Finally, I must thank my wife. I know that it has become almost *de rigueur* for authors to do this, so much so that one now and then hears jokes made about it. But in this case it is no mere formal gesture designed, perhaps, to keep peace in the family. The typing of the manuscript was begun by Mrs. Franklin S. Clark, who had so willingly and efficiently assisted me in this regard for a period of more than twenty years. When sudden death took her from our midst early in 1975, the task was carried forward for a while by various persons who had been secured on a temporary basis. But it was my wife who brought the typing of the first draft of the manuscript to a conclusion and also placed it in its revised and final form. She has also assisted in the reading of the proof and the preparation of the indexes. Without her help I do not know when the job would have been finished. The thanks that I express to her is, therefore, both richly deserved and most sincerely intended.

J.B.

Abbreviations

1. Books and Periodicals

AB   *The Anchor Bible*, W. F. Albright and D. N. Freedman,
              eds. (New York: Doubleday & Company, Inc.)

ANET   J. B. Pritchard, ed., *Ancient Near Eastern Texts Relating
              to the Old Testament* (Princeton University Press, 1950;
              Supplementary Texts, 1969)

ATD   *Das Alte Testament Deutsch*, V. Herntrich and A. Weiser,
              eds. (Göttingen: Vandenhoeck & Ruprecht)

BA   *The Biblical Archaeologist*

BASOR   *Bulletin of the American Schools of Oriental Research*

BAT   *Die Botschaft des Alten Testaments* (Stuttgart: Calwer
              Verlag)

BKAT   *Biblischer Kommentar, Altes Testament*, M. Noth, S.
              Herrmann, and H. W. Wolff, eds. (Neukirchen-Vluyn:
              Neukirchener Verlag des Erziehungsvereins)

BWANT   *Beiträge zur Wissenschaft vom Alten und Neuen Testa-
              ment* (Stuttgart: W. Kohlhammer)

BZAW   *Beihefte zur Zeitschrift für die alttestamentliche Wissen-
              schaft* (Berlin: Walter de Gruyter & Co.)

CBQ   *The Catholic Biblical Quarterly*

FRLANT   *Forschungen zur Religion und Literatur des Alten und
              Neuen Testaments* (Göttingen: Vandenhoeck & Ru-
              precht)

HAT   *Handbuch zum Alten Testament*, O. Eissfeldt, ed. (Tübin-
              gen: J. C. B. Mohr)

HTR   *Harvard Theological Review*
IB   *The Interpreter's Bible*, G. A. Buttrick, ed. (New York
             and Nashville: Abingdon Press)
IDB   *The Interpreter's Dictionary of the Bible*, G. A. Buttrick,
             ed. (New York and Nashville: Abingdon Press)
JBL   *Journal of Biblical Literature*
JNES   *Journal of Near Eastern Studies*
JSS   *Journal of Semitic Studies*
KAT   *Kommentar zum Alten Testament*, E. Sellin, ed.; new
             series, W. Rudolph, K. Elliger, and F. Hesse, eds.
             (Gütersloher Verlagshaus Gerd Mohn)
OTL   *The Old Testament Library*, P. R. Ackroyd, J. Barr, G. E.
             Wright and J. Bright, eds. (London: SCM Press;
             Philadelphia: The Westminster Press)
ThLZ   *Theologische Literaturzeitung*
VT   *Vetus Testamentum*
WMANT   *Wissenschaftliche Monographien zum Alten und Neuen
             Testament* (Neukirchen-Vluyn: Neukirchener Verlag
             des Erziehungsvereins)
ZAW   *Zeitschrift für die alttestamentliche Wissenschaft*
ZThK   *Zeitschrift für Theologie und Kirche*

2. Texts and Versions of Scripture

BH³   *Biblia Hebraica*, R. Kittel, ed.; 3d ed., A. Alt, O. Eissfeldt,
             and P. Kahle, eds. (Stuttgart: Privilegierte Württem-
             bergische Bibelanstalt)
BHS   *Biblia Hebraica Stuttgartensia*, K. Elliger and W. Ru-
             dolph, eds. (Stuttgart: Württembergische Bibelanstalt)
EVV   English Versions generally
JB   *The Jerusalem Bible*
LXX   The Septuagint (i.e., the Greek translation of the Old
             Testament made between the third and the first
             centuries B.C.)
MT   The Masoretic Text (the received Hebrew text of the Old
             Testament)
NEB   *The New English Bible*
RSV   *The Holy Bible, The Revised Standard Version*
Vrs.   The ancient versions generally

1

The Future Hope
of Early Israel

As its subtitle indicates, we shall be concerned in this book with a central feature in the message of the pre-exilic prophets. Specifically, we shall be concerned with their understanding of what the future—both the immediate future and the farthest future—had in store for their people. As every reader knows, the prophets were anything but optimists with regard to the immediate future. On the contrary, they attacked the religious, social, and moral abuses of which their nation was guilty, and they criticized in the strongest terms the policies of state which its leaders followed, and declared that the nation was under the judgment of God and facing imminent disaster. But their message of judgment was not their last word. Virtually all of the pre-exilic prophets, albeit by no means in identical ways, looked beyond the judgment they were compelled to announce to a farther future when God would come once again to his people in mercy, restore their fortunes, and establish his rule over them in righteousness and peace. This promise of future salvation is one of the most distinctive features in the message of the prophets, and it is this perhaps more than anything else that serves to bind the Old Testament unbreakably with the New in a single canon of Scripture. An understanding of it is therefore of the first importance for the understanding of the message of the Bible as a whole.

Although it may seem illogical to do so (it is certainly not to begin at the beginning), we shall take our start with the prophet Jeremiah. The subject of the lectures upon which this book is based was, in fact, first suggested to me by a problem that arises in connection with that prophet's career. This was a problem that plagued Jeremiah through-

out his entire life. It was a problem that arose from the fact that his
view of his country's future and that of the vast majority of his
contemporaries was simply not the same, and from his inability to
convince very many of his fellow citizens that his view might well be
the correct one. Our study will have that problem as its focus and will
seek to give it clarification.

Jeremiah lived, of course, in the last days of the Kingdom of
Judah. All his life the burning question before the nation was that of
survival. From the time of the collapse of the Assyrian Empire,
through the dark days of the Babylonian advance into the west, and
down to the end, the question was always: What course ought this
nation to follow in order to secure its future? What must it do if it is
even to survive? Would it survive? Jeremiah clearly became convinced that it would not survive. As the years wore on he said so ever
more plainly, until in the end his message became the flat announcement that the Babylonians would destroy the nation, bring the
Davidic dynasty to an end, carry the people into exile in a far country,
and that in so doing they acted as God's own agents of judgment upon
the nation for its refusal to heed his word.

But what is equally clear is that this was not the majority opinion.
Indeed, it was dangerous to express such an opinion; on various
occasions Jeremiah nearly lost his life for expressing it. Instances
leap to the mind. When he declared that God would cause the Temple
to be destroyed because of the crimes of those who worshiped there
(Jer. 7:1–15), he was set upon by the crowd and narrowly escaped
being put to death (cf. ch. 26). In the attempt to warn his fellow
citizens, he dictated certain of his prophecies to his friend Baruch,
who wrote them down in a scroll and subsequently read them publicly
in the Temple; when the scroll was brought to the king's attention,
the king destroyed it and sought to have Jeremiah and Baruch
arrested, undoubtedly with the intention of executing them (ch. 36).
And in the end, because of his preaching, Jeremiah was placed in a
waterless cistern with deep mud at the bottom and left to die; and he
certainly would have died had not a certain palace servant interceded
with the king in his behalf and gained for him more lenient treatment
(38:1–13). In a word, Jeremiah's opponents had radically other views
than his regarding the nation's future, and they found Jeremiah's
view unacceptable, false, dangerous, blasphemous.

So explosive a tension cannot be explained merely as a difference
of political opinion, a disagreement regarding what policy the nation
ought to follow. To be sure, it was at least that. And Jeremiah's

opponents—who, whatever else one might say of them, were ardent patriots—clearly regarded him as a defeatist and a traitor. But this was no mere clash between patriotic men who had calculated the odds and believed the nation could win through and a pessimist who had likewise weighed the odds and thought that it stood no chance. Least of all was it a collision between a man of sincere theological convictions and men who had no convictions. Whatever we may think of those individuals who persecuted Jeremiah, and of those prophets who contradicted him, there is not the slightest reason for saying that they were insincere. Jeremiah himself made no such accusation. Indeed, on one occasion (Jer. 28:6) he indicated that he wished he could share their optimistic confidence regarding the nation's future.

The truth is that Jeremiah and his opponents held equally strong theological convictions. Jeremiah was convinced—on theological grounds—that the nation had fallen under God's judgment and would be destroyed if it continued in its course. His opponent's were convinced—again on theological grounds—that such a thing could never happen: God would not allow it! On the contrary, he would come to the defense of the nation, intervene in the nick of time with a miracle and save it. The fact that they drove the nation to suicide does not alter the sincerity of their convictions. It was a collision precisely in the realm of theology. It was a collision between two understandings of the nation's relationship to God and its future under God, a clash regarding the nature of God's promises to the nation and the extent to which he was committed to its defense. The fate of the nation was at stake. On the one side stood men who apparently believed that the nation's survival was unconditionally assured by the promises of God; against them stood a prophet who was clearly convinced that it was not. The former seem to have had every confidence in the nation's future; the latter rejected that confidence completely and reserved what hope he offered (for Jeremiah did offer hope, as we shall see) for an indefinitely farther future, the eschatological future. One is moved to ask how two such diametrically opposite views of the matter could ever have arisen within the same religious community.

I

The question just raised is one that can be answered only when we have gained some perspective, for both Jeremiah and his opponents could claim the support of ancient theological traditions. We have therefore to go far back and inquire after the nature and origins of expectations with regard to the future in Israel. We have to ask: What was the source of that stubborn confidence in the future which seems to have been characteristic of ancient Israel at all periods and which misled Jeremiah's opponents into their foolhardy course of action? What were the grounds for the prophetic rejection of that confidence? What were those factors in ancient tradition that caused the prophets—who, in spite of their rejection of the popular hope, did not abandon hope—to shape their respective visions of the farthest future, their eschatology, as they did?

1. But we should do well to begin with a definition: In what sense are we using the word "eschatology" in this connection? A clear definition of terms is always desirable, and that is especially the case here, for the word "eschatology" as it relates to the Old Testament has been used in more than one way, and this has not infrequently created confusion in the minds of students. The student, as he reads, discovers that while one scholar will discuss the eschatology of the eighth-century prophets—perhaps will even speak of a pre-prophetic eschatology—another, equally competent, will declare that Israel had no eschatology until well on in the post-exilic period. Yet he senses that both are covering much the same ground and discussing much the same topics. It is simply that they are operating with different sets of definitions.

If we define the word narrowly, much as it would be understood in dogmatic theology, it is probably improper to speak of eschatology in connection with the pre-exilic prophets. Thus, for example, S. Mowinckel defines eschatology as a more or less developed doctrine, or complex of ideas, about the "last things" which includes a dualistic conception of the course of history, the conflict of divine and demonic powers, and which looks for the end of this present world order through a cosmic catastrophe, and for the ushering in of a new, entirely different and suprahistorical world order by the power of God. In accordance with this definition, Mowinckel refuses to speak of eschatology until toward the very end of the Old Testament period.[1] And it must be admitted that if this definition is correct (and it is essentially the one found in my English dictionary), eschatology

[1] S. Mowinckel, *He That Cometh* (Eng. tr., Oxford: Basil Blackwell; Nashville: Abingdon Press, 1956), pp. 125 f. With a somewhat similar definition, G. Fohrer would likewise restrict eschatology to the exilic and post-exilic periods; "Die Struktur der alttestamentlichen Eschatologie" (*Studien zur alttestamentlichen Prophetie* [BZAW, 99, 1967], pp. 32–58).

is indeed a late phenomenon in Israel. Early Israel had no doctrine of the end of the world, the last judgment, resurrection to eternal life beyond the grave, and the like. But one wonders if such a definition is not too narrow to do justice to what we find in the Old Testament. One wonders if it is not to impose our definition of eschatology on the Old Testament, and then to discover that the Old Testament has relatively little eschatology as *we* understand the term.

In common with perhaps the majority of scholars, we shall be using the word "eschatology" in a much broader sense. As virtually all would agree, Israel's faith had from a very early period an orientation toward the future, a future hope, that was characteristic and unique. Perhaps in the popular mind this was no more than the expectation of better times to come, of blessing, prosperity, and victory for the nation. But with the pre-exilic prophets there had already emerged the anticipation of a definitive divine intervention through which God would first bring judgment on his people and then, in the farther future, would deliver them and restore them, and bring his purpose for them to a triumphant conclusion. Moreover, the eighth-century prophets developed certain definite patterns to describe this expected consummation. These became classic and retained their validity through the centuries to come, and were taken up and used by later prophets in a variety of ways. One thinks, for example, of Isaiah's expectation of an ideal king of David's line (the "Messiah") who, ruling as God's viceroy, would bring justice and peace to the earth. Or one thinks of Hosea, who looked, beyond the judgment that was imminently coming, for the reestablishment of the covenant bond between God and people in a profounder and more permanent way and for the renewal of the covenant blessings.

This is certainly not eschatology in the later Jewish, or Christian, sense. There is no suprahistorical termination of things, no end of the world (end of the age). On the contrary, the terminus is on this earth, within history. But it is a terminus, the introduction of a situation discontinuous with the current evil one, the consummation of the divine purpose beyond which there was no need to look, and beyond which the prophets in fact did not look. (What can one imagine Isaiah as expecting *after* the kingly figure whom we see described in the pages of his book? Obviously his thoughts ran no farther. This was, to him, the "last thing"; it would endure forever [Isa. 9:7; cf. Hos. 2:19].) Since this is so, it is proper to speak of eschatology as far back as the eighth-century prophets.[2]

[2] Among recent scholars who define eschatology similarly, cf. J. Lindblom, *Prophecy in Ancient Israel* (Oxford: Basil Blackwell, 1962), pp. 360–362; G. von Rad, *Old*

2. But although eschatological expectations may be said to have begun with the eighth-century prophets, it is clear that the prophets did not originate Israel's future hope. The people whom they addressed already had a lively hope for the future. To mention but one example, Amos cries out, "Ah you that eagerly desire the day of Yahweh!" (Amos 5:18). This is chronologically the first mention of the day of Yahweh in the Bible. But it is clear from Amos' words that he was not introducing some new concept thitherto unknown to his hearers, but rather was addressing people in whose minds the expectation of a day of Yahweh was already firmly entrenched. They were looking forward with eager anticipation to a day when God would once again intervene in history, smash the enemies of Israel and bring victory, deliverance, and blessing to his people.

It is worth noting that Amos did not in any way dispute the validity of the concept of the day of Yahweh. He neither denied that there would be such a day, nor that it would be a day of disaster for the enemies of Yahweh. Rather, he took the popular hope for that day and stood it on its head. He said in effect: There will indeed be a day of Yahweh, but it will be a black day for Israel—for God regards Israel as an enemy, not as his people!

> Amos 5:18   Ah you that eagerly desire the day of Yahweh!
>   What do you want with the day of Yahweh?
>   It is darkness, not light.

Amos by no means denied the validity of the notion of the day of Yahweh; but in his thinking it was no longer a day to be hoped for, but a day to be feared. Nor did any of the other pre-exilic prophets deny the validity of the concept, but rather adapted it along the same lines as Amos had. In fact, the day of Yahweh occupied a central position in prophetic eschatology from the eighth century onward.

The popular hope for the day of Yahweh, which Amos attacked, is in no sense to be thought of as an eschatology. It did not look for a definitive consummation of the divine purpose in history, but was rather the confident belief that God would in the future, as he had in the past, come ever and again to the aid of his people, defend them,

Testament Theology, Vol. II (Eng. tr., Edinburgh and London: Oliver & Boyd; New York: Harper & Row, 1965), pp. 114–116; R. E. Clements, _Prophecy and Covenant_ (London: SCM Press, 1965), pp. 103–107; H. D. Preuss, _Jahweglaube und Zukunftser-wartung_ (BWANT, 7, 1968), pp. 205–214. See also the excellent article of Th. C. Vriezen, who likewise argues for a broad definition of eschatology but prefers to speak of the expectations of the pre-exilic prophets as "proto-eschatological"; cf. "Prophecy and Eschatology" (VT, Suppl. Vol. 1, 1953, pp. 199–229).

and make good his promises to them. The prophets radically reinterpreted that hope—indeed demolished it—and developed those patterns for describing what the future—both the immediate future and the farthest future—had in store that became normative. But in doing so they worked with concepts, beliefs, traditions already at home in the minds of the people.

3. But where did this hope of future salvation, so characteristic even of popular Israelite belief before the first of the classical prophets appeared on the scene, have its origin? How is it that, of all the peoples of the world of her day, Israel alone developed what can properly be described as an eschatology? Various answers to these questions have been attempted. We cannot pause to discuss them in detail; we can only take position.[3]

Some have sought to explain Israel's eschatological expectations in terms of a borrowing from outside, from the pagan environment.[4] This view may with confidence be rejected, and it would in fact find few defenders today. It is true that various features in the prophetic vision of the future have parallels in the pagan myth (a time of blessedness following a time of disaster, miraculous fertility of the soil, the destruction of weapons of war, peace in the animal kingdom, etc.). It can hardly be doubted that certain of the forms in which the Old Testament's eschatology found expression were shared with the pagan environment.[5] But Israel's eschatological hope cannot itself be explained in terms of borrowing, if only because not one of the ancient paganisms, from which such concepts were supposedly borrowed, ever developed anything that can properly be spoken of as an eschatology. Being polytheisms, keyed to the rhythm of nature, dedicated to serve the well-being of the existing order, without sense of a divine guidance of history toward a goal in accordance with a long-range purpose announced in advance,[6] they could hardly have

---

[3] On this section see especially W. Eichrodt, *Theology of the Old Testament*, Vol. I (Eng. tr., OTL, 1961), pp. 494–501, with whose position I am in agreement.

[4] So notably H. Gressmann, *Der Messias* (Göttingen: Vandenhoeck & Ruprecht, 1929); earlier, H. Gunkel, *Schöpfung und Chaos in Urzeit und Endzeit* (Göttingen: Vandenhoeck & Ruprecht, 1895).

[5] On the manner in which Israel's faith adapted concepts originally at home in the world of myth, cf. F. M. Cross, *Canaanite Myth and Hebrew Epic* (Cambridge, Mass.: Harvard University Press, 1973).

[6] The uniqueness of Israel's understanding of God's activity in history has been disputed; cf. B. Albrektson, *History and the Gods* (Lund: C. W. K. Gleerup, 1967). The contrast between Israel's faith and the ancient paganisms in this regard must not be stated too sharply, for the pagan conceived of his gods as acting in events, and doing so for a reason. But this must not lead to a minimizing of the manifest differences that exist.

done so. The hope of the pagan was a hope of better times, of victory, plenty, and peace—a hope that is common to all men. One finds in the ancient paganisms no anticipation of a goal toward which all things move, of the "last things." However much Israel may have borrowed from the world of her environment, it is impossible that her eschatological hope, or her peculiar orientation toward the future, could have had its origin there.

Others would give to Israel's eschatological expectations a political explanation, and would argue that these arose as a reflex of the frustration of national ambition by bitter reality.[7] There is certainly an element of truth in this view. Israel knew one brief period of imperial power, and the recollection of this was never erased from her memory. As we shall see, she continued to entertain political aspirations for her king and for the nation so sweeping that they might readily seem to us pretentious. In the days of the divided monarchy, as these aspirations came to correspond less and less to reality, it would be understandable that men should begin to look forward to a better day in the future which would bring them realization. It can hardly be regarded as an accident that eschatological patterns should have emerged for the first time in Israel coincident with the Assyrian invasions of the latter part of the eighth century. Yet Israel's eschatological hope cannot itself be explained in this way. It leaves us asking why other nations of the ancient world—whose political aspirations (whatever they may have been) were likewise sooner or later frustrated—did not also develop an eschatology. Yet the fact remains that they did not. Political reversals may well have provided an impetus for the development of an eschatology, but they cannot in themselves explain the phenomenon.

Finally, there are those who would give to Israel's eschatological hope a cultic explanation. These would suppose that eschatology emerged as the result of a projection into the future of cultic experiences and cultic affirmations—specifically, affirmations regarding the kingly rule of God and regarding the earthly king—which because of cultural changes, shifts in the social structure and,

---

[7] This view was advocated by various scholars of an earlier generation; cf. Eichrodt, *Theology of the Old Testament*, Vol. I, p. 498. More recently, M. Buber has written that hope "becomes eschatologized only through growing historical disillusionment. In this process faith seizes upon the future as the unconditioned turning point of history, then as the unconditioned overcoming of history." Cf. Buber, *Kingship of God* (Eng. tr. of 3d German ed. [1956], New York: Harper & Row, 1967), p. 14. But Buber is careful to relate Israel's future hope to the distinctive nature of her faith.

finally, the nations' decline and fall, had lost their present reality.[8] Now it is certainly true that Israel's cult expressed lofty ideals and aroused hopes that far exceeded reality, and thus pointed men out toward the future. The kingly ideal as affirmed in the cult was indeed the seedbed of the Messianic hope, as we shall see. And again and again the prophets, in seeking to give expression to their vision of the farthest future, adapted cultic forms and employed concepts at home in the cult. But the cult cannot of itself explain Israel's eschatological hope. Leaving aside the fact that the ritual of the Enthronement Festival as Mowinckel reconstructs it is a highly debatable question, we are again forced to ask why, of all the nations of the ancient world, Israel alone developed an eschatology. Why did not other nations, which also had official cults in which the king occupied a central position, likewise do so? In addition to this, history and present-day experience teach us that when affirmations of faith made in public worship lose their immediacy and no longer seem real to the worshipers, they are *not* projected into the future, but rather are given up in favor of rationalism, skepticism, superstition, or some substitute religion. Nor can we seek to explain Israel's becoming an apparent exception to the rule by appealing to some special vitality supposedly inherent in her spirit,[9] for this is simply to substitute one x quantity for another.[10]

Let it be repeated that none of the foregoing explanations is entirely without merit; each contains an element of truth. But they leave questions unanswered. Above all, they do not answer the central question: Why eschatology in Israel, and in Israel alone? So unique a phenomenon is not to be explained in terms of borrowing from the outside (though Israel borrowed much from outside), nor in terms of the reversals that befell the nation (though these must certainly have caused men to long with heightened intensity for a better future), nor in terms of any particular one of the nation's institutions (though what was affirmed in the cult helped to shape the eschatological patterns that emerged). The origin of the prophetic

---

[8] First advanced by S. Mowinckel (*Psalmenstudien* II, 1922 [repr., Amsterdam: Verlag P. Schippers, 1961]), this view has found many adherents. Mowinckel has restated his position in later works: *He That Cometh* (cf. esp. pp. 149–154); *The Psalms in Israel's Worship* (2 vols., Eng. tr., Oxford: Basil Blackwell, 1962), esp. Vol. I, Ch. 5.

[9] S. Mowinckel, *Psalmenstudien* II, pp. 323 f.

[10] Eichrodt (*Theology of the Old Testament*, Vol. I, p. 497) with justice makes these points regarding Mowinckel's position. It is my impression that in his later works (cf. *He That Cometh*, p. 153) Mowinckel does not appeal to this psychological explanation, but rather stresses Israel's "unique conception of God as the God of history" as the ultimate root of eschatology.

eschatology, and of the popular hope for the future which was present before the classical prophets appeared and which their preaching presupposed, must be sought at a far deeper level. It must be sought in Israel's understanding of her God and his activity in history, and specifically in her belief that God had chosen her to be his people, delivered her from bondage, entered into covenant with her, and extended to her his promises.[11] In a word, the roots of Israel's future hope, and the ultimate roots of her later eschatology, are to be found in the essential nature of the faith that called her into being as a people in the first place.

II

The confidence that the future was secure in the promises of God—and, therewith, a remarkable openness toward the future—seems in fact to have been characteristic of the Israelite mentality from the beginning. It cannot be our task here to discuss the nature of earliest Israel's faith in general: that would take us too far afield. Enough to say that it was a phenomenon unique in the ancient world, fundamentally different from the pagan religions in its essential structure. It was not keyed to the rhythm of nature, the fertility of the soil, and the cycle of the seasons, but to unrepeatable events of history in which God had acted marvelously and graciously in behalf of his people. Israel's relationship to her God—indeed her existence as a people—was not based in the nature of things, in blood and soil, but in the memory of historical experience. It is of this historical experience that we read in the first six books of the Bible. The overarching theme of the story told in these books is one of promise moving to fulfillment. We read how God called Abraham and promised him land, posterity, and blessing; how his descendants went down to Egypt and suffered hard bondage there; and how God led them forth in the exodus miracle, gave them his covenant and law at Sinai, and then led them through the desert to give them the Promised Land. The whole story of the exodus, the wilderness experience, and the giving of the land is seen as the fulfillment of the promise made to the fathers.

The Hexateuchal account thus presents the reader with what appears to be a theologically harmonious and coherent picture:

---

[11] A similar understanding of the matter has many representatives today. As examples, see the works of von Rad (pp. 99–119 *et passim*), Clements (pp. 112–114 *et passim*), and Preuss (pp. 71–108, 205–214 *et passim*) listed in note 2, above.

promises are made, and the story of their fulfillment is told. Yet at the same time one may see in the narrative hints of two conceptions of God's election of Israel, and of Israel's relationship to God, that are quite different, and that might readily give rise to different ways of viewing the future. They are not intrinsically incompatible; rather, so we shall argue, they are complementary, and both are essential to the structure of Israel's faith. But they differ so markedly in emphasis that the possibility of a certain tension between them is present. Both are very ancient, and both are associated with the word "covenant." [12]

1. On the one hand, there is the covenant with Abraham. The theme of God's promise to Abraham is one that is sounded again and again throughout the book of Genesis. We first encounter it at Abraham's call (12:1-3), where God says to him:

> (Gen. 12:1-3) Go from your country and your kindred and your father's house to the land that I will show you. (v. 2) And I will make of you a great nation, and I will bless you, and make your name great, so that you will be a blessing. (v. 3) I will bless those who bless you, and him who curses you I will curse; and by you all the families of the earth will bless themselves.

This promise is repeated in 18:17-19, in 22:15-18 (as a solemn oath) and elsewhere, and is resumed to Isaac (26:2-5) and to Jacob (28:13 f.; 35:11 f.). But the most instructive example is surely in ch. 15, where the transaction is called a "covenant" (v. 18). The story is familiar. Abraham questions the promise, complaining in effect that it is impossible that his descendants should become a great nation, since he is already advancing in years and God has not yet given him a son. But God renews the promise and assures Abraham that his descendants would be as numerous as the stars (v. 5). And we read that Abraham believed God, and God "reckoned it to him as righteousness" (v. 6). Then follows a solemn ceremony, with the sacrificial animals slaughtered and divided into two parts, in the course of which God assures Abraham that, after generations of hard bondage, his descendants would possess the land.[13]

It is to be noted that this covenant is depicted simply as a binding

---

[12] On covenant forms in Israel, see the works cited in note 36, below.

[13] We cannot delay on the literary structure of the chapter, which is complex. It seems to come basically from the Yahwist, but various traditions have been worked together; vs. 13-16, which interrupt the description of the covenant ceremony, serve to relate the story to the Egyptian bondage and to explain why the promise was so long in being fulfilled.

promise—or, better, a promissory oath—on the part of God. No particular conditions are attached to it. True, it is assumed that Abraham would continue to trust God and walk before him in righteousness and obedience, and the point is now and then made that Abraham did so (e.g., 22:16; 26:5). But the giving of the promise itself is not made subject to conditions. There is no list of commandments that Abraham must obey, or obligations that he must fulfill, if it is to be made good. In fact, in the covenant ceremony (15:7–12, 17) Abraham is depicted as passive: he is in a trance (v. 12). God himself, his presence symbolized by the smoking fire pot and the flaming torch (v. 17), passes between the parts of the slaughtered animals, thus binding himself by a solemn self-curse to make his promises good. The patriarchal covenant thus rests in God's unconditional promises for the future, and it asks of the recipient only that he trust.

The belief that God had chosen the patriarchs, singled them out as the objects of his especial favor, and promised to their descendants the land which they now possessed, seems to have been current in Israel at a very early period. It is true that the documents in which we read of this, commonly referred to as J (the Yahwist) and E (the Elohist), were first set down in the days of the monarchy, and that their accounts have been colored by later experience—not least by the glories of the Davidic-Solomonic Empire.[14] (Note how the dimensions of the Promised Land in Gen. 15:18 correspond to those of the empire, which the Yahwist apparently regarded as the fulfillment of the promise.) But the belief itself is surely much older. Since it is a central theme in both of the oldest strands of the Hexateuchal narrative, and since these appear to be variant forms in prose of an older cycle of epic traditions already in existence in the days of the Judges, it seems clear that at a very early period the belief had established itself among Israelites that their God had singled out their ancestors for special blessing and had promised them land and a numerous posterity. Indeed, the theme of blessing, which we encounter for the first time at the call of Abraham ("I will bless those who bless you, and him who curses you I will curse," Gen. 12:3), is already to be found in certain of the earliest poems preserved in the Bible:

Num. 24:9   Blessed be every one who blesses you,
             And cursed be every one who curses you.[15]

---

[14] The Yahwist is commonly believed to have worked in Jerusalem in the days of David or Solomon, the Elohist somewhat later and in the north. But exact dates cannot be assigned.

[15] The Balaam poems in Num., chs. 23 to 24, are older than the tenth century and may be as early as the twelfth; cf. W. F. Albright, "The Oracles of Balaam" (JBL, 63 [1944],

It would seem, then, that a belief in God's election of the patriarchs, and his promises to them, was present in Israel from the beginning. In any event, the covenant with Abraham, as it is described in Genesis, can hardly be regarded as a later retrojection of the Sinaitic covenant into the more distant past, as some have been inclined to do, for, as we shall see in a moment, the two are of markedly different types. Indeed, it has been cogently argued that the picture found in Genesis of a personal relationship between the clan head and his God, a relationship supported by promise and sealed by covenant, is an authentic reflection of the religion of those wandering Northwest-Semitic herdsmen who were Israel's remotest ancestors.[16] We cannot attempt here to discuss the religion of Israel's ancestors or the historical process that brought these people to Palestine from their original homeland in Upper Mesopotamia: that would take us much too far afield.[17] But it appears that the belief that their God had promised them land and a numerous posterity may indeed have been an original and central element in the patriarchal religion. Perhaps this was in the first instance understood by these wandering herdsmen as a promise that they would one day have land of their own and become a very large clan indeed. Perhaps, too, as they—or their descendants—gained a foothold in Palestine, established themselves there and began to increase in number, they related the promise to the limited area in which they had settled and regarded it as fulfilled. But, later, as Israel took shape as a people, as clans with patriarchal traditions were absorbed into its structure and their deities worshiped in identification with Yahweh, the promise was extended by a process that can be reconstructed only conjecturally (perhaps not least as it was reaffirmed in the cult of the tribal league) to refer to the whole of the Land of Canaan.[18] And the Yahwist, as we saw, understood it as embracing the entirety of the Davidic-Solomonic Empire at its widest dimensions.

pp. 207–233); *idem, Yahweh and the Gods of Canaan* (New York: Doubleday & Co., 1968); pp. 15 f. The same theme recurs (with the clauses reversed) in the ancient poetic piece in Gen. 27:27–29 (v. 29); cf. also Num. 23:8, 20.

[16] See the basic monograph of A. Alt, *The God of the Fathers* (1929; Eng. tr., *Essays on Old Testament History and Religion* [Oxford: Basil Blackwell, 1966], pp. 1–77). Alt's conclusions have been supplemented and modified by various scholars; cf. especially F. M. Cross, "Yahweh and the God of the Patriarchs" (HTR, 55 [1962], pp. 225–259); more recently and at greater length, *idem, Canaanite Myth and Hebrew Epic*, esp. pp. 1–75.

[17] For my own understanding of the matter, I refer the reader to my book, *A History of Israel* (Philadelphia: The Westminster Press; London: SCM Press, 2d ed., 1972), Ch. 2.

[18] We really cannot move beyond conjecture at this point. The process was assuredly complex. For an interesting attempt at a reconstruction, cf. R. E. Clements, *Abraham and David* (London: SCM Press, 1967), esp. Chs. 4 and 5.

As we have said, it is impossible to say with assurance precisely among which groups in earliest Israel the traditions of the patriarchal covenant were cherished and transmitted. But they seem to have been present from the beginning, and they ultimately became the property of Israel as a whole. Though belief in these traditions need not have led to complacency with regard to the future, it must have served to engender a certain confidence. Those who cherished such belief could feel assured that their God had chosen them to be his people, had promised them blessing, and intended that they should become a great nation. They could view the land they occupied—and much more besides—as Promised Land; they could see their title to it as resting in the sure promises of God to their ancestors, and their possession of it for all the future as secured by the same unconditional promises. A certain long-range optimism must inevitably have resulted.

2. But we also encounter another, and markedly different, pattern of covenant in the Hexateuch: that of the covenant made at Sinai. According to the Bible's own witness, this covenant was constitutive of Israel: it called her into being as a people. This is not described as a promissory covenant. Rather, it created a bond between God and people which was based in gracious and saving actions of the Deity already performed, and it laid upon the recipient (Israel) the binding obligation to obey the divine commandments under threat of the severest penalties in the event of failure to do so.

a. We cannot here attempt a reconstruction of those historical realities which lie behind the stories of the exodus of the Israelites from Egypt, of their experiences in the desert and at Sinai, and of their entry into the Land of Canaan. That would lead us into a veritable minefield of disputed issues and would involve us in a lengthy discussion that would be out of place in a book of this kind.[19] Suffice it to say that it is accepted here that, at some time in the thirteenth century B.C., a party of Hebrew slaves made their escape from Egypt under the leadership of Moses; that these fugitives then made their way by a route that can no longer be traced with assurance to Mt. Sinai (itself of uncertain location), where they underwent those experiences which gave them their distinctive faith and welded them together as a people;[20] and that they subsequently,

---

[19] For my own reconstruction, admittedly tentative and subject to correction, I again refer the reader to my book, *A History of Israel*, cf. Ch. 3.

[20] Some scholars separate the exodus traditions from those of Sinai and posit that these experiences befell different groups of people: cf. G. von Rad, *The Form-Critical*

by a process far more complex than the schematized narrative of the Bible allows us to see, made their way into Palestine, where they became the nucleus of the Israelite tribal system which we see established there in the days of the Judges.

But however the formation of the Israelite people may have come about from a historical point of view, Israel early and late remembered the exodus events as the supreme exhibition of the divine grace whereby her God had delivered her from bondage and established her in her land. Her very earliest poems—the Balaam poems (in Num., chs. 23 to 24), the Song of Miriam (Ex. 15:1–18)—celebrate these events.[21] And at all periods Israel recollected them and reaffirmed them as the basis of her bond with Yahweh and of her obligation to him. This is illustrated again and again throughout the Old Testament. One sees it in the Decalogue (Ex. 20:1–17), which—whatever the origin of the piece in its present form may have been (I see no reason why the various commandments may not come from the earliest period)—was in all likelihood used for cultic recitation in Israel. Here, preceding the commandments and providing the motivation for obeying them, there stands the divine word reminding the hearers of God's prevenient grace to them: "I am Yahweh your God, who brought you out of the land of Egypt, out of the house of bondage" (v. 2). One sees this also in certain pieces of a "confessional" nature embedded in the book of Deuteronomy: in Deut. 6:20–25, where the events of exodus and land-giving are advanced as the basis of one's obligation to obey the divine commandments; and in

Problem of the Hexateuch (1938; Eng. tr., _The Problem of the Hexateuch and Other Essays_ [Edinburgh and London: Oliver & Boyd; New York: McGraw-Hill, 1966], pp. 1–78); M. Noth, _A History of Pentateuchal Traditions_ (1948; Eng. tr., Englewood Cliffs, N.J.: Prentice-Hall, 1972), cf. pp. 59–62. (Noth does not regard Moses as original in either of these blocks of tradition.) This view is rejected here. It has been contested by various scholars through various lines of reasoning: e.g., A. Weiser, _The Old Testament: Its Formation and Development_ (4th ed., 1957; Eng. tr., New York: Association Press, 1961), pp. 81–99; W. Beyerlin, _Origins and History of the Oldest Sinaitic Traditions_ (1961; Eng. tr., Oxford: Basil Blackwell, 1965); S. Herrmann, _A History of Israel in Old Testament Times_ (1973; Eng. tr., London: SCM Press; Philadelphia: Fortress Press, 1975), Part I; cf. also H. B. Huffmon, "The Exodus, Sinai and the Credo" (CBQ, 27 [1965], pp. 101–113). In fact, the themes of exodus, Sinai, and entry into the land seem already to be linked together in the ancient (possibly twelfth-century) poem of Ex. 15:1–18; cf. E. F. Campbell, _Interpretation_, 29 (1975), pp. 143 f., and the reference to the yet unpublished article of D. N. Freedman there.

[21] On the Balaam poems, see above, note 15. On the Song of Miriam, cf. F. M. Cross and D. N. Freedman, JNES, 14 (1955), pp. 237–250; more recently, Cross, _Canaanite Myth and Hebrew Epic_, pp. 112–144; Freedman in H. N. Bream, R. D. Heim, and C. A. Moore, eds., _A Light Unto My Path: Old Testament Studies in Honor of Jacob M. Myers_ (Philadelphia: Temple University Press, 1974), pp. 163–203.

26:5–10, where the Israelite farmer, having brought the gift of his firstfruits to the shrine, recites the saving events as his motivation for bringing them:[22]

> (Deut. 26:5) A wandering Aramean was my father. He went down to Egypt and took up residence there, few in number. But there he became a nation, great, strong, and numerous. (v. 6) And the Egyptians treated us harshly, humiliated us, and inflicted upon us cruel bondage. (v. 7) Then we cried to Yahweh, the God of our fathers; and Yahweh heard our cry, and saw our humiliation, our hardships and our distress. (v. 8) And Yahweh brought us out of Egypt with a mighty hand, with irresistible power,[23] with great terror, with signs and wonders. (v. 9) He brought us to this place and gave us this land, a land flowing with milk and honey. (v. 10) And now, see! I have brought the first-fruits of the soil, which thou, O Yahweh, hast given me. . . .

But perhaps the clearest example of all of the way in which the ancient Israelite looked upon the saving deeds of Yahweh as the basis of his people's bond with him, and the ground of their obligation to him, is to be found in the account of the covenant ceremony at Shechem in Josh. 24:1–28. This passage, though it has been transmitted to us as a part of the so-called Deuteronomic historical corpus (Joshua through II Kings) and has doubtless been shaped by the composers of that work, is not to be regarded as a free creation of the Deuteronomists, as some have thought. Rather, it preserves an ancient tradition at home in northern Israel which, though it may have been shaped, as a number of scholars have believed, by a ceremony of covenant renewal that was periodically conducted there, may be assumed to have its roots in the memory of historical events. Here Joshua, speaking in the name of Yahweh, recites the *magnalia dei* beginning with the call of Abraham and ending with the giving of the land and, on the basis of this, challenges the people to choose whether they will serve Yahweh or some other god, announcing as he does so that his own choice has already been made. When the people

---

[22] The setting, function, and age of these passages is disputed. Von Rad, *The Form-Critical Problem of the Hexateuch* (see note 20) regarded them as very ancient cultic confessions. Others disagree: e.g., Th. C. Vriezen, "The Credo in the Old Testament" (*Papers Read at the Sixth Meeting of Die Ou-Testamentiese Werkgemeenskap in Suid Afrika* [Potchefstroom: Pro Rege Pers-Beperk, 1963], pp. 5–17); L. Rost, *Das kleine Credo und andere Studien zum Alten Testament* (Heidelberg: Quelle & Meyer, 1965), pp. 11–25. Though their style and vocabulary is Deuteronomic, it is unlikely that these pieces are free creations of the Deuteronomist. I should regard them as lying relatively far back in the stream of tradition upon which Deuteronomy drew.

[23] Lit., "with an outstretched arm."

declare that they choose Yahweh, Joshua, after solemnly reminding them of the gravity of the step they are taking and warning them to put aside all other gods, enters into covenant with them to serve Yahweh, and him alone. The account, as we said, may be assumed to rest on the memory of historical events. A number of scholars have believed—and it is by no means unreasonable or impossible—that it preserves the memory of the formation of the Israelite tribal league in its normative form on the soil of Palestine. Certainly, it reaches back to some occasion upon which elements that had not previously been worshipers of Yahweh were drawn into the Israelite tribal structure through solemn covenant.

b. Israel seems in fact to have entered history as a covenant society. For some two hundred years after her first appearance in Palestine, she had no statehood, no organized government, no administrative machinery and, above all, no king. She was a sacral league of tribes united in covenant with Yahweh.[24] The focal point of the league was the shrine that housed its most sacred object, the Ark of the Covenant, the portable throne of the invisible Deity, which at least by the end of the earliest period was located at Shiloh. There, we may suppose, the tribal representatives would gather on feast days to seek the presence of Yahweh and renew their allegiance to him, and also to adjust matters of controversy and mutual interest among themselves. Though it was continually menaced by hostile neighbors, the league had no standing army. In times of danger there would arise a judge who, seized by "the spirit of Yahweh," the charismatic fury, would call out the clans to battle and repel the foe. But though his victories won him prestige, the judge was in no sense a king; his authority was neither absolute, nor permanent, nor in any case hereditary. The whole notion of monarchy was rejected as improper. One has only to recall stout Gideon's rejection of a crown in order to sense this. When, after his brilliant victory, the people wished to make him their king, he is said to have replied (Judg. 8:23): "I will not rule over you; my son will not rule over you. Yahweh rules over you." He addresses them as if they should have known that Israel's structure allowed no place for a king! Or, one thinks of Jotham's biting fable (9:7–15) about the trees who wanted to elect a king. After they had approached the olive tree, the fig tree, and the grapevine, and these had refused on the grounds that they had more useful things to do, they turned to the bramblebush—and the

---

[24] This is, of course, a disputed subject. We shall return to it in a moment.

bramble gladly accepted! Can anyone miss the irony of it? Only a worthless bramble of a man would want to be a king!

Passages such as these are not to be dismissed as reflections of later generations' disillusionment with the monarchy, for they embody an ancient and authentically Israelite sentiment.[25] The league had no king save Yahweh.[26] He was its sole and sovereign Overlord. It was obligated to adjust its affairs in accordance with his stated will; its wars were his wars, and it was he who won the victory.[27] The clansmen were obligated to come to his aid and were roundly cursed if they did not:

> Judg. 5:23   Curse Meroz, said Yahweh's angel,
> Curse bitterly its inhabitants,
> Because they came not to the aid of Yahweh,
> To the aid of Yahweh among the warriors.

But the victory did not depend on human strength, or on the number of troops that responded. Indeed, as the narrator sometimes tells it, large numbers of troops were not desirable, since this might readily lead to boasting. (7:2.) Nor were large numbers needed, since it was Yahweh, and not they, who struck terror in the hearts of the foe (v. 22) and drove them in panic.

It must in fairness be said that the understanding of earliest Israel which we have followed here is warmly disputed today. The classical statement of this understanding was advanced a generation ago by Martin Noth, who argued that early Israel existed as a sacral

---

[25] There is really very little evidence of a consistent rejection of monarchy in later Israel. Some have argued that Hosea was opposed to the institution of monarchy as such (though, to me, this is dubious); and there were groups in Israel (the Rechabites; cf. Jer., ch. 35) who turned their backs on the sedentary way of life and all its institutions and who, presumably, had little love for the monarchy. But with the possible (and very doubtful) exception of Hosea, no prophet can be found who condemned the institution of monarchy in principle, however severely the prophets may have criticized the kings of their day. Nor does later literature in general offer clear examples of this—not even Deuteronomy, however firmly it places the king in subjection to a higher order (cf. Deut. 17:14–20). (I Sam., ch. 8 and 12:1–18, could be argued to be exceptions; but these too may well reflect an ancient sentiment.) North Israel, it is true, did reject the Davidic monarchy, but in doing so, it did not reject the institution itself, for it set up its own monarchy.

[26] Cf. G. E. Mendenhall, *The Tenth Generation* (Baltimore: The Johns Hopkins University Press, 1973), Ch. I ("Early Israel as the Kingdom of Yahweh"); also G. E. Wright, *The Old Testament and Theology* (New York: Harper & Row, 1969), pp. 104–112.

[27] With E. F. Campbell (*Interpretation*, 29 [1975], p. 142), I am not inclined to agree that the wars of Yahweh were not a function of the league, as R. Smend argues in his stimulating book, *Yahweh Wars and Tribal Confederation* (1963; Eng. tr., Nashville: Abingdon Press, 1970).

confederation of twelve tribes united about the worship of Yahweh, after the analogy of the amphictyonies which appear in Greece and Italy at a somewhat later period.[28] So ably and so persuasively was Noth's thesis presented that it carried widespread conviction and became for a time well-nigh the consensus. But in recent years it has been the target of a veritable barrage of criticism from scholars who deny that such an amphictyony (or even a sacral league of any sort) ever existed, and who in some cases even deny that the very notion of covenant was determinative in Israel until a much later date.[29] But, although Noth's reconstruction is admittedly a hypothetical one, and is subject to criticism and correction at a number of points,[30] it seems to me that to posit a sacral league of some sort best accounts for the evidence and affords the only satisfactory explanation of the phenomenon of early Israel as we see it in the Bible. It also seems to me that those who have contested Noth's position have failed to offer any convincing alternative explanation of that very same phenomenon.[31]

How are we to understand earliest Israel? That the entity called "Israel" did not come into being for the first time with the rise of the monarchy in the tenth century may be regarded as certain. Whatever its components and its nature may have been, such an entity had already existed, clearly set off from its neighbors, for many generations prior to that time. This would be quite generally agreed.[32] But what sort of entity was this? What created it? What was it that imparted to these Israelite tribesmen a feeling of self-conscious unity

---

[28] Cf. M. Noth, *Das System der zwölf Stämme Israels* (1930; repr., Darmstadt: Wissenschaftliche Buchgesellschaft, 1960). For a briefer statement in English, cf. Noth, *The History of Israel* (1950; Eng. tr. of 2d ed., London: Adam & Charles Black, 1958), Part I.

[29] Among those who from various points of view have disputed Noth's conclusions the following may be mentioned: H. M. Orlinsky, "The Tribal System of Israel and Related Groups in the Period of the Judges" (*Oriens Antiquus* I [1962], pp. 11–20); G. Fohrer, "Altes Testament—'Amphiktyonie' und 'Bund'?" (ThLZ, 91 [1966], cols. 801–816, 893–904); G. W. Anderson, "Israel: Amphictyony: 'am; kāhāl; 'ēdāh" (H. T. Frank and W. L. Reed, eds., *Translating and Understanding the Old Testament: Essays in Honor of Herbert Gordon May* [Nashville: Abingdon Press, 1970], pp. 135–151); A. D. H. Mayes, *Israel in the Period of the Judges* (London: SCM Press, 1974). See also the works of E. Kutsch and L. Perlitt listed in note 42, below.

[30] I should myself now prefer to avoid use of the word "amphictyony" in this connection, since the parallels, while illuminating, are not exact and are, moreover, drawn from another culture at a later period. Tribal confederations of one sort or another, however, seem to have been common among Israel's neighbors at approximately the time when she took shape as a people.

[31] R. E. Clements makes the same point in his brief notice of Mayes's book (reference in note 29); cf. *Society for Old Testament Study Book List*, 1975, pp. 31 f.

[32] Many of those who dispute Noth's thesis of a sacral league explicitly concede the point: e.g., Mayes, *Israel in the Period of the Judges*, pp. 1–7.

that held them together as a definable entity through the first two hundred years of their history without a king or any machinery of state to impose it? Certainly a mere feeling of kinship will not suffice to explain it. True, the Bible traces the descent of all the tribes from the patriarch Jacob (Israel). But the Bible also offers clear and abundant evidence that Israel included, or came to include, elements of the most heterogeneous origin who could not possibly have been descendants of a single family tree. And, on the other hand, it is clear that from the beginning, and throughout her history, Israel was not set off from her immediate neighbors (Canaanites, Moabites, Ammonites, Edomites, etc.) either in her general racial stock or by language. Early Israel was not a unit that was based merely in a feeling of blood kinship. Indeed, common descent and common language have rarely in all of history been a major factor in the formation and preservation of larger social and political units.[33]

What shall we say then? Were the Israelite tribes progressively driven into unity as they were again and again forced to line up back to back, as it were, to beat off common danger? This must certainly have been a factor in strengthening a feeling of unity, at least among certain of the tribes. But it is hardly a sufficient explanation of it. Common danger may frequently create temporary alliances (and the memory of these may linger for generations) but, the danger removed, these have seldom, unless other factors are also operative, issued in the formation of lasting political units[34] (and, let it be said, early Israel, though not a state, was a sort of political unit, and one of considerable tenacity). Common dangers may well have intensified Israel's feeling of unity, but they scarcely created it. Indeed, there were occasions, as the ancient Song of Deborah (Judg., ch. 5) shows us, when tribes which already had bonds of unity with those most immediately threatened, and which were for this reason felt to be under obligation to send help, nevertheless failed to do so. In this case it was not the common emergency that created unity. A feeling of unity was already present before the danger struck, and it survived, as later history shows, in spite of the fact that certain parties to this unity failed to do what was expected of them. Early

[33] Cf. Mendenhall, *The Tenth Generation*, p. 174 and Ch. 7 *passim*.

[34] For example, Canaanite city-states frequently formed temporary coalitions, but no lasting political unity ever resulted. Again, in the ninth century a large coalition of Syro-Palestinian states was formed to resist Assyria; but whenever the danger was relaxed, the coalition tended to fall apart as its members resumed their private quarrels. Such has been the history of military alliances throughout the centuries and down to the present day.

Israel cannot be understood merely as a miscellaneous collection of tribes that were driven into unity in the face of danger.

Can we, then, appeal to common religion—that is, to the worship of Yahweh that was common to the tribes, and specifically to the memory of those experiences which certain of their forebears had undergone in the wilderness—as an explanation of the phenomenon of early Israel? Certainly this is a factor that is on no account to be minimized or slighted. One believes that had not a party of Hebrews undergone the experiences of exodus and Sinai, and had they not then—in whatever way and by whatever route—made their way into Palestine bringing their new faith with them, the catalyst that precipitated the formation of Israel would not have been present, and the Israel that we see in the Bible would never have existed. Let that be affirmed with all clarity. But can the mere fact of common religion of itself serve to explain the phenomenon that was Israel? In all of history common religion has seldom of itself created lasting political unity (and, let it be repeated, early Israel was a sort of political unit, and one that lasted for some two centuries). On the contrary and sadly, history teaches us that coreligionists are as likely to fight with one another as not. Where political unity among coreligionists has existed, it has usually not been created by religion in the abstract, but by other factors and forces. In the society of the day in which Israel came to birth, relationships between tribal groups, regardless of their religious beliefs, were always parlous. When one group confronted another, either some formal agreement would be arrived at enabling them to live side by side in peace, or there would be war. As for Israel, her various tribes did indeed have, or come to have, a unity in their common religion. But it is doubtful that such unity could ever have translated itself into fact had there not been some solemn treaty, or covenant, to enforce it.[35]

It is for this reason difficult to understand early Israel in any other way than as a sacral league, or confederation, formed in covenant with Yahweh and under the rule of Yahweh. Various details with regard to this league and its institutions will doubtless always remain hypothetical and subject to debate. We cannot say with assurance just how, or when, the league came into being, or whether it consisted of twelve tribes from the beginning or was originally smaller and experienced a gradual filling out of its structure in the course of the years. Nor can we determine just how its components may have

---

[35] On the point, cf. Mendenhall, *The Tenth Generation*, p. 16 and Ch. 1 *passim*.

fluctuated, or which tribes may have been its members at one time or another (though I myself believe that it consisted of the classical twelve at least from a very early period). Moreover, many of the institutions, customs, and practices of the league remain hypothetical and obscure. We cannot delay on these questions here. But the view that Israel emerged into history as a sacral, covenant league may with some confidence be accepted. It is the view, one believes, that accords best with the Biblical evidence. Only so, indeed, can earliest Israel be understood.

c. But what was the nature of the covenant that brought the Israelite tribes together in this sacral league? Here, once again, we enter disputed territory. Some years ago G. E. Mendenhall pointed out the remarkable similarities that exist between the Sinaitic covenant as this is described for us in the Bible and certain suzerainty treaties (i.e., treaties between the Great King and his vassals) which we know from texts of the Hittite Empire.[36] He argued that the covenant brought the Israelite tribes together as vassals of the divine Overlord, Yahweh. To be sure, the Israelite covenant can hardly have been adapted directly from Hittite models, for the infant Israel had no contacts with the Hittite Empire, which fell shortly before she came into existence as a people. But it is all but certain that treaties of this type were not specifically Hittite in origin, but rather represent a treaty form which was widely used in the ancient Orient in the second millennium B.C., but which is so far known to us in that period only from texts of the Hittite Empire. Moreover, there is growing evidence that as the Late Bronze Age ended (thirteenth to twelfth centuries B.C.) Palestine and the surrounding lands were heavily influenced by elements coming from the north (Anatolia and other lands once a part of the Hittite Empire),[37] so that even if the treaty form just mentioned was specifically Hittite in origin (which it probably was not) there is no reason a priori why the founders of Israel may not have known of it.

Though the Hittite treaties do not follow a rigidly stereotyped

---

[36] Cf. G. E. Mendenhall, *Law and Covenant in Israel and the Ancient Near East* (Pittsburgh: The Biblical Colloquium, 1955). This had appeared a year earlier in the form of two articles, cf. BA, 17 (1954), pp. 26–46, 50–76. The correspondences were noted nearly simultaneously, and apparently independently, by K. Baltzer; cf. *The Covenant Formulary* (Eng. tr. of the 2d ed., Oxford: Basil Blackwell, 1971). The literature is now extensive; cf. D. J. McCarthy, *Old Testament Covenant* (Oxford: Basil Blackwell; Richmond: John Knox Press, 1972) for a summary. For a useful popular presentation, parallel to that of Mendenhall, cf. D. R. Hillers, *Covenant: The History of a Biblical Idea* (Baltimore: The Johns Hopkins Press, 1969).

[37] Cf. especially Mendenhall, *The Tenth Generation*, Ch. 6.

form, certain features are normally present (though not always in the same order). There is a preamble in which the Great King identifies himself by giving his name and titles, after which he proceeds to speak to the vassal directly, using the "I-Thou" form of address. Normally there follows a historical recital in which the Great King reviews past relationships between himself and the vassal, stressing his various benevolent acts toward the vassal, which should move the latter to perpetual gratitude. Then come the stipulations, which set forth in detail what the Great King expects of the vassal if the treaty relationship is to be maintained. Naturally, these can vary greatly depending on the situation. But, typically, the vassal is forbidden to engage in foreign relations with rulers other than the Great King, as well as to indulge in hostilities with others of his vassals; all controversies between vassals are to be submitted to the Great King for adjudication. Further, the vassal must respond to the call to arms, and he must do so wholeheartedly ("with all your heart"). He is to repose unlimited trust in the Great King, and he is on no account to utter or tolerate unfriendly words about him. And he is to appear regularly before the Great King with the stipulated tribute. Following the stipulations it is sometimes directed that a copy of the treaty be deposited in the vassal's shrine and read publicly at regular intervals. Various gods, both of the Hittite lands and the vassal's own country—as well as others (mountains, rivers, heaven, earth, etc.)— are then invoked as witnesses to the treaty. Finally, sanctions are supplied the treaty in the form of a series of blessings and curses which the gods are summoned to bring on the vassal, the blessings in the event of obedience, the curses in the event of disobedience. It may be assumed that the treaty was ratified through a religious ceremony in the course of which the vassal took his solemn oath of allegiance to the Hittite king.

Most of the features just noted have their parallels in the covenant form as we know it from the Bible. The divine Overlord's self-identification is present (e.g., "I am Yahweh your God," Ex. 20:2a; or, "Thus says Yahweh, the God of Israel," Josh. 24:2a), as is the historical recital reviewing the Overlord's past beneficent acts toward his people. This last can be very brief (cf. "who brought you out of the land of Egypt, out of the house of bondage," Ex. 20:2b) or quite lengthy (cf. the long recitation of Yahweh's gracious acts in Josh. 24:2b–13). Furthermore, as vassals of the Hittite Empire are forbidden to conclude alliances independently of the Great King, so Israelites are forbidden to make commitments to any god-overlord save Yahweh. As Hittite vassals are to maintain internal peace and submit all controversies with other vassals to the Great King for adjustment, so Israelites are to regulate all dealings with fellow Israelites in accordance with Yahweh's covenant law. Likewise, response to the call to arms was clearly recognized as obligatory in the early Israelite league (cf. Judg. 5:14–18, 23; 21:8–12). Moreover, as the vassal was to appear before the Great King with the stipulated tribute, so the Israelite was to appear regularly before Yahweh, and he was not to do so "empty-handed" (Ex. 23:14–17; 34:18–20). The provision that a copy of the treaty be deposited in the shrine and periodically read in public likewise has its parallel in Israel (Deut. 10:5; 31:9–13).[38] The invoking of various gods as witnesses to the treaty could, of course, have no place in the Biblical covenant (but see Josh. 24:22, 27, where first the people themselves, then the sacred stone, are called to witness). Yet reminiscences even of this feature may be seen in certain "covenant lawsuits" in the prophetic books and elsewhere (e.g., Isa. 1:2 f.; Micah 6:1 f.; also Deut. 32:1), where heaven and earth, mountains and hills, are called upon to bear witness to the people's derelictions.[39] As for the blessings and curses, they occupy a prominent place especially in Deuteronomy (cf. chs. 27 to 28), but they were certainly known much earlier, as is evidenced by reminiscences of the covenant curses in the preaching of even the earliest of the prophets.[40] Indeed, Judges 5:23 would indicate that to call down curses on those who had defaulted on covenant obligation was the accepted practice in the very earliest period.

Parallels such as these are striking, and they would seem to argue powerfully both for the extreme antiquity of the covenant in Israel and its central importance in her corporate life. It would appear that from the very beginning of her existence as a people Israel understood her relationship to her God after the analogy of the international suzerainty treaty form, as that of vassal to overlord. She had been the recipient of Yahweh's especial favor and had therefore bound herself to acknowledge him as her sole and supreme Overlord,

---

[38] The fact that Joshua is said to have written the words of the covenant in a book (Josh. 24:26) suggests a tradition that a covenant document was kept in the shrine at Shechem; cf. Hillers, *Covenant*, p. 64.

[39] There is a considerable literature on these "lawsuit speeches"; cf. J. Harvey, *Le Plaidoyer prophétique contre Israël après la rupture de l'alliance* (Bruges and Paris: Desclée de Brouwer; Montreal: Les Éditions Bellarmin, 1967); see the bibliography at the back of Harvey's book for further literature.

[40] See especially D. R. Hillers, *Treaty-Curses and the Old Testament Prophets* (Rome: Pontifical Biblical Institute, 1964).

and she had shouldered the obligation to live in obedience to his stipulations under threat of his extreme displeasure in the event of failure to do so.

d. But persuasive as this line of argument may seem, it must be said that a number of scholars are not convinced by it, but rather argue that the treaty form was taken over by Israel as a means of expressing her relationship to her God at a relatively late period in her history. Their reasons for taking this position are various and they are by no means to be brushed aside as entirely without merit. Perhaps the most important of these reasons are the following. For one thing, it must be admitted that the treaty form just described did not disappear with the fall of the Hittite Empire in the thirteenth century B.C., for many of its essential features continue to be seen in Aramean and Assyrian treaties down to as late as the seventh century. Is it not possible—indeed more likely—that Israel learned of this form, and adapted it for her purposes, late in the days of the divided monarchy, rather than at the beginning of her history? To this must be added the fact that in the Bible the covenant receives by far its clearest formal expression in the book of Deuteronomy (which critics customarily date to the seventh century)—much clearer than in those portions of Exodus that tell of the events at Sinai, where the covenant form has to be pieced together from isolated fragments. Moreover, it is also the fact that the word "covenant" (b°rît) occurs with relative rarity in literature that is uncontestably to be dated before the seventh century. (Of prophets prior to that time only Hosea uses the word, and he perhaps twice.) Considerations such as these have led various scholars to the belief that Israel adapted the treaty form as a means of expressing her relationship to her God at a relatively late date.[41] Some have even argued that the very notion of covenant was of little importance in Israel until the days of the Deuteronomic writers in the seventh century.[42]

The above considerations are weighty, and they deserve more extended discussion than it is possible to give them here. But one may doubt, as many scholars do, that they are as compelling as they may seem on the surface to be. There are strong objections to supposing that the covenant-treaty form became known to Israel only

[41] The literature is too extensive to list here. See McCarthy, *Old Testament Covenant* (reference in note 36) for a survey of the discussion. McCarthy himself doubts the antiquity of the treaty form in Israel.

[42] Cf. especially L. Perlitt, *Bundestheologie im Alten Testament* (WMANT, 36, 1969); E. Kutsch, *Verheissung und Gesetz: Untersuchungen zum sogenannten "Bund" im Alten Testament* (BZAW, 131, 1973); see also the article of G. Fohrer cited in note 29.

in the days of the divided monarchy. It is true that the suzerainty-treaty form described above is not found only in documents of the second millennium B.C., but continues to be seen in Assyrian texts as late as the seventh century. But there are important differences between the treaties of the second millennium and those of the first, and these must not be overlooked or minimized. Most important of these differences is the fact that the historical prologue outlining past relationships between the suzerain and his vassal, which is a standard feature both in the Hittite treaties and in all of the classical covenant formulations of the Bible, is lacking in the first-millennium treaties known to us,[43] while the curses enforcing the treaty become much more elaborate and lurid, and the blessings tend to disappear. A different conception of the suzerain-vassal relationship has emerged, one based on threats and naked force rather than on conciliation and persuasion, and as different in spirit from the Biblical covenant as possible. It is difficult to believe that Israel's conception of covenant could have been drawn from treaties like these. No doubt the Assyrian treaties did influence Israel's thinking in the seventh century; but it is unlikely that this influence would have been effective had not Israel already conceived of her relationship to her God as that of vassal to overlord. To be sure, we cannot *prove* that the treaty form was known to Israel at an early date, and new evidence may at any time put a different face on the matter. But at present it can be said that the Israelite covenant is far closer in its form and in its spirit to the Hittite treaties of the second millennium than to any later treaties known to us.

The fact that the covenant form is given its clearest expression in Deuteronomy, while presented in broken fashion in the Sinai pericope of Exodus, and elsewhere, cannot of itself be regarded as decisive. Nowhere in the Old Testament do we have a covenant-treaty document in its original form. We have only narrative accounts of the making of covenants and, perhaps, of their ritual reenactment. This, together with the new content that Israel's faith injected into it, would of itself have necessitated that the form to some degree be broken. One must also remember that the Sinai pericope as we find it in our Bibles is the end product of an exceedingly long and complex

---

[43] A damaged fragment of a treaty between Asshurbanapal and the people of Qedar seems to contain a brief allusion to past relationships and may constitute an exception to this statement; cf. K. Deller and S. Parpola, *Orientalia*, 37 (1968), pp. 464–466. But the lengthy historical recital reviewing the past benevolent acts of the suzerain is certainly not a characteristic feature of the Assyrian treaties as we know them.

process of transmission and reworking, in the course of which material has been displaced from its original context and the ritual pattern of the tradition thereby dissolved.[44] Under such circumstances unbroken forms are hardly to be expected. Nevertheless, even in the Sinai pericope most, if not all, of the standard features of the treaty form described above may be detected, either explicitly or by inference, as all may be in the narrative of Joshua, ch. 24,[45] which, in my opinion as in that of many others, is not to be dismissed as a creation of the Deuteronomists, but is surely much older. It appears, then, in every way more likely that, though the covenant receives its clearest expression in Deuteronomy, the treaty form which it adapted was known in Israel at a much earlier date.

The relatively limited occurrence of the word for "covenant" ($b^e r\bar{\imath} t$) prior to the seventh century is likewise not decisive. (How limited this occurrence is will depend, of course, on one's critical presuppositions. If one regards certain key passages in the Hexateuch and elsewhere in which a covenant between God and people is mentioned as Deuteronomic or later,[46] as some scholars do, then occurrences of the word in its theological sense are few indeed. But if one takes a contrary position, as I should with many others, there are many more of them.) We cannot delay upon the question of whether the word $b^e r\bar{\imath} t$ is best translated as "covenant" or in some other way,[47] or why it was that the earlier prophets avoided the word (as we said, only Hosea uses it, and he rarely). But a concept may well be present even when no fixed terminology has been developed to express it. For example, the standard terminology for expressing the concept of election seems likewise to have become firmly fixed in the seventh century and after;[48] yet few would wish to argue that Israel began to understand herself as a chosen people, singled out by Yahweh for especial favor, only at that relatively late date. On the contrary, as

---

[44] Cf. Cross, *Canaanite Myth and Hebrew Epic*, pp. 83–86, on the point.

[45] See conveniently Campbell, *Interpretation*, 29 (1975), p. 150.

[46] One thinks of such passages as Gen. 15:18; Ex. 19:5; 24:7 f.; 34:27 f.; Josh. 24:1–28; also II Sam. 23:5; Ps. 89; etc.

[47] E. Kutsch (reference in note 42) contends that the German word *Bund* (and presumably the English word "covenant") is in most cases a misleading translation, and prefers *Verpflichtung* ("obligation") and the like. On this point, see the judicious remarks of M. Newman in his review of Kutsch in JBL, 94 (1975), pp. 118–120.

[48] Cf. Th. C. Vriezen, *Die Erwählung Israels nach dem Alten Testament* (Zurich: Zwingli Verlag, 1953). As Vriezen shows, the use of the root *bāḥar* as the standard election term seems to have achieved currency in the Deuteronomic literature and after. It probably had, however, antecedents in the cult as its use in the psalm literature suggests; cf. G. E. Mendenhall, "Election," IDB, Vol. II, pp. 76–82, on the subject.

far as we can tell, she so thought of herself from the beginning, although she used no fixed set of words to express that conviction. Just so, the notion of a covenant with Yahweh may well have been, and apparently was, present in Israel perhaps long before any fixed theological vocabulary had been developed to describe it. The early prophets may have avoided use of the word "covenant" for a variety of reasons, not least because it may have acquired in the popular mind connotations with which they could not operate.

In any event, it seems certain that long before the seventh century there existed in Israel the awareness of a bond with Yahweh which, in its essential features, is at least reminiscent of the treaty form described above. It was a bond that rested in Yahweh's gracious favor in bringing his people from bondage and giving them their land, and it involved the people in the obligation to serve him alone and to live in obedience to his righteous commandments (stipulations). The entire prophetic preaching, as will become more clear in subsequent chapters, presupposes such a notion. The prophets from the beginning attacked the people for their worship of gods other than Yahweh and for their flagrant disregard of his commandments, reminding them as they did so of his gracious favor to them which should have moved them to more perfect obedience. And, in doing this, the prophets did not propose to inform the people of an obligation of which they had thitherto been unaware, but rather to remind them of an obligation that they should have known very well, but had forgotten. Many specific features in the prophetic preaching presuppose an awareness on the part of the people of a bond with Yahweh which had committed them to absolute loyalty to him, and to obedience, under threat of his extreme displeasure. Hosea's metaphor of marriage to describe the God-people relationship, carrying with it, as it did, the obligation on the part of Israel of absolute faithfulness to her divine "Husband" under threat of "divorce," does so. The frequent use of the treaty curses by the prophets as they announced the divine judgment on the people[49] would seem to indicate that knowledge of the covenant-treaty form was widespread in Israel, for, if it had not been, such ways of speaking would not have been understood. The pattern of the divine lawsuit, which is employed by the earliest prophets and also in Deuteronomy, ch. 32,[50]

---

[49] On this feature, see Hillers, *Treaty-Curses and the Old Testament Prophets* (reference in note 40). This feature is more prominent in Hosea than in any other prophet, with the possible exception of Jeremiah.

[50] Cf. Hos. 4:1–3; Isa. 1:2 f.; 3:13–15; Micah 6:1–5; etc. The poem in Deut., ch. 32, is still more ancient. Some scholars would date it to the eleventh century; cf. O. Eissfeldt,

likewise presupposes awareness of a prior legal relation between God and people, for in these speeches Yahweh brings suit against his people for their failure to live up to obligations that they have assumed.[51] When one adds to this the way in which early and late terminology with treaty connotations pervades legal, prophetic, and other material in the Bible outside specific covenant formulations, one finds it difficult to believe that the covenant-treaty form in which this terminology was at home was not also widely known in Israel from a very early period.[52]

When all has been said, it must be admitted once again that we have been moving in the realm of the hypothetical and the inferential. The evidence is such that it does not allow us to march ahead to complete certainty. The nature of the constitution of earliest Israel, and of her understanding of her relationship to her God, will probably always remain subjects of debate. But the probability seems to me, as it does to others, to lie strongly on the side of the reconstruction that has been adopted here. The notion of a covenant bond between God and people seems clearly to antedate the earliest of the prophets, and it was presumably much older still. The considerations advanced above—plus the difficulty (I had almost said, the impossibility) of understanding earliest Israel in any other way than as a league of tribes bound to one another by some sort of agreement, or treaty (covenant)—make it in every way reasonable to suppose that the covenant had been a determinative factor in Israel's life from the beginning. We may with some confidence believe that Israel did in fact come into being as a sacral confederation formed in covenant with Yahweh, and that this covenant followed broadly the pattern of those international suzerainty treaties that are known to us from texts of the second millennium B.C.

Das Lied Moses Deuteronomium 32:1–43 und das Lehrgedicht Asaphs Psalm 78 samt einer Analyse der Umgebung des Mose-Liedes (Berlin: Akademie-Verlag, 1958); W. F. Albright, VT, 9 (1959), pp. 339–346. Others prefer the ninth century; cf. G. E. Wright, "The Lawsuit of God: A Form-Critical Study of Deuteronomy 32" (B. W. Anderson and W. Harrelson, eds., *Israel's Prophetic Heritage: Essays in Honor of James Muilenburg* [New York: Harper & Brothers, 1962], pp. 26–67).

[51] It is true that use of this pattern does not necessarily imply knowledge of the treaty form described above; but it is best explained so.

[52] The evidence is too massive to be ignored. It includes such terms as "to hear (i.e., obey) the words," "to love," "to fear," "to hate," "to know," "to remember," etc. Literature on the subject is widely scattered and need not be cited here; cf. Campbell (reference in note 45), for a brief summary.

III

1. If early Israel's understanding of her God, and of her relationship to him and position under him, was at all as we have described it above, it must have awakened in her a remarkable openness toward the future. This would certainly have been true, as we have said, of those elements in Israel which cherished patriarchal traditions and remembered the sure promises that their God had made to their ancestors. These could always regard the land that they occupied (and, later, all the territory occupied or claimed by Israel) as Promised Land; they could see their title to it as validated, and their continuing possession of it as assured, by those same unconditional promises, and they could therefore look forward to a future that would bring them increase and great blessing.

But the Sinaitic covenant, no less than the patriarchal, by its very nature must have pointed men toward the future. True, it offered no unconditional promises. Still less was it a bargain between equals which might be terminated at the request of either party, or altered through arbitration. It was a vassal's acceptance of the Overlord's terms. It rested in the recognition on Israel's part of the gracious favor of Yahweh to her in the past, and it bound her to acknowledge him as her sole and supreme Overlord. And though the divine Overlord had extended his promises to the lesser party to the covenant, his vassal Israel, these were by no means unconditional; the vassal was obligated to full compliance with the covenant stipulations under threat of the Overlord's wrath in the event of disobedience: "If you forsake Yahweh and serve foreign gods, then he will turn and do you harm, and consume you, after having done you good" (Josh. 24:20). The future is not assured by the promises: it may be blessing, or it may be curse. All depends on Israel's faithfulness to the covenant. One might say that the future and the promises are laid under the little word "if":

> (Ex. 19:4) You have seen what I did to the Egyptians, and how I bore you on eagles' wings and brought you to myself. (v. 5) And now, *if* you will really obey me and keep my covenant, you shall be my own possession among all the peoples. . . .[53]

As long as such a view of the God-people relationship was kept in

---

[53] The date and provenience of this passage is much disputed. Though it *may* have received touches at the hands of Deuteronomistic editors, as many believe, it is not to be dismissed as their free creation. See the commentaries for discussion.

mind and not forgotten, there would seem to be no place in Israel for complacency with regard to the future.

Still, the future is left open. If there was the threat of the curse in the event of disobedience, there was also the explicit assurance that, if the terms of the covenant were met, the divine Overlord's favor would be endlessly continued. The future might therefore be faced with assurance. One could be confident that the God who had showed himself to be gracious and powerful in the past would show himself to be equally gracious and powerful in the future, and that he would neither break covenant nor be false to his promises. Israelites then could, as long as they accepted the rule of this God and obeyed his commandments—or convinced themselves that they were doing so—feel assured of his continuing protection and expect of him yet greater blessings. Such an understanding of the relationship of God and people does not make for complacency, no, but it does not make for despair either. The future is always open under God, who is both mighty and faithful.

2. In any event and whatever its source, earliest Israel did in fact exhibit a remarkable openness toward the future, a confidence that the future was not to be feared, but rather held good things in store. We see this confidence reflected in certain of the most ancient poems preserved in the Bible: the oracles of Balaam (in Num., chs. 23 to 24), the Blessing of Moses (Deut., ch. 33), the Blessing of Jacob (Gen., ch. 49), the Song of Miriam (Ex. 15:1–18), and the Song of Deborah (Judg., ch. 5), as well as others.[54] These poems tell how God delivered his people from bondage in Egypt that he might lead them triumphantly to the land that he would give them (Ex. 15:1–18; cf. Num. 23:22; 24:8). They describe Israel as a people set apart (Num. 23:9), the recipient of God's promises (v. 19), blessed with a blessing that no one can revoke (vs. 20 f.); who blesses her will be blessed, who curses her will be cursed (24:9; cf. Gen. 12:3). Since God has blessed her, no enchantment can avail against her, nor can any foe stand against her; she will rend her foes like a lion or a lioness, gore them like a wild bull (Num. 23:22–24; 24:8 f.; Deut. 33:17). Protected and blessed by her God, Israel dwells in safety (Deut. 33:12, 28), on a land that will yield unimagined material plenty (Gen. 49:22–26; Deut. 33:13–16; Num. 24:5–7).

---

[54] The literature on these and other ancient poems is extensive, technical, and widely scattered. Some of it has already been cited. For a selection of it, the reader is referred to my book, *A History of Israel*, p. 143 and the footnotes there. More recently, see D. A. Robertson, *Linguistic Evidence in Dating Early Hebrew Poetry* (SBL Dissertation Series, 3 [Missoula: University of Montana, 1972]).

Deut. 33:13   Blessed by Yahweh is his land
               With the abundance of heaven above,
               And of the deep that couches beneath.
     14   With the abundance of the yields of the sun,
               The abundance of the produce of the months,
     15   With the abundance of the ancient mountains,
               The abundance of the everlasting hills.[55]

An exuberant confidence indeed! One almost gains the impression that the poet is not speaking of Palestine at all, but positively of paradise. To be sure, we have no way of saying how many in Israel shared the assurance expressed in poems such as these, whether the majority or relatively few. But so from earliest times her bards and seers encouraged her, assuring her of the continued possession of her land, and the protection and blessing of her God.

When one considers early Israel's actual situation, such confident assurance seems well-nigh incredible. The actual situation held little, one would think, that would tend to awaken optimism, and certainly nothing to foster complacency. Israel had neither great military might nor material plenty, nor any reasonable hope of achieving such things in the foreseeable future. She was a loose confederation of tribes, poorly armed, without central authority, continually threatened by enemies from every side, continually having to fight for her life. She lived on a land—call it "a land flowing with milk and honey" if you will—poor in comparison with others, which allowed her an existence that even later generations of Israelites would probably have regarded as marginal; she had few material comforts, almost no luxuries, and nothing that could be described as great wealth. She knew peace and physical security only intermittently, danger and violence constantly, and in the end she found herself confronted in the Philistines with an enemy with whom she could not cope. One marvels that such a people could face the future with any confidence at all. One marvels that they did not face it with misgiving, if not with fear.

Yet the confidence is there. It was a confidence that rested in the memory of historical experience, an experience that Israelites interpreted as an experience with their God, Yahweh. It was Yahweh who

---

[55] On the poem in Deut., ch. 33, see F. M. Cross and D. N. Freedman, "The Blessing of Moses" (JBL, 67[1948], pp. 191–210). I find their reconstruction of the text at most places convincing and I have followed it at various places. But not wishing to engage in a discussion of textual minutiae in a book of this sort, I have allowed the wording of my translation to conform more closely to that of RSV.

had brought them from slavery in Egypt and destroyed the army of
the Pharaoh. It was he who had led them to the land that he would
give them, paralyzing their enemies with terror before them (Ex.
15:1–18). And he had given them the land as he had promised their
fathers. And it was he who in subsequent years had again and again
come to them in times of emergency with awesome portents, and
saved them from their foes (Judg., ch. 5). Yahweh is the heavenly
Warrior (Ex. 15:3),[56] irresistible in might, incomparable among the
gods (v. 11). And Israel is his special possession, his people (v. 16),
over whom he "will reign for ever and ever" (v. 18). With such a God
as their protector and Overlord, why should Israelites not with
confidence entrust the future to him and face it without fear?

> Deut. 33:26 There is none like the God of Yeshurun,
> Who rides the heavens to your help,
> In his majesty the clouds.
>
> 27 The God of old is your refuge,
> Underneath are the Eternal One's arms.
> He drove out the foe before you,
> He gave the word to destroy.
>
> 28 So Israel encamps in safety,
> Jacob dwells securely alone,
> On a land of grain and wine;
> Yes, his heavens drip down dew.
>
> 29 Happy are you, O Israel! Who is like you?
> A people saved by Yahweh,
> Whose shield is your help,
> Whose sword is your glory.
> Your enemies come fawning to you,
> And you shall tread upon their backs.[57]

Thus the confidence of earliest Israel with regard to the future.
Let it be repeated that this is not to be thought of as an eschatology
in any sense of the word. Not only does it develop no doctrine of the
"last things"; one cannot even find in it the anticipation of some
radical turning point within history, some goal toward which the
divine purpose is moving, which might qualify as eschatology in a
limited sense. Rather, it is the unshakable confidence that the God
who has given the land in accordance with his promises would secure
his people in the possession of it and continue his protection and

---

[56] On this concept, cf. P. D. Miller, Jr., *The Divine Warrior in Early Israel*
(Cambridge, Mass.: Harvard University Press, 1973); in a briefer and more popular
form, cf. Wright, *The Old Testament and Theology* (reference in note 26), Ch. 5.

[57] See note 55, above.

blessing into the indefinite future. It is the sublime assurance that the God who acted mightily and graciously in the past is Lord also of the future, and will in the future continue to exhibit his might and gracious favor toward his people always. This is not eschatology; but this abounding confidence in the future, as a future under the protection and blessing of God, was the seedbed from which Israel's unique eschatological expectations were later to grow.

2

Yahweh's Election of
Mt. Zion and of David

In the preceding chapter we observed that exuberant confidence in the future which, judging from certain of the most ancient poems preserved in the Bible, seems to have been characteristic of Israel since the earliest period of her life as a people. This was a confidence that can hardly be explained in terms of early Israel's actual situation—which was for the most part parlous, insecure, and most unpromising of future opulence and greatness. Rather, it must be assumed to have rested in the essential nature of the faith that called Israel into being as a people in the first place. Specifically, it rested in Israel's conviction that her God, Yahweh, was a mighty God above all gods, and that he had singled her out for special favor, had chosen her to be his people, entered into covenant with her, and extended to her his promises. It was her understanding of her God, and of her relationship to him, that gave to Israel her unique openness toward the future. Not, of course, that the covenant that was constitutive of Israel allowed any rightful place for optimistic complacency with regard to the future! By its very nature it did not, for its stipulations were stringent, and there was always the threat of the divine Overlord's wrath in the event of disobedience. But the door to the future was left open. As long as Israelites were faithful to their God, and obedient to his commandments, they might feel confident of his continuing protection and a future filled with blessing.

I

But Israel's hope for the future was shaped by yet another factor: the great achievement of royal David and the indelible impression

that this made on the minds of his people. Under David and his son
Solomon, Israel reached its golden age of power and glory. Later
generations would always remember that age and would look back
upon it with nostalgia and with pride.

1. We cannot pause to trace the history of the rise of the monarchy
in Israel.[1] But readers familiar with the Bible's account will recall
that, after some two hundred years of existence, the tribal confeder-
acy was broken by the Philistines; Israel's army was cut to pieces, the
Ark—which had been brought into battle in the hope that Yahweh's
presence would turn defeat into victory—was captured, and its
priests were slain. The Philistines then proceeded to follow up their
advantage by occupying as much of Israel's territory as they could;
the shrine of Shiloh was destroyed, and Philistine garrisons were
placed at strategic points in the land. It was Israel's shameful
position that finally led to the demand for a king—and a king was
elected: Saul. But Saul's reign did not end auspiciously. Though he
won initial victories which gave to Israel a respite and new hope, he
soon became insanely jealous of the young hero, David, and ended his
career in mental disintegration, defeat, and tragic death. Israel was
once again at the mercy of the Philistines.

In this time of emergency, it was David who took hold of beaten
Israel and in a few short years transformed it into the dominant
power in all of Palestine and Syria. Again, we cannot dwell on the
details of David's brilliant career. Suffice it to say that he united
Israel in his person as it had never been united before. With his tough
little army he broke the power of the Philistines, drove them back
into a narrow strip along the seacoast, and confined them there; they
would never be a serious menace to Israel again. Indeed, Philistine
mercenaries thereafter formed the core of David's professional
soldiery. Early in his reign David took the Jebusite city of Jerusalem
and, since he did so with his own personal troops, it became his
personal holding; David then made the city his capital. Meanwhile,
other Canaanite cities up and down the land, most of which had
apparently been under Philistine domination, likewise came under
David's control.

As a matter of fact, David actually completed the conquest of
Canaan. Though Israel had occupied Palestine some two centuries
earlier, a careful reading of the books of Joshua and Judges makes it

[1] For the details, and for further literature, the interested reader is referred to my
book, *A History of Israel* (Philadelphia: The Westminster Press; London: SCM Press,
2d ed., 1972); see Ch. 5.

clear that this occupation had been far from complete. Actually, Israelite holdings were confined to the central mountain range of western Palestine and the highlands east of the Jordan. Israel had never been able to master the Coastal Plain or the Plain of Esdraelon, while even in the mountains a number of Canaanite enclaves (such as Jerusalem) remained out of Israelite control. Under David all this was changed; every inch of Palestinian soil was now Israel—or under Israelite domination.

More than this, David went on to win a considerable foreign empire. The Transjordanian states—Moab, Edom, and Ammon—were conquered, as were the Aramean states of southern and central Syria, while the kingdom of Hamath, still farther to the north along the Orontes River, yielded tribute. In the end, David ruled a domain which reached from the Gulf of Aqabah and the Sinai desert in the south to the center of Syria in the north, with his control extending northeastward along the caravan routes across the Syrian desert as far as the Euphrates River. What had been in one generation a loose confederation of tribes ground under the heel of a foreign oppressor had in the next become a sizable empire. A new Israel had emerged.

2. What is more, David was able to found a dynasty: he passed his power on to his son. This was a new thing in Israel. The Judges of old had been charismatic leaders, men inspired by the spirit of Yahweh, who came to the fore in times of emergency and rallied the clans to battle. The charisma was their only badge of leadership; the emergency over, none had ruled Israel as a king, still less had any attempted to pass his power on to his son.[2] Saul, too, had risen like the Judges before him; the spirit of Yahweh had rushed upon him and, under the impulse of the divine fury, he had assumed the leadership and called out the clans to battle (I Sam. 11:6 f.). In his case, to be sure, there was a difference in that he was anointed by the prophet Samuel and acclaimed by the people as king: his authority was recognized as permanent. But he, too, could not pass his power on to his son. True, after his death, the attempt was made to set up his son Eshbaal (Ish-bosheth) as king in his place. But the people, apparently because they saw in Eshbaal no evidence of charismatic gifts, never followed him, and soon went over to David, whom they

---

[2] The case of Abimelech, the son of Gideon, who had himself made king after his father's death (Judg., ch. 9), is no exception. Abimelech did not rule all the tribes of Israel, but was a city-state king after the Canaanite pattern. Moreover, his reign was brief and ended in failure. Nor is there anything in the text to suggest that Gideon desired his son to act as he did, or encouraged him to do so.

regarded as God's designated leader. The principle of dynastic succession was not recognized.

With David it was different. It had to be! The structure he had built was so much his personal achievement, and so centered in his person, that only an heir could hold it together. One must recall that the union of Judah (which David already ruled) with northern Israel (which Eshbaal had claimed) was a union in the person of David. The United Monarchy in Israel was a dual monarchy. Moreover, the capital city, Jerusalem, had been taken by David's personal troops and belonged to David personally: it was "David's city" (cf. II Sam. 5:7). And the other Canaanite cities of the land which had come under Israelite control gave their allegiance not to the tribes of Israel, but to the crown. The backbone of Israel's fighting force came increasingly to consist of professional soldiers, and these were responsible, through their commanding officer, to the king personally. It was thanks chiefly to these professional troops that David's foreign empire was won and held; the various conquered territories in the empire were governed by the crown and yielded tribute to the crown, not to the tribes of Israel. It must soon have become evident to all that, if David should die, only an heir could hold such a patchwork structure together.

Probably the majority of Israelites understood this, and acquiesced in it. Certainly not all of them *liked* it. But by the time David grew old, the question was really no longer *whether* a son would succeed him, but *which* son would. And though Solomon took the throne through palace intrigue, and without any real pretense of charismatic gifts, the people seem to have accepted him. After all, the empire had to be held together, and through dynastic succession it *was* held together. And because it was, Israel entered her golden age of wealth, power, and glory. We cannot dwell on Solomon's many achievements: in the realm of international relations, in industry, commerce and trade, his lavish building programs, the cultural flowering that accompanied his reign. Suffice it to say that he reaped the fruits of David's achievement. His reign brought to Israel a material prosperity and a physical security such as she had never dreamed of before, and was never to know again. And though his stupidly harsh policies alienated many of his subjects and hastened the day when the proud structure would collapse, the achievement had been so impressive, so dazzling, that many in Israel regarded the continuance of the Davidic dynasty as both a necessity—and the will of God.

3. But far the most significant—and enduring—achievement of the monarchy lay in the realm of religion. Once again, David began it. Early in his reign, David brought the Ark of the Covenant—which, since the Philistines had captured it more than a generation previously, had lain neglected at Kiryat-yearim—with great ceremony and rejoicing to Jerusalem and established it in a tent-shrine erected for the purpose there (II Sam., ch. 6). As one of the two chief priests of the new shrine he appointed Abiathar, a descendant of the house of Eli, which had ministered before the Ark in the shrine of Shiloh. (The other was Zadok, whose origins are obscure.) This action of David's was both politically wise and of incalculable significance. The Ark, the portable throne of the invisible Deity, had been the focal point of the old tribal league, the symbol of God's presence among his people. In bringing it to Jerusalem, David made that city the religious, as well as the political, capital of his realm and, what is more, forged a link between the newly created state and Israel's ancient order which enabled him to advertise the state as the legitimate successor of the tribal league and the patron and protector of the sacred institutions of the past. His action must have served to bind the affections of large numbers of his people to Jerusalem in a way that we can hardly imagine.

Solomon, of course, put the seal on this when he replaced the tent-shrine with his magnificent Temple. It must be realized that in all of the ancient Orient the temple was conceived of as the house—the palace—of the god. So it was in Israel too. The Temple was the earthly palace of the heavenly King where, enthroned in the awful darkness of the inner sanctuary, the Holy of Holies, he dwelt among his people, ruling them and protecting them. To be sure, sophisticated Israelites did not suppose that Yahweh was physically present in the Temple. Indeed, later theologians were so concerned to combat such a notion that they avoided speaking of Yahweh as dwelling in the Temple, but rather spoke of him as having caused his "name" to dwell there (so especially in the Deuteronomic corpus of literature). One sees this clearly in the prayer (I Kings 8:22–53) said to have been offered by Solomon at the dedication of the Temple (which consistently speaks of the Temple as a house for Yahweh's "name") where the king cries out:

> (I Kings 8:27) But will God indeed dwell on the earth? Behold, heaven and the highest heaven cannot contain thee; how much less this house which I have built!

Nevertheless it was believed that Yahweh was really present in the Temple. We read that, when it was dedicated, the glory of Yahweh, symbolized by a great cloud (of smoke?) filled the house to the extent that the priests could not stand and perform their duties (I Kings 8:10 f.): Yahweh had in a real, if not in a literal, sense taken up his residence there. Then we read (vs. 12 f.) how Solomon said:

> I Kings 8:12   Yahweh has set the sun in the heavens,[3]
>   But has said that he would dwell
>   in thick darkness.
>   13   I have built thee a lofty house,
>   A place for thee to dwell forever.

The Temple was intended to serve as a permanent dwelling place for Yahweh.

But if this be so, does it not follow that Yahweh has taken the initiative in all of this? The ancient mind would certainly have reasoned so. How could it possibly be otherwise? Is it really possible that God could have been seized by the collar, as it were, brought to Jerusalem, and then installed in a new house *against* his will? Unthinkable! If God really dwells in this place, it is because he first indicated through some prophetic oracle or sign his desire to do so. It is because he *wills* to dwell in this place, has chosen it as his abode.

4. Of course, we are not to suppose that everyone in Israel approved of the changes that the monarchy brought. Changes as radical as these inevitably evoked tensions, and the monarchy never succeeded in overcoming them. There was tension with the very notion of dynastic kingship, which many, especially in northern Israel, were not prepared to accept. There was tension over the growing power of the crown and the loss of individual and tribal freedom, as well as a continuing tension between the claims of the house of David and those of the house of Saul, many of whose adherents believed that David had cynically tried to exterminate them. And, not least, there was tension between northern and southern Israel, a tension always latent which Solomon's harsh policies aggravated beyond endurance. And more. And it was in good part because it could not resolve these tensions that the Israelite Empire did not long endure. Sons of men who had helped to build it lived to see its collapse. As soon as Solomon was dead the whole structure fell apart, to be replaced by two petty states of third-rate importance. The glories of the empire became no more than a fond memory, a memory that with

---

[3] The colon is added on the basis of LXX; cf. RSV.

the passage of time receded ever farther and farther into the past.

Yet David's achievement had been so brilliant that it impressed itself indelibly on the minds of his people and was never forgotten. David himself was transfigured in the national memory; his many sins forgotten, he came to be remembered as the ideal king, the embodiment of all that a king ought to be, one who was in every respect pleasing in the sight of God. It is understandable that it should have been so. Not only did David bring Israel to heights of power and glory undreamed of before and only to be dreamed of afterward; all the land by the wildest stretch of imagination thought of as "promised," "from the river of Egypt to the great river, the river Euphrates" (Gen. 15:18), was for the first and last time in Israel's control. Israel was for the first and last time a great and mighty nation "like the sand on the seashore" in number (22:17). It must have seemed to many in Israel that the promises of God to Abraham, Isaac, and Jacob had at last been fulfilled, and amply fulfilled, in great David.[4] And if Israelites might view the Davidic Empire as the fulfillment of the promises to the fathers, might they not also look to the God of the promises, whose earthly habitation was in their midst on Mt. Zion, to continue to protect them and bless them, and grant them a glorious future?

II

In view of what has just been said, it is scarcely surprising that a theology—or, as some might prefer to say, an ideology—should have grown up about Jerusalem and David which soon became official in the cult of the Jerusalem Temple. This, too, was a theology associated with the word "covenant." It combined within itself two related complexes of ideas, both of which, we may believe, were given shape by David's great achievement. On the one hand, it was believed that Yahweh had chosen Mt. Zion as the seat of his earthly rule, there to dwell among his people forever and protect them from their foes; and it was likewise believed that he had chosen David as his designated king and had promised him through an everlasting covenant that his dynasty would never end. True, kings were

---

[4] The Yahwist apparently felt so, as we have said. And note how the author of I Kings 4:20 f., in describing the reign of Solomon (who, as we said, reaped the fruits of David's achievement), says that "Judah and Israel were as many as the sand by the sea" (cf. Gen. 22:17), and then adds that Solomon ruled all the kingdoms from the Euphrates to the border of Egypt (cf. Gen. 15:18).

expected to rule justly, and otherwise to obey the divine commandments, and there is the explicit warning that if a king should fail to
do this he would bring chastisement on himself and his people. But no
conditions attached to the promise itself: the dynasty would be
eternal. God would never take his gracious favor from it but would,
on the contrary, give it victory over all of its foes, and a wide domain,
with the kings of the earth fawning at its feet.

1. This theology seems to have established itself early. The Zion
tradition is assuredly very old, it being widely believed among
scholars that it had its roots in the cult of pre-Israelite Jerusalem.[5] In
any event, David's transfer of the Ark to Jerusalem, followed by
Solomon's erection of the Temple there, must inevitably have given
rise to the belief that Yahweh had chosen Mt. Zion as his abode. The
belief in Yahweh's election of David and his house is likewise old. It
is given classical expression in the well-known oracle of Nathan to
David found in II Sam. 7:1-17. Here we read how David, who had
already built a palace for himself in Jerusalem, conceived the idea of
building a temple for Yahweh. He consulted with Nathan the
prophet, who at first—whether out of genuine enthusiasm for the
project or, as seems more likely, out of deference to the king's
wishes—gave his assent. But then, having received in the night a
word from Yahweh, Nathan must go back to the king and command
him to desist, reminding him that up until then Yahweh had always
had a tent as his dwelling place and had never requested anyone to
build him a fine house of cedar. In effect, Nathan says that David has
gotten matters reversed. He had wanted to build Yahweh a house
when, in fact, it is Yahweh who will build him a house (v. 11): His son
will succeed him and his dynasty will endure forever (vs. 12, 14–16):

(II Sam. 7:12) When your days are finished and you lie down with your
fathers, I will raise your offspring after you, who shall come forth from
your own body, and I will establish his kingdom.[6] (v. 14) I will be his
father, and he shall be my son. If he commits iniquity, I will chasten him
with the rod of men, with the stripes of the sons of men; (v. 15) but I will
not take my gracious favor[7] from him, as I took it from Saul, whom I

---

[5] But unfortunately we know very little about this cult. Recently J. J. M. Roberts
(JBL, 92 [1973], pp. 329–344) has advanced strong arguments for finding the original
setting of the Zion tradition in the Davidic-Solomonic Empire. (Relevant literature on
the subject is referred to in this article.)

[6] We omit v. 13, which says that this son will build a house for Yahweh. This verse
may belong to a later stratum of the tradition; cf. JB.

[7] So with LXX, certain other Vrs., and I Chron. 17:13; MT, "my gracious favor shall
not depart."

removed from before you. (v. 16) Your house and your kingdom shall be made sure forever before me;[8] your throne shall be established forever.

It is true that the date and literary history of this passage is a much-debated question. Some scholars regard it as a mixed composition that was given its present form at a relatively late date, while others believe that it comes substantially from the tenth century.[9] We cannot debate the matter here. But though it seems certain that the piece has received editing at the hands of those writers who gave us the Deuteronomic historical corpus (Joshua through Kings), there is little reason to doubt that it develops an ancient nucleus which in all likelihood is as old as the days of David or Solomon.[10] Be that as it may, the belief that Yahweh had chosen David and made a covenant with him is certainly very old. We find it mentioned in the archaic poem in II Sam. 23:1–7, the so-called "Last Words of David," which is in all probability of tenth-century date.[11] In this poem David appears as the speaker, and in v. 5 he says:

II Sam. 23:5   Yes, surely my house is right with God ('$\bar{E}l$)
Yes, an eternal covenant he has made with me.[12]

The permanency and the legitimacy of the Davidic line seems to have been generally accepted in Judah, and with little question. The very fact that throughout the entire history of the Southern Kingdom no attempt to overthrow the Davidic dynasty was ever made[13] (contrast the many and violent dynastic changes in northern Israel) would seem to indicate that, even in the earliest days of the monarchy in Judah, the belief had entrenched itself that only a Davidic king might legitimately rule. An unpopular king might be assassinated, but the

---

[8] So with some MSS., LXX; MT, "before you."

[9] Among those who take the latter position, cf. M. Noth, "David and Israel in II Samuel VII" (*The Laws in the Pentateuch and Other Studies* [Eng. tr., Edinburgh and London: Oliver & Boyd, 1966; Philadelphia: Fortress Press, 1967], pp. 250–259); A. Weiser, "Die Tempelbaukrise unter David" (ZAW, 77 [1965], pp. 153–168).

[10] Cf. especially the treatment of F. M. Cross, *Canaanite Myth and Hebrew Epic* (Cambridge, Mass.: Harvard University Press, 1973), pp. 241–264 (p. 241, n. 95, for further literature on the subject). Cross makes clear the extent of Deuteronomistic editing, but sees an ancient poetic oracle as underlying the present prose form.

[11] A number of scholars have defended this date; most recently, Cross, *Canaanite Myth and Hebrew Epic*, pp. 234–237.

[12] It is uncertain whether the second colon speaks of an "eternal covenant" or not, for it could equally well be translated, "Yes, the Eternal ('$\bar{O}l\bar{a}m$) has made a covenant with me"; cf. Cross, *Canaanite Myth and Hebrew Epic*, p. 236. I had earlier heard D. N. Freedman make the same point orally.

[13] The case of Athaliah (II Kings, ch. 11) is no exception. She usurped the throne by criminal violence and apparently had very little support among her subjects, for she was removed from the throne and put to death at the earliest opportunity.

people would immediately take his son, even if only a child, and place
him on the throne; Judahites found it unthinkable that any but a
Davidide should sit there.

It was, indeed, through this theology of kingship that the institution of dynastic monarchy, a thing totally foreign to earlier Israelite
tradition, was integrated with Israel's normative faith. Divine
designation and charismatic gifts, the principle upon which leadership
had been selected in earlier times, had, in theory, been transferred to
the Davidic dynasty in perpetuity.[14] The king ruled as Yahweh's
deputy, the earthly representative of the heavenly King. He was
Yahweh's "anointed" (Ps. 2:2; 18:50; 20:6), his "son" (Ps. 2:7; II Sam.
7:14)—not of course in a physical, but in an adoptive, sense—his
"first-born" (Ps. 89:27), his rule given legitimacy by Yahweh's
unconditional promise to David.

2. The belief that Yahweh had chosen Mt. Zion as his permanent
abode, and had promised to David a dynasty that would never end,
was affirmed in the cult of the Jerusalem Temple and became, indeed,
a central feature in the official theology of the monarchy in Judah.
This is evidenced by the fact that it finds expression in various of the
psalms which were composed for use on certain solemn festal
occasions which were celebrated in the cult of the Temple. Notable
among these are the so-called Royal Psalms.[15] These Psalms, which
are of various types, cannot be dated with precision but, since all of
them have the king as their central figure, they may confidently be
assumed to be of pre-exilic origin. They therefore provide us, as it
were, with a window looking in upon beliefs with regard to kingship
that were held in the days of the monarchy in Judah.

Of all the Royal Psalms, the one most closely parallel to the oracle
of Nathan, mentioned above, is Psalm 89. This psalm, which is a long
one, falls into three well-defined parts. It opens with a hymn (vs.
1–18) extolling the might and the faithfulness of Yahweh as creator
and lord of the universe; then follows a lengthy section (vs. 19–37)
recapitulating the promises he has made to David and his dynasty;
and finally there is a bitter lament (vs. 38–51) occasioned by some
disaster that has befallen the nation.[16] The motif of the covenant

---

[14] Cf. A. Alt, "The Monarchy in the Kingdoms of Israel and Judah" (*Essays on Old
Testament History and Religion* [Eng. tr., Oxford: Basil Blackwell, 1966], pp. 239–259);
see pp. 256 f.

[15] See Ps. 2; 18; 20; 21; 45; 72; 89; 101; 110; 132; 144. Though we can touch upon only
a few of these psalms here, the reader would do well to study them all carefully. Cf.
Keith R. Crim, *The Royal Psalms* (Richmond: John Knox Press, 1962), for an excellent
introduction.

[16] It is not necessary to identify this disaster with the fall of Jerusalem in 587 B.C.,
and to assign to the psalm—or at least its concluding portion—an exilic or post-exilic

with David appears in all three of these parts and is the thread that binds them together. It appears in the prelude to the hymn, where the speaker (perhaps a priest) cites words spoken by Yahweh himself:

> Ps. 89:3   I have made a covenant with my chosen one,
>   Have sworn to David my servant:
>   4   "I will establish your line forever,
>   Will build your throne for all generations."

The same motif underlies the concluding lament, for the disaster the nation had suffered had made it seem that the covenant with David had been voided (cf. v. 39). But it is in the middle section that the theology of the Davidic covenant receives its clearest, most extended, and most confident expression. Here the speaker (very probably the king) recalls and recapitulates a prophetic revelation through which Yahweh had made known his sure promises to David and his dynasty:

> Ps. 89:19   Then you spoke in a vision
>   to your faithful one, and said:
>   "I have made a lad to rule over the warrior,[17]
>   Have exalted a youth above the people.
>   20   I have found David my servant,
>   With my holy oil have anointed him."

Then (vs. 21–23) Yahweh goes on to promise David that he will always be with him to strengthen him, so that no enemy can get the better of him, for he, Yahweh, will strike down all who oppose him. The oracle then continues:

> Ps. 89:24   My faithfulness and gracious favor will be with him;
>   In my name will his horn be exalted.
>   25   I will set his hand on the sea,
>   His right hand on the river.[18]
>   26   He shall cry to me, "My Father art thou,
>   My God, the Rock of my salvation."
>   27   As for me, I will make him my first-born,
>   The highest of the kings of the earth.

---

date, as many commentators have done. Though the king has clearly suffered defeat and humiliation, there is nothing tangible to indicate that he has been taken prisoner and carried into exile together with his people. A pre-exilic date is preferable; cf. A. Weiser, *The Psalms* (Eng. tr., OTL, 1962), p. 591; H.-J. Kraus, *Die Psalmen* (BKAT, 1961), p. 617.

[17] On the translation of this colon, cf. Cross, *Canaanite Myth and Hebrew Epic*, p. 258.

[18] Perhaps we should have written "Sea" and "River" (with capitals) in this verse, for we probably have an allusion to the myth of the warrior god vanquishing the watery chaos. In the Ugaritic texts Baal gained his eternal dominion by conquering "Sea" and "River"; cf. M. Dahood, *Psalms II* (AB, 1968), p. 317.

28   My gracious favor I will keep for him always,
      My covenant with him shall stand firm.
29   I will establish his line forever,
      His throne as the days of heaven.

Then, as in the oracle of Nathan, there follows the warning that if a
king should disobey Yahweh's commandments, he will receive chastisement; but the promise of the eternity of the dynasty is reaffirmed
unconditionally—and in the strongest language:

Ps. 89:30   If his children forsake my law
             And do not follow my decrees,
      31   If they violate my statutes,
             And do not keep my commandments,
      32   I will punish their rebellion with the rod,
             Their iniquity with the whip;
      33   But my gracious favor I will not remove from him,
             Nor be false to my faithfulness.
      34   I will not violate my covenant,
             Nor alter what passed from my lips.
      35   Once for all I have sworn by my holiness;
             Never would I lie to David.
      36   His line shall continue forever,
             His throne like the sun before me,
      37   Like the moon established forever,
             Standing firm while the skies endure.[19]

Those are strong words. Nor are they to be dismissed as mere
hyperbole, for they were *believed*. The Davidic dynasty would endure
forever, secure in the promises of God who is both mighty and true to
his word.

In Psalm 78 the double theme of Yahweh's choice of Mt. Zion as his
permanent abode and of his election of David as king finds an
unusually clear expression. This is not a Royal Psalm but a long
reflection on the history of God's dealings with his people beginning
with the deliverance from Egypt and culminating in David.[20] It tells
how God had given his covenant and law to his people and had
repeatedly done marvelous things in their behalf in bringing them

---

[19] The reading of this colon is uncertain. MT has, "a witness in the skies (clouds)
standing firm," which does not fit the context very well. The reading adopted (and cf.
RSV) involves the alteration of but two letters.

[20] O. Eissfeldt has argued that Ps. 78 dates to the tenth century, before the division
of the monarchy; cf. *Das Lied Moses Deuteronomium 32:1–43 und das Lehrgedicht
Asaphs Psalm 78 samt einer Analyse der Umgebung des Mose-Liedes* (Berlin:
Akademie-Verlag, 1958). The psalm is in any case pre-exilic.

from bondage and preserving them in the desert, but how the people
had just as repeatedly rewarded him with ingratitude and rebellion
and had again and again incurred his wrath. Even after he had
settled them safely in their land their rebellion continued; disobeying
his commandments, they worshiped on high places and bowed down
to graven images (vs. 56–58). The psalm then continues:

> Ps. 78:59   God heard and was enraged;
>   He rejected Israel completely.
>   60   He forsook his dwelling in Shiloh,
>   The tent where he dwelt among men,
>   61   Handed over his might to captivity,
>   His glory to the clutch of the foe.
>   62   To the sword he consigned his people,
>   On his heritage vented his rage.

The allusion to the fall of Shiloh and the loss of the Ark to the
Philistines is unmistakable.[21] But be it noted that, to the mind of the
psalmist, the Philistines did not simply overpower Israel and capture
the Ark. God himself caused the defeat of his people and of his own
volition handed the Ark over to the foe; and they were able to take
and destroy Shiloh only because he had himself first abandoned it.

But the psalm does not end on this doleful note. Rather, it tells
how God once again roused himself and acted in behalf of his people.
And it is with this that the psalm reaches its climax: God's choice of
Mt. Zion as his new and permanent dwelling place, and his election of
David as king.

> Ps. 78:67   He rejected the tent of Joseph,
>   He chose not the tribe of Ephraim.
>   68   He chose the tribe of Judah,
>   Mt. Zion, which he loved.
>   69   He built his shrine like high heaven,
>   Like the earth, which he founded forever.
>   70   He chose David his servant,
>   And took him away from the sheepfolds;
>   71   From tending the ewes he brought him
>   To shepherd Jacob his people,
>   Israel his heritage.
>   72   And with singleness of mind he tended them,
>   With a skillful hand he led them.

---

[21] "His glory" and "his might" (v. 61) refer to the Ark; cf., e.g., "The Ark of thy
might" in Ps. 132:8.

Be it noted once again that though David erected the tent-shrine that first received the Ark in Jerusalem, and though Solomon built the Temple that replaced it, to the psalmist's mind it was God himself who built the Temple, and (the language is borrowed from the world of myth) as a copy of his dwelling place in the heights of heaven. And David did not owe his rise to the throne to good fortune or cleverness; God himself brought him all the way from the sheepfold to that position because he had chosen him.

The same two motifs likewise find expression in Psalm 132, albeit in a somewhat different context. The psalm seems to be very old.[22] It celebrates David's bringing of the Ark to Jerusalem, and it may have served, though it is impossible to be certain, as the text for the ritual reenactment of this event, in the course of which the Ark was carried in procession to its new home.[23] In any event, it apparently served as part of the liturgy for some festal occasion—probably the great autumnal feast at the New Year—a central feature of which was the cultic reaffirmation of Yahweh's election of David and his line as rulers forever and his coming to Mt. Zion to take up his permanent residence there. The psalm begins with David's expression of concern for the homeless Ark and his determination not to rest until he had provided for it an appropriate shrine.

Ps. 132:1   Remember, Yahweh, of David
        All his pious devotion;[24]
    2   How he swore to Yahweh,
        Made a vow to the Champion of Jacob,
    3   "I will not enter my canopied room,
        Nor mount my cushioned bed;[25]
    4   I will give my eyes no sleep,
        Nor my eyelids[26] slumber,
    5   Till I find a place for Yahweh,
        A dwelling for the Champion of Jacob."

---

[22] Archaic features have been pointed out by M. Dahood (*Psalms III* [AB, 1970], pp. 241 f.), who dates the psalm to the tenth century, and by F. M. Cross (*Canaanite Myth and Hebrew Epic*, p. 97, n. 24). On the basis of these and certain ideas that it expresses (see further below), Cross argues that the piece had its origin in the cult of David's day, though later adapted for use in the royal cult of the Temple (*ibid.*, pp. 233 f.).

[23] On the point, cf. D. R. Hillers, "Ritual Procession of the Ark and Ps. 132" (CBQ, 30 [1968], pp. 48–55), who finds such a procession neither proved nor disproved.

[24] Pointing the last word as '*anwātō* following LXX ("his humility"). But perhaps "his piety," "his pious devotion" would catch the force better; cf. Hillers, "Ritual Procession of the Ark and Ps. 132," p. 53.

[25] The translation of this verse follows Cross, *Canaanite Myth and Hebrew Epic*, p. 244.

[26] Perhaps better, "pupils"; cf. Dahood, *Psalms III*, p. 244.

Then, apparently, a search had to be made, for it seems that in the tradition behind Psalm 132 the whereabouts of the Ark was unknown. In this the psalm differs from the account in I Sam. 7:1 f. and II Sam., ch. 6. There we read that when the Philistines released the Ark, it was brought to Kiryat-yearim and placed in the house of one Abinadab, where it remained for some twenty years until David sent to get it; there is no hint that its location was not well known.[27] But in the psalm a search is made, and the Ark is found at Kiryat-yearim.[28] Whereupon the worshipers proceed thither and prostrate themselves before it.

> Ps. 132:6   Look! We heard of it in Ephratah,
> We found it in the fields of Yaar.
> 7   Let us go to his dwelling,
> Let us worship at his footstool.

They then beg Yahweh to come with them to the new dwelling place that has been prepared for him. In its original reference, this would have been the tent-shrine erected by David, but in later years, as the psalm was used in the royal cult, it would have been understood as the Temple.

> Ps. 132:8   Arise, Yahweh, to thy resting place,[29]
> Thou and the Ark of thy might.
> 9   Let thy priests be clothed with righteousness,
> Thy devout ones shout for joy.
> 10   For the sake of David thy servant
> Refuse not thy anointed king.

This last has an almost wheedling tone, as if the speaker were saying: "Please, Yahweh, don't disappoint us! Don't say you won't come!" Yet the plea was necessary, for to the ancient's mind it would have been unthinkable to move the Ark, Yahweh's portable throne and symbol of his presence, from one place to another unless Yahweh had

[27] On these differing traditions, cf. Cross, *Canaanite Myth and Hebrew Epic*, pp. 96 f.

[28] "The fields of Yaar" ("the fields of the forest") in v. 6 can only be a name for Kiryat-yearim ("the town of the forests"). Whether Ephratah refers to Bethlehem, as various scholars believe, or is the name of a clan in the vicinity of Kiryat-yearim, cannot be debated here. But the latter seems far more likely; cf. Cross, *Canaanite Myth and Hebrew Epic*, pp. 94 f., n. 16, for the evidence.

[29] Or, "from thy resting place." The preposition can be translated either way. Hillers ("Ritual Procession of the Ark and Ps. 132," pp. 49–51) gives strong arguments for reading "from," and he is followed in this by Cross (*Canaanite Myth and Hebrew Epic*, p. 95, n. 20). I am unable to reach a decision. If it is "from," Yahweh is begged to leave his temporary abode at Kiryat-yearim; if "to," he is invited to go to David's new shrine in Jerusalem (the same word, "resting place," is used for it in v. 14).

first, through some oracle or sign, given his permission. To gain that permission was therefore of vital concern. But permission was granted, for there follows a reiteration of Yahweh's sure promise to David. But with a difference! The continuance of the dynasty is made subject to conditions!

> Ps. 132:11   Yahweh has sworn to David
>   An oath which he will not break:
>   "One of your very own sons
>   I will place upon your throne.
>   12   If your sons keep my covenant,
>   My stipulations which I teach them,
>   Their sons in turn forever
>   Will sit upon your throne."

In such a context this seems surprising, for it is quite unlike other formulations of the Davidic covenant such as those found in Nathan's oracle in II Samuel, ch. 7, and in Psalm 89. There, though it is explicitly stated that a disobedient king will bring severe chastisement upon himself, the continuance of the dynasty is affirmed without qualification. Here its continuance is made dependent upon obedience to the stipulations of Yahweh's covenant. The reason for this may well be that the psalm in its original form stems from a very early stage in the development of the royal theology, before the later ideology of kingship with its notion of an unconditional decree granting the Davidic house an eternal rule had taken hold, and while the idea of a conditional decree of kingship still prevailed.[30] Even so, it is to be doubted that, as the psalm was used in the official cult of the Temple, worshipers felt the dynasty to be seriously threatened by this conditional element. For one thing, they could fall back on other formulations of the Davidic covenant where the continuance of the dynasty is explicitly assured. For another, they could probably tell themselves that through the elaborate cultus of the Temple, which the kings supported, whatever conditions might attach to the promises were being met. In any event, in the psalm in its present form the conditional element is somewhat blunted in that it is immediately followed by Yahweh's announcement of his choice of Mt. Zion as his eternal abode (vs. 13–16)—and this carries with it no conditions. And then (vs. 17 f.) further promises are extended to David: of prosperity, a continuing dynasty,[31] and victory over all his

---

[30] See the arguments of Cross, *Canaanite Myth and Hebrew Epic*, pp. 94–97, 232–234, etc. Cross dates the original poem, from which he excludes vs. 10, 13–18 (*ibid.*, p. 232, n. 56), to the reign of David.

[31] The "lamp" which Yahweh will trim for David (v. 17) is a metaphor for the

foes—and these too are without condition.

Ps. 132:13   For Yahweh has chosen Zion;
           He has wanted it for his home:
     14   "This is my resting place forever;
           Here I will dwell, for I have wanted it.
     15   I will richly bless her provisions;
           Her poor I will satisfy with food.
     16   Her priests I will clothe with salvation;
           Her devout ones will shout for joy.
     17   I will renew there the line of David,[32]
           Will trim a lamp for my anointed.
     18   His enemies I will clothe with shame,
           While on his head his crown will sparkle."

But although it was believed that the Davidic house had been guaranteed a perpetual rule through the promises of God, it was not expected that the king should rule arbitrarily or despotically. On the contrary, a lofty ideal of justice, especially justice toward the weak and helpless, was held before the king, to which it was hoped that he would conform. The king's obligation to rule justly, and actively to restrain evildoers, finds expression in various of the psalms (see, for example, Psalm 101, where the king announces that he will do this); but nowhere is this note sounded more clearly than in Psalm 72. This psalm is a prayer for the king, probably used as a part of the liturgy for the day of his enthronement. It begins:

Ps. 72:1   Give to the king thy judgments, O God,
         Thy righteousness to the royal son!
    2   May he judge[33] thy people with righteousness,
         Thy poor with justice!
    3   May the mountains bring peace to the people,
         And the hills righteousness!
    4   May he defend the poor of the people,
         Deliver the sons of the needy,
         And crush the oppressor!

Following this come prayers that the king might enjoy a long and

preservation of the dynasty; cf. I Kings 11:36; 15:4; II Kings 8:19, and the comments of Dahood, *Psalms III*, p. 248.

[32] A paraphrase following NEB; lit., "I will make a horn to sprout for David"—i.e., renew its prosperity. It is interesting that the verb "to sprout" is of the same root as the noun *ṣemaḥ*, which later became a title for the expected Messianic king; cf. Jer. 23:5; Zech. 3:8; 6:12.

[33] Or, "to judge (govern)"; i.e., "that he may . . ." (cf. LXX), and take the verse as the continuation of v. 1.

beneficent reign (vs. 5–7), and rule a vast domain with foreigners bringing him tribute (vs. 8–11; we shall return to this). Then (vs. 12–14) the king's concern for the helpless once again receives stress:

> Ps. 72:12 For he rescues the needy when he calls,
>   The distressed who has no protector.
>   13   He pities the weak and the needy,
>   And the lives of the needy he saves.
>   14   He redeems them from lawless oppression,
>   For their lives are precious to him.[34]

A noble ideal indeed! Would that all rulers were like that! Yet, lofty though it is, it is not an ideal that is impossible of fulfillment. Rather, it is one that an able and just ruler might conceivably live up to, at least with relative success. It is when we read vs. 8–11, alluded to above, that the prayer seems to outrun all reality:

> Ps. 72:8 May he rule from sea to sea,
>   From the River[35] to the ends of the earth!
>   9   May his foes[36] bow down before him,
>   His enemies lick the dust!
>   10   May the kings of Tarshish
>   and the isles render tribute,
>   The kings of Sheba and of Seba offer gifts!
>   11   May all kings pay him homage,
>   All nations render him service!

This does outrun reality—both present reality and anything that might reasonably be hoped for in the foreseeable future. May the king rule an empire as great as that of David and Solomon—and greater! May he rule a world empire! Tarshish lay perhaps in Spain, perhaps in Sardinia, whence the Phoenicians imported their copper; it was, in any event, at the western limit of the world within the ken of Biblical man. And Sheba was in southernmost Arabia, the fabled source of spices and incense, whence came the Queen of Sheba to visit Solomon (I Kings 10:1–10). When was there ever the remotest realistic hope that any king in little Judah would rule such an empire? Even allowing for conventional court language, and for Oriental

---

[34] Lit., "For precious is their blood in his sight."

[35] I.e., the Euphrates.

[36] The word (Heb., *ṣiyyîm*) denotes animals or demons of the desert; cf. Isa. 13:21; 34:14; Jer. 50:39; etc. Perhaps it is used here as a figure for the king's foes or, more specifically, the "desert dwellers." Various scholars emend to *ṣārāw* ("his foes"; and so RSV). We have adopted this translation for the sake of the parallelism, but with misgivings. LXX reads, "the Ethiopians" (and so NEB).

hyperbole, such words seem not short of fantastic. Certainly they pointed beyond existing realities to a future no human eye could see.

But if so grandiose a wish for the king is not to be found elsewhere in the Royal Psalms, the assurance of divine aid and protection is a constant feature. Again and again in these psalms the king is promised, or expresses the conviction, that God will deliver him from danger, give him victory over his foes, and cause foreign kings to come to him in submission. This note is sounded in Psalm 2, in Psalm 20, in Psalm 21, in Psalm 89, in Psalm 110, in Psalm 144—indeed in almost all of the Royal Psalms. But perhaps the best example is Psalm 18 (also to be found at II Samuel, ch. 22). The psalm appears to be an old one.[37] It is very long, and we cannot quote from it at length. But the reader will observe how, after an opening stanza of praise, the king tells how, in mortal danger, he cried to his God for help, and how God heard him from his Temple (vs. 4–6). He then tells how God intervened in an awe-inspiring theophany and saved him (vs. 7–19). Then, after speaking at length of the justice of God (vs. 20–30), he once again praises God for having trained him for war and sustained him, given him victory over all his foes, and caused foreign peoples to come cringing to him in submission (vs. 31–45). The psalm then concludes with further praise to Yahweh:

Ps. 18:50   Who gives his king great triumphs,
             Who shows to his anointed gracious favor,
             To David and his line forever.[38]

Kings in whose cult such a theology was affirmed, and who themselves took that theology seriously, certainly need not face the future with fear!

3. But it is not only in the Royal Psalms that we find expressions of that peculiar theology of election that was affirmed in the cult of the pre-exilic temple. There are other psalms as well. One thinks in particular of the so-called Hymns of Zion (especially Ps. 46; 48; 76), which, though precise dates cannot be assigned to them, seem to develop an ancient Jerusalem tradition.[39] In these psalms the king

---

[37] Cf. F. M. Cross and D. N. Freedman, "A Royal Song of Thanksgiving" (JBL, 72 [1953], pp. 15–34), who date the psalm not later than the ninth to eighth centuries. Cross now prefers a tenth-century date; cf. *Canaanite Myth and Hebrew Epic*, p. 123.

[38] Cross and Freedman ("A Royal Song of Thanksgiving," p. 34) doubt that this last colon was an original part of the hymn. But, even so, it may be assumed to have been added as the hymn was used in the cult of the pre-exilic Temple.

[39] Some scholars, it is true, deny this and place these psalms, and others of similar character, in the post-exilic period; e.g., G. Wanke, *Die Zionstheologie der Korachiten* (BZAW, 97, 1966). But this does not seem likely.

plays no role—indeed, is not even mentioned. But everywhere one sees expressed the unshakable assurance of God's presence in Zion, his chosen dwelling place, protecting his people from all danger.

It is with such a note of confident trust that Psalm 46 begins:

> Ps. 46:1   God is our refuge and strength,
> A well-tried help in time of trouble.
> 2   Therefore will we not fear though the earth
> give way,
> Though the mountains collapse in the depths
> of the sea,
> 3   Though its waters roar and foam,
> And the mountains quake with its heaving.

The ground of this confidence is Yahweh's presence in Zion, his chosen dwelling place (Ps. 76:2), the city which he has established forever (Ps. 48:8). The same thought is expressed in the strange language of Psalm 46:4:

> Ps. 46:4   There is a river whose streams make glad
> the city of God,
> Which the Most High has set apart as his dwelling.[40]

Manifestly the first colon is not to be taken literally, for Jerusalem, as everyone knows, has no river. Allusion can only be to the river of Paradise which appears in the Bible at Genesis 2:10–14, and in various texts describing the felicity that will obtain when God's saving purpose has triumphed on earth (e.g., Ezek. 47:1–12; Zech. 14:8; cf. Rev. 22:1): Jerusalem, as God's holy abode, is watered by the streams of Paradise. Similar language is found in Psalm 48:2, where Mt. Zion is described as being "in the far north" ("in the recesses of Zaphon"). Taken literally, this is a geographical absurdity, for Jerusalem is *not* in the far north—either of Palestine or of the world known to Old Testament man. But the language is once again drawn from the world of myth. Allusion is to the mythical mountain of the gods in the far north, the Mt. Zaphon which is known from the Ugaritic texts and mentioned at various places in the Bible (e.g., Isa. 14:13 f.; Ezek. 28:14–16).[41] The temple mountain, as God's chosen abode, *is* the holy mountain "in the far north."

Since God dwells on Mt. Zion, the people have nothing to fear. The

---

[40] Our reading follows LXX; cf. BHS. MT is obscure; RSV reads, "the holy habitation of the Most High."

[41] Cf. R. J. Clifford, *The Cosmic Mountain in Canaan and the Old Testament* (Cambridge, Mass.: Harvard University Press, 1972), esp. pp. 131–160.

nations may rage and storm, and close in on Jerusalem with fearsome power, but God intervenes and breaks them, and sends them reeling in rout. Indeed, he shatters their weapons, brings wars to an end, and shows himself to be all-powerful in the earth and his people's sure defender. This note is sounded in various of these psalms (Ps. 48:4–8; 76:1–6), but nowhere more clearly than in the concluding stanzas of Psalm 46 (cf. vs. 5–11):

Ps. 46:5 God is in her midst, she shall not be moved;
    God will help her by break of day.
  6 Nations rage, kingdoms totter;
    He loudly shouts, the earth melts.
  7 Yahweh of Hosts is with us,[42]
    The God of Jacob is our stronghold.

  8 Come and see what Yahweh has done,
    The marvels he has wrought upon earth.
  9 He stamps out wars to the earth's farthest bounds;
    He breaks the bow, he snaps the spear,
    And casts the shields[43] in the fire.
 10 Be still and know that I am God,
    Exalted above the nations,
    Exalted over the earth.
 11 Yahweh of Hosts is with us,
    The God of Jacob is our stronghold.

Such affirmations, insofar as they were truly believed, must have given to the nation an enormous sense of security, an abounding confidence in the future. God has chosen Mt. Zion as his dwelling place, and he will never abandon it to its foes. Let the nation but entrust itself to this God and face the future without fear. As the psalmist expresses it (Ps. 48:12–14):

Ps. 48:12 Go around Zion, walk about her,
    Number her towers,
 13 Take note of her ramparts,
    Pass her citadels in review,
 14 That you may tell the next generation
    That this is God,
    Our God for ever and ever.
    He will be our guide for ever.

---

[42] The refrain, "Yahweh of Hosts is with us" (*yhwh ṣᵉbā'ōt 'immānū*), which concludes the last two stanzas of the hymn (vs. 7 and 11) and may originally have concluded the first, reminds one of the name of the royal child Immanuel (*'immānū 'ēl*) announced by Isaiah (Isa. 7:10–17).

[43] So with various commentators (and cf. NEB and JB) following LXX. MT apparently reads "chariots."

III

There are, of course, still other psalms that allow us to see features
of the beliefs held by the worshiping community in Judah in the days
of the monarchy. But these must suffice. They make it clear that the
belief that Yahweh had chosen Mt. Zion as his permanent abode,
there to dwell among his people and defend them from their foes, and
that he had promised to David a dynasty that would never end, was
officially affirmed in the cult of the Jerusalem Temple and, we may
suppose, firmly entrenched in the minds of large segments of the
population.

1. Now it will be evident that, in its essential features, the
covenant with David follows the pattern of the patriarchal covenant.[44] To be sure, there are differences, and these are perhaps not
unimportant. Most noteworthy is the fact that the obligations laid on
the recipient of covenant, which in the accounts of the Abrahamic
covenant are at best implicit, are in the case of the Davidic king
clearly and explicitly stated. The king was obligated to do justice (as
all ancient kings in theory were) and otherwise to obey the divine
commands, and he was threatened with chastisement if he did not.
Nor was there any specification short of the fall of the dynasty as to
how severe that chastisement might be. Moreover, the king's
responsibility seems clearly to have been conceived of in terms of
Yahweh's covenant law, his statutes and his ordinances (Ps. 18:21 f.;
89:30 f.; etc.). The king did not rule autonomously or willfully, but as
God's deputy, responsible to the divine Suzerain for his conduct.
Nevertheless, stress falls upon the promises, and these are unconditional and without qualification. Though the divine chastisement
remains an ever-present possibility in the event of disobedience, the
dynasty will nevertheless continue. The nation is therefore secure
because God has so promised (II Sam. 7:15 f.; Ps. 89:33–37; etc.); he
may discipline both king and people, and discipline severely, but he
will never remove his gracious favor from the Davidic line or be false
to his promises. And in this God, and in these promises, the king (like
Abraham in Genesis 15:6 and elsewhere) was supposed to trust.

This note of trust is one that is struck again and again in the Royal
Psalms—for example in Psalm 21:7, where we read:

    Ps. 21:7   Yes, the king puts his trust in Yahweh;

---

[44] First pointed out, so far as I am aware, by G. E. Mendenhall, *Law and Covenant in
Israel and the Ancient Near East* (Pittsburgh: The Biblical Colloquium, 1955); cf. pp.
45 f.

> Through the gracious favor of
> the Most High he stands unshaken.

Or in Psalm 20, where the king is represented as saying:

> Ps. 20:6 Now I know that Yahweh saves his anointed;
> From his holy heaven he will answer him
> With mighty victories by his own right hand.
> 7 Some boast of chariots, some of horses;
> But we boast in the name of Yahweh our God.

This is a note that Isaiah will later play upon, as we shall see.

The nature of the historical relationship between the Abrahamic covenant and the Davidic remains a matter of dispute. In view of the limitations of the evidence available to us, this will probably continue to be the case. We cannot enter into the discussion here.[45] On the one hand, the belief that Yahweh had unconditionally promised the ancestors land and numerous posterity is certainly older than the monarchy—indeed, was very probably an original feature in the religion of the patriarchs themselves. The traditions of these promises were doubtless preserved and handed down at various places in Palestine (Hebron, etc.); with the rise of the Davidic state they became known in Jerusalem also, and they may well have influenced the theology of kingship that was developed there. But, on the other hand, it is evident that the accounts that we have in the Bible of God's promises to the ancestors were given literary form at a time later than David, and that they reflect and were shaped by his brilliant achievement. (As was noted above,[46] the dimensions of the land promised to Abraham in Genesis, ch. 15, correspond to the dimensions of the Davidic-Solomonic Empire at its greatest extent, rather than to the actual holdings of the Israelite tribes at an earlier period.) A reciprocal influence of the two traditions of covenant is in every way likely.

But, whatever their historical relationships may have been, it appears that in the course of time the Davidic covenant came to be viewed, in some circles at least, as no less than a renewal and extension of the promises to Abraham. This we may judge from certain allusions in the psalms. Whether or not we should lay weight on the fact that God is frequently referred to in the psalms as the

---

[45] For recent discussions of the subject, aside from Mendenhall (see preceding note), cf. R. E. Clements, *Abraham and David* (London: SCM Press, 1967), Ch. 5; Cross, *Canaanite Myth and Hebrew Epic*, Ch. IV:9 (esp. pp. 260–273).

[46] Cf. Ch. 1, p. 26.

"shield" of his people is uncertain. This is an epithet for the Deity that occurs numerous times in the psalm literature (in the Royal Psalms, cf. Ps. 18:2, 30; 144:2), while very rarely elsewhere; and it is the word by which God is described in Genesis 15:1 ("Fear not, Abram, I am your shield . . ." [47]). In any event, such a text as Psalm 47:9 ("The princes of the peoples gather with[48] the people of the God of Abraham") indicates that the traditions of Abraham occupied a place in the cult of the Jerusalem Temple, and that the universalism of the promises to him (Gen. 12:1–3; 22:18; etc.) had apparently been brought into connection with the royal ideology developed under the monarchy.[49] But it is in Psalm 72 that the case is clearest of all. Here at the end of the psalm—which is a prayer for the king—after petitions that the king might enjoy a long and beneficent reign, we read:

> Ps. 72:17   May men bless themselves by him,
> All nations call him blessed.

The allusion to the promise to Abraham in Genesis 12:1–3 ("By you will all the families of the earth bless themselves") is unmistakable. It is as if the psalmist were saying: May the sure promises of God to Abraham, Isaac, and Jacob, fulfilled in the giving of the land, and amply fulfilled in great David, be extended through David to this king who now takes the throne, and to every descendant of his who shall rule in Judah throughout all the future.

2. Such a theology must have enabled the nation—or at least such elements in the nation as were committed to it and affirmed it—to march toward the future with an unshakable confidence. Let it be repeated that this is not to be thought of as an eschatology, at least not in any proper sense of the word. It was not the expectation of a catastrophic divine intervention in the future, which would replace the present order with a new and better order and bring God's purpose in history to a triumphant conclusion. Rather, it was the cultic affirmation of an immutable reality, the expression of a sublime confidence in the permanence and ultimate triumph of the existing order. It affirmed that the promises of God, already made good in

---

[47] M. Dahood, *Psalms I* (AB, 1966), pp. 16–18, argues that the word should be translated as "your suzerain," "your benefactor"; cf. also Cross, *Canaanite Myth and Hebrew Epic*, p. 4, n. 4. Some have even surmised that "the Shield of Abraham" was the appellation of Abraham's God; cf. A. Alt, *The God of the Fathers* (Eng. tr., *Essays on Old Testament History and Religion* [Oxford: Basil Blackwell, 1966], pp. 1–77), p. 66.

[48] Cf. LXX.

[49] Cf. H.-J. Kraus, *Die Psalmen*, p. 353; Clements, *Abraham and David*, p. 64.

David, had been extended through him to every descendant of his who should sit on the throne of Judah, while time endures. The existing order of the nation was willed by God and founded by God; it is therefore secure forever in his immutable promises. Troubles, reversals, it may experience, but final catastrophe it need never fear, for God will never be false to his sure covenant with David.

One must agree that there are manifest dangers in such a theology. It called for implicit trust in the promises of God—and that is good. But trust can readily lapse into complacency—and apparently it did. As the sure promises of God to David were reaffirmed in the cult of the Temple, we may assume that the Sinaitic covenant with its stern stipulations tended to be thrust into the background.[50] To be sure, we cannot document this as we should like; but it was almost certainly the case. Certainly Isaiah and Micah were to face many people in Judah who were living in high disregard of covenant law, yet without any apparent thought that the future of the nation, or their own relationship to their God, might be endangered thereby. Enough that they brought lavish sacrifices to the Temple and paid homage to the God whose earthly habitation was there. Apparently they had little awareness of, or concern for, the stringent moral demands that their faith laid upon them. One must assume that they regarded their relationship to God, and the nation's future under God, as something based in the nature of things and to be taken for granted.

To be sure, we must not generalize about this. Not only were the traditions of exodus, wilderness wandering, and conquest, and of the covenant made in the desert with its stern stipulations, never forgotten either in Israel or in Judah;[51] there were parts of Israel where the theology of the Davidic covenant had never been accepted. This was emphatically true of northern Israel, where the claims of the Davidic house to rule in perpetuity had always been rejected. Indeed, the first king of northern Israel, Jeroboam, was obliged to set up a

---

[50] The relationship of the Davidic covenant to the Sinaitic is a disputed subject that cannot occupy us here. Significant discussions include L. Rost, "Davidsbund und Sinaibund" (ThLZ, 72 [1947], cols. 129–134); A. H. J. Gunneweg, "Sinaibund und Davidsbund" (VT, 10 [1960], pp. 335–341); H.-J. Kraus, *Worship in Israel* (rev. ed., 1962; Eng. tr., Oxford: Basil Blackwell; Richmond: John Knox Press, 1966), pp. 189–200; R. de Vaux, "Le Roi d'Israël, vassal de Yahvé" (1964, repr., *Bible et Orient* [Paris: Les Éditions du Cerf, 1967], pp. 287–301); R. E. Clements, *Prophecy and Covenant* (London: SCM Press, 1965), pp. 56–66; Cross, *Canaanite Myth and Hebrew Epic*, Ch. IV:9.

[51] Rost (*art. cit.* in preceding note) surely goes too far in suggesting that the Sinaitic covenant was of negligible importance in Judah until a relatively late date.

state cult of his own to counteract such notions and to give his rule legitimacy (I Kings 12:26–33). Not only did northern Israel reject the Davidic dynasty; it resisted the principle of dynastic succession as such, preferring that kings be selected by divine (prophetic) designation and popular acclamation, following the pattern of the kingship of Saul.[52] Only so can we explain the extreme instability of the monarchy in northern Israel, with its many revolutions and throne changes by violence,[53] in contrast with the situation in Judah, which stuck with the Davidic dynasty throughout its entire history. This feeling with regard to the proper way of selecting kings persisted in northern Israel until a relatively late date.[54] Attempts to establish a dynasty were repeatedly made, but none was permanently successful; only one (the dynasty of Jehu) lasted beyond the second generation.

Now we know too little of the official state cult of northern Israel to say very much about it. But it is probable that, insofar as it was not paganized, its ritual centered about the traditions of exodus and land-giving, the Sinaitic covenant and the tribal league. Certainly the Sinaitic tradition was very much alive in prophetic circles in northern Israel, as a reading of the stories of Elijah (cf. I Kings, ch. 19), as well as the prophecies of Hosea, makes clear. The traditions of the tribal league and its holy wars likewise lived on. (Note how a prophet rebuked King Ahab for not executing his enemy Ben-hadad, when he had captured him, in accordance with the rules of holy war [20:35–43]).

Yet, in spite of this, it seems that in northern Israel too the moral demands of the covenant had been widely forgotten. This is clear from the preaching of Amos and Hosea, to which we shall return. The traditions of exodus and conquest were cultically recited and feasts of covenant renewal were no doubt periodically held. But the whole concept of covenant seems to have been externalized and perverted. The feeling seems to have been general that its stringent

---

[52] On this point, cf. A. Alt, "The Monarchy in the Kingdoms of Israel and Judah" (*Essays on Old Testament History and Religion*, pp. 239–259). Alt's thesis has been criticized, but it seems to me that it is fundamentally correct.

[53] Note how Jeroboam, who had been designated by a prophet (I Kings 11:29–39) and acclaimed by the people (12:20), reigned throughout his life; but when his son Nadab attempted to succeed him, he was assassinated by Baasha, apparently with prophetic instigation (15:25–30). Baasha ruled until his death, but when his son Elah tried to succeed him, he was in turn assassinated, apparently again with prophetic prompting (16:1–10). The principle of dynastic succession was not recognized.

[54] Note how Jehu (ca. 842–815) struck to seize the throne after having been anointed by a prophet (II Kings 9:1–10) and acclaimed by the army (v. 13)—which last at least preserved the fiction of popular acclamation.

demands could be met by sacrifice and cultic observance alone; and, since this was being done, men could feel that the stipulations of covenant were being met, and the covenant bond maintained. The notion that the nation could, by its paganism and its crimes against justice, break covenant with Yahweh and come under his judgment seems not to have been entertained. The very theology of covenant, which should have been a warning to the nation, had become the earnest of its security as Yahweh's people: Yahweh is our God, and we are his people—and that will always be the case! As in the past, so in the future, he will come to our aid with his mighty acts, defend us from our foes, and secure us in the possession of the blessings promised to our fathers!

3. Such a view of the nation's relationship to its God, and its future under God, must inevitably lead to disappointment: it collided with harsh reality. The events of the ninth and eighth centuries must have placed it under a fearful strain. The great days of the Israelite Empire were now no more than a fond memory. Israel and Judah were two petty states, harassed by foes, at times invaded and humiliated; and finally they saw themselves menaced by the rising power of Assyria and threatened with total destruction. The ideal affirmed in the cult and present reality did not in the least correspond! Under such circumstances men could not be satisfied with a continuation of the existing state of affairs. They must reach out for a better future, a future that would amount to a radical improvement—if not the reversal—of the existing situation. There seems to have grown up—though we cannot document it in detail—a longing for the lost glories of the (idealized) past, and a yearning for a divine intervention that would recapture them, and perhaps exceed them. And to express this longing, men reached back to those factors in the national tradition in which confidence had originally inhered and projected them onto the future.

In Judah, quite naturally, this took the form of a yearning for the lost glories of David. There were many in Judah who, as Isaiah seems to have (Isa. 7:17), regarded the secession of northern Israel after the death of Solomon as the greatest calamity that had ever befallen the nation, and who longed for the time when the damage would be repaired and the empire once ruled by David would be recovered. It is possible that we see a reflection of such a hope in one of those short sayings near the end of The Book of Amos (Amos 9:11 f.) which, though its authorship is disputed, may well come from the eighth century (or even earlier).[55]

> Amos 9:11 "On that day I will raise up
> The tumble-down hut of David,[56]
> Will repair its yawning gaps,
> Raise up its ruins,
> And rebuild it as in the days of old;
> 12 That they may possess what is left of Edom
> And all the nations that are rightfully mine"—[57]
> Word of Yahweh, who will do this.

What had been the memory of an idealized past has become the pattern of hope for the future.

It was probably within this same context, too, that the hope for the day of Yahweh arose. As we noted above, this was an entrenched popular hope in northern Israel at least as far back as the eighth century (Amos 5:18–20). But it was alive in Judah too, for Isaiah likewise plays upon it (Isa. 2:6–22). The origins of the concept are obscure and have been much debated; we cannot enter into the discussion here. But von Rad is almost certainly correct that it reached back to the memory of the holy wars of the old tribal league when Yahweh would come to the aid of his people with awesome power and strike terror in the hearts of their foes, and it looked forward to the coming of another such day in the future.[58] It was the yearning for God to come again to the aid of his people with irresistible might, win them victory, and put things right again.

So it was that the very theology affirmed in the cult, and entrenched in the popular mind, must in the end point toward the future and engender the hope of a better day. This was not, let it be repeated, an eschatology in any proper sense of the word. The

---

[55] The passage is usually denied to Amos, but its genuineness has been defended by G. von Rad, *Old Testament Theology*, Vol. II (Eng. tr., Edinburgh and London: Oliver & Boyd; New York: Harper & Row, 1965), p. 138; cf. Clements, *Prophecy and Covenant*, p. 49; H. D. Preuss, *Jahweglaube und Zukunftserwartung* (BWANT, 7, 1968), pp. 140 f. One cannot be certain. But the passage certainly need not be of exilic or post-exilic date. It does not presuppose that the Davidic house has fallen, but only that it is in a most decrepit condition.

[56] Lit., "The hut of David that is falling," or ". . . is fallen." The participle can be translated either way.

[57] Lit., "And all the nations over which my name has been called." The expression has a legal background and denotes something or someone to which one lays legal claim. Here the nations once included in the Davidic empire are referred to.

[58] Cf. G. von Rad, "The Origin of the Concept of the Day of Yahweh" (JSS, 4 [1959], pp. 97–108); also *Old Testament Theology*, Vol. II, pp. 119–125. Cross (*Canaanite Myth and Hebrew Epic*, p. 111) sees in the day of Yahweh a wedding of the theme of holy war with that of the ritual reenactment of the conquest in the cultus.

expected day of Yahweh was not *the* final day, but *a* day: a day of God's intervention like the great days of the past (cf. "the day of Midian," Isa. 9:4; cf. 10:26). The popular expectation did not reach out for the consummation of the divine purpose in history, for some new order that God would create, but rather was the hope for a turning of fortune to the better, a putting of things back as they ideally should be and as they were cultically affirmed to be. This was not an eschatology; but the very traditions upon which the popular hope rested would profoundly shape the vision of God's decisive intervention, and his final provision for his people, as the prophets were given to see it. And to that we must now turn.

3

The Future in the Theology of
the Eighth-Century Prophets:
The Beginnings of Eschatology

U p to this point we have been dealing with the origins and background of eschatological expectations in Israel. So far we have spoken only of background, for at least until the eighth century Israel had no eschatology in any proper sense of the word. But she did have from earliest times onward an orientation toward the future, a hope and confidence in the future, which was characteristic and unique. And we saw that this rested in her understanding of her God, and of her relationship to him, specifically in her belief that God had chosen her, made convenant with her, and extended his promises to her. But we also saw that the nature of God's covenant with Israel, and therewith of Israel's future under God, could be conceived of in more than one way. These were not—so we shall argue—intrinsically incompatible, but rather complementary. But the balance between them was delicate and easily upset, and the possibility of a tension between them was certainly present.

I

1. In the preceding chapter we observed the great achievement of David and the theology that grew up about him and about Jerusalem, namely, that of God's choice of Mt. Zion as his earthly abode and of the covenant that he had made with David. The covenant with David was a promissory covenant. It was, in effect, a binding promise on the part of God that, having chosen Mt. Zion as the seat of his earthly rule, he would dwell there forever among his people, protecting them from their foes, and that he would give to David a dynasty that would

never end. Of course, there was the understanding that a king might, through his sin, bring chastisement on himself and on his people. But no condition attached to the promise itself: the dynasty would endure and be given victory over its foes and a wide domain, with the kings of the earth fawning at its feet.

Such a theology must have allowed for an enormous optimism regarding the future. Though it left room for the possibility that the nation might have to face troubles, reversals, problems, as all nations do, there was in the final analysis no *ultimate* need to worry about the future, for it is secure in the promises of God. Indeed, in difficult times, it gave rise to a reaching out *toward* the future—toward better times, victory, prosperity, the recovery of the lost glories of David— for, according to what was affirmed in the cult, this was what the future held. This reaching out for the future, let it be repeated, was in no sense an eschatology. It looked for no consummation of the divine purpose in history, no new order that God would create; rather, it was a sublime confidence in the continuation and ultimate triumph of the existing order, which might readily lapse into complacency.

2. But we also observed another, and far older, notion of God's covenant with his people that was abroad in Israel, namely, the covenant made in the desert and periodically reaffirmed by the Israelite tribes. This understanding of the God-people relationship had never been entirely forgotten. No doubt it had been thrust into the background in the cult of the Jerusalem Temple, where the theology of the Davidic covenant had become official. But it was very much alive among the population of Judah, especially of rural Judah, and also in prophetic and Levitic circles in northern Israel. Indeed, the traditions of the exodus and the conquest of the land, of the old covenant league and of Yahweh's holy wars, probably formed the basis of the ritual of the official state cult of northern Israel, where the theology of the Davidic covenant had never been accepted.

This view of covenant ought to have allowed no complacency whatever with regard to the future. As was noted, the Sinaitic covenant followed the pattern of an international suzerainty treaty; it knew of *no* unconditional promises. Rather, it was based in the recollection of God's prevenient grace to his people in calling them from bondage, guiding them through the desert, and giving them the Land of Promise; and it issued in the unconditional acceptance on the part of Israel of the divine Overlord's binding stipulations under the threat of the covenant curses in the event of disobedience. Far from leading to complacency, such a notion of the God-people relationship should have called the nation to continual self-examination and penitence.

But, as we said, it seems that by the eighth century the whole concept of covenant had been widely externalized and perverted. The notion seems to have established itself that the stipulations of covenant could be met by sacrifice and cultic observance alone. Since the cultus was lavishly supported, men might assure themselves that the covenant bond was being maintained, and might feel confident of the continuation of the covenant blessings and of God's continued protection of the nation. Indeed, in dangerous times men could look forward eagerly to a great day of Yahweh, when God would come again to the aid of his people, strike terror in the hearts of their foes, win great victories and bring realization to their fondest hopes of national aggrandizement and well-being. This expectation of a day of Yahweh, again, was in no sense an eschatology. It was not a hope for the definitive consummation of the divine purpose in history, some new order that God would create. Rather, it was the confidence that as in the past, so in the future, God would always come to the rescue of the present order and secure his people in the possession of their land and the promised blessings.

3. Such optimism regarding the future was a facile, fragile thing, one must agree. It simply could not last. It might survive through times of prosperity, or limited emergency, but it could never survive the eighth century. It is not our task to trace the history of the period.[1] Enough to say that the latter half of the eighth century saw the beginning of Assyria's period of empire, and a time of sheer terror for the petty states of western Asia. Assyria, long a menace on the horizon, had now—with the accession of Tiglath-pileser III in 745—come to conquer, occupy, and rule. The little nations of the area had just one choice: to surrender and pay tribute, or resist—and die. Northern Israel chose to resist, and within twenty-five years had been wiped from the map. Though Judah submitted and yielded tribute, and so survived, she was not to be a free country again for more than a hundred years. When, late in the eighth century, Hezekiah attempted rebellion, it was put down to the accompaniment of a frightful bloodbath in the "best" Assyrian tradition. It was a time of shameful servitude, onerous tribute, the attendant recognition of Assyria's gods even in the Temple itself,[2] and the ever-present threat

[1] For the details, I again refer to my book, *A History of Israel* (Philadelphia: The Westminster Press; London: SCM Press, 2d ed., 1972); see Ch. 7.

[2] It has recently been argued that there is no convincing evidence that the Assyrians required vassal states to worship their gods; cf. M. Cogan, *Imperialism and Religion:*

of Assyrian reprisals for the least attempt to alter the situation. The great-grandchildren of men alive when it began would not live to see the end of it.

In such a time facile optimism regarding the future simply had no place. The events gave the lie to whatever optimistic confidence there may have been. Obviously God was not always going to come to the defense of his people: he had not done so! Obviously he was not always going to give the Davidic king victory over his foes and cause conquered kings to grovel at his feet: the Davidic king was a helpless vassal, the lackey of a foreign power. And what shall one say of Yahweh's kingly and worldwide rule on Mt. Zion, when he must move over and make place for other gods in his very own house? What indeed? The popular confidence in the promises of God, and the continuing protection of God, must have seemed questionable in the face of what the nation was undergoing. Some profounder explanation of God's dealings with his people, and of what the future had in store for them, was urgently needed. If this had not been provided, it is difficult to see how any conclusion could logically have been drawn save that God is powerless—or unfaithful to his promises. And surely if any hope for the future was to be offered at all, it had to be something profounder than facile optimism regarding God's continuing protection of the existing order.

4. Providentially, it was just at this time that the first of the classical prophets stepped on the scene. They brought the needed word. They provided an understanding of the immediate future that was completely different from the popular one and, at the same time, they offered a vision of the farthest future, of God's final provision for his people, that became classical and that dominated the thinking of the Israelite people through the centuries to come. It was with the eighth-century prophets that true eschatological patterns first emerged.[3]

The prophets were of all things not facile optimists. Their word was first of all not a word of promise at all, but of judgment. They

---

Assyria, Judah and Israel in the Eighth Century B.C.E. (SBL Monograph Series, 19, 1974); J. McKay, *Religion in Judah Under the Assyrians* (London: SCM Press, 1973). This may well be correct. But vassals had to take their oath of loyalty by the overlord's gods, and thus acknowledge their supremacy, and it would certainly have been politic of them to show these gods respect. This, plus a general loss of confidence in Yahweh's power, may go far to explain why periods of subservience, such as the reigns of Ahaz and Manasseh, should have been characterized by the infiltration of pagan cults, both native and foreign.

[3] We use the word "eschatology," of course, in the sense defined above; cf. Ch. 1, pp. 18 f.

were rooted in the sacred traditions of Israel's past if anything more deeply than their contemporaries were, but they rejected the popular hope drawn from those traditions completely. Indeed, they made those very traditions the basis and norm of their evaluation of the national policy and character and, in the light of them, they saw the nation as under the judgment of God for its violation of his commandments and heading for disaster. And when they attempted to describe the disaster that they saw coming, they frequently did so in terms of those same sacred traditions, the very ones that the people had made the basis of their hope. (Recall, for example, how Amos upended the popular hope of the day of Yahweh and announced it not as a day of victory, but as a day of catastrophe.)

But the prophets did not see the judgment as involving the revocation of promise—as the *end*. All of them had hope for the farther future—although it is true that some of them, like Amos, had little of a tangible nature to say about it. But this hope did not lie in straight-line continuity with the existing order, as the popular hope did. On the contrary, it lay beyond a radical break, God's imminent judgment on the existing order, and it would come through a new and decisive divine act in the yet farther future, an act that would reestablish the relationship between God and people in a new and profounder way and bring God's purpose for his people to a triumphant conclusion. And to describe this new divine act the prophets reached back—once again—to those factors in the nation's history and sacred tradition that had been the basis of its existence and self-understanding, and projected them onto the future as patterns of God's final provision for his people.

Just here we may speak of the beginnings of eschatology in Israel. This new divine act, though described in terms of patterns drawn from the past, was not thought of as a mere repetition of the past, a reestablishment of things as they once had been. Rather, it was to be something new, something that would exceed the past, that would make actual the true intention of the past, and the promises of the past, in a new and profounder way. And it would introduce a state of affairs that would be final. Nothing was looked for beyond it; it would endure forever, it would never end.

But, in view of what has been said, it is not surprising that the eschatology of the eighth-century prophets did not follow any single pattern, but several. At the risk of oversimplification we can say that two patterns stand out, corresponding to the two views of election and covenant already observed. On the one hand, we see a reaching back to the traditions of exodus and conquest and the old covenant league, which conceived of the immediate future in terms of national destruction, the bringing down of the covenant curses and ejection from the land, which would be followed in the farther future by a new entrance into the land and the restoration of the covenant bond on a deeper level. And, on the other hand, we see a reaching back to the traditions of Jerusalem and David, which viewed the immediate future in terms of a terrible chastisement, to be followed in the farther future by the vindication of God's kingly rule on Mt. Zion and the coming of an ideal king of the line of David who would fulfill the dynastic ideal and make all the dynastic promises actual.

II

The first of these patterns finds its classical expression in northern Israel's great prophet, Hosea. No prophet was more deeply rooted in the traditions of Israel's beginnings than was he.

1. To be sure, Amos' preaching was also rooted in the traditions of exodus, wilderness wandering and conquest, and in the stipulations of Yahweh's covenant law. Amos, of course, preached in the middle of the eighth century before the storm broke, at a time when Israel and Judah had reached heights of physical expansion and prosperity unknown since the days of Solomon. He spoke to a nation proud of its military strength, untroubled by any immediate external threat, and confident of the future. He addressed an affluent society which enjoyed every luxury money could buy. Yet it was a sick society: at the top the privileged rich, at the bottom the hopelessly poor. And the rich were not only careless of the plight of the poor; they missed no opportunity to crowd them, cheat them, and rob them of their rights.

Amos' attack on the crimes of society is too well known to require extended review: it is the classical prophetic attack. He savagely assailed the oppression of the poor and the cheating of the poor, as well as the corrupt judicial system which denied them any hope of obtaining justice (Amos 2:6–8; 3:9–11; 5:7, 10–12; 8:4–6; etc.). With equal vehemence he attacked the pampered upper classes, who enjoyed every comfort and luxury, but who could not have cared less for the plight of the poor, or for the fracture that their careless and selfish behavior had precipitated in the texture of society (6:1–7;

4:1–3; etc.). Amos' entire preaching is dominated by a righteous indignation against the crimes against justice which the prophet observed on every hand (e.g., 5:7, 10–12):

> Amos 5:7 Ah,[4] these who turn justice to poison,
> Thrust righteousness down to the ground!
> 10 They hate him who pleads in the court,[5]
> Abhor him who speaks with integrity.

This note is fully typical of Amos; as we have said, it pervades his entire message.

But Amos did not attack crimes against justice merely out of personal outrage, or for humanitarian reasons; his attack was deeply rooted in theology. Although he nowhere uses the word "covenant," it is clear that the crimes he attacks are infractions of covenant law; as such Amos views them, and as such he pronounces judgment on them.[6] Moreover, on occasion he throws these crimes against the backdrop of the events of the exodus and the giving of the land—and the continuing tradition of these events—and evaluates them as crimes against grace (e.g., 2:9–12).[7] The election favor which Israel has received, and which ought to have moved her to more perfect obedience, has had no such effect; it therefore stands over her and pronounces upon her a double condemnation. In Amos' view, God demands of his people justice—first, last, and always. The busy cultus whereby they think to satisfy his demands is a fraud of which he wishes no part (5:21–24):

> Amos 5:21 I hate, I despise your pilgrim feasts,

---

[4] "Ah" is added conjecturally to conform to 5:18; 6:1. Verse 7 is to be brought into connection with vs. 10–12, as most commentators agree.

[5] Lit., "who argues the case (i.e., strives to see justice done) in the gate." The town gate was the place where legal cases were heard and decided—thus, the court.

[6] That Amos' accusations presuppose some commonly known tradition of Yahweh's commandments seems certain, else they would have carried little weight. Whether or not this was the Book of the Covenant as we know it (Ex., chs. 21 to 23) may be left an open question, though it is entirely likely that both Amos and his hearers knew of these laws. It has been argued that Amos derived his norms of evaluation from the ethos of the rural society in which he had been raised; cf. H. W. Wolff, *Amos' geistige Heimat* (WMANT, 18, 1964); also *Amos* (BKAT, 14/2, fasc. 6–9, 1967–69.). One may agree in this, but only if it is recalled that instruction by family heads may have been one of the important channels through which knowledge of the sacred traditions of the past, and of Yahweh's covenant stipulations, was handed down; cf. my remarks in JBL, 92 (1973), pp. 203 f.

[7] I am unable to agree that vs. 10–12 are to be assigned on form-critical and other grounds to a later stratum of the Amos tradition, as some have argued; cf. Wolff, *Amos*, pp. 172, 205–207; J. Vollmer, *Geschichtliche Rückblicke und Motive in der Prophetie des Amos, Hosea und Jesaja* (BZAW, 119, 1971), pp. 24 f. Cf. on the point W. Rudolph, *Joel-Amos-Obadja-Jona* (HAT, 13/2, 1971), pp. 146 f.

> Take no pleasure in your high holy days.
> 22 Though you offer me burnt offerings,
> . . . .[8]
> Your cereal offerings I will not accept,
> And your peace offerings of fatted beasts I will not regard.
> 23 Take away from me the noise of your songs;
> To the melody of your harps I will not listen.
> 24 But let justice roll down like water,
> Righteousness like a perennial stream.

In the light of the above convictions, Amos completely rejected the popular confidence that because Israel is God's chosen people, God will always protect her. Israel, said he, has indeed been elected, and has been the recipient of grace; but it is precisely *because* she has been the recipient of grace that she will be judged (3:1 f.):

> Amos 3:1 Hear this word which Yahweh has spoken against you, O Israelites—against the whole family which I brought up out of the land of Egypt:
> 2 "You only have I recognized
> Out of all the families of the earth;
> Therefore I will punish you
> For all your crimes." [9]

Israel does not, because of her election, occupy a favored position in the eyes of God, exempt from responsibility. On the contrary, Israel in this regard is no better than any other nation whose fortunes God has likewise guided:

> Amos 9:7 Are you not like the Ethiopians to me,
> O Israelites?—Yahweh's word—
> Did I not bring Israel up from the land of Egypt—
> And the Philistines from Caphtor,
> and the Arameans from Kir?

This is no denial of the historic fact that Yahweh had brought Israel from bondage in Egypt to her present land, but rather its affirmation. But it is a denial of the popular conceit that God's grace to his people had conferred upon them a special, protected status above all other

---

[8] A colon seems to have been lost here; cf. BH³, BHS, and the commentaries.

[9] Whether or not v. 1b is to be regarded as an expansion, as many believe, need not be debated here (it is an expedient that does not seem to me necessary). God's election of Israel is in any event clearly affirmed. On the background of the verb "recognize" (lit., "know") in treaty (covenant) terminology, see especially H. B. Huffmon, BASOR, 181 (1966), pp. 31–37.

nations. God, who judges the nations for their crimes, will judge
Israel also (chs. 1 to 2). In attempting to describe the judgment he
saw coming, Amos, as we have seen, seized upon the popular hope of
the day of Yahweh and stood it on its head: it will be a black and
terrible day (5:18–20). God will declare holy war against Israel, will
smite her armies with panic (2:13–16), will nine times decimate them
(5:3). He sends the covenant curses on his people (4:6–12)[10] and, in the
end, will deport them from their land, destroy them. And it is on this
note that Amos' preaching reaches a thundering climax: "See, the
eyes of Lord Yahweh are on the sinful kingdom, and I will destroy it
from off the face of the earth" (9:8a).

Amos offered no hope whatever for the immediate future; it held,
so far as he could see, only "black darkness with not a ray of light in
it" (5:20). But did he have no hope for the farther future? One is
constrained to believe that he did. But it must be admitted that it
plays no clear role in his book. We have only the two brief sayings at
the end of ch. 9 (vs. 11 f., and vs. 13–15), both of which are widely
questioned by scholars. The first of these expresses a theology that
was certainly widespread in Judah in the eighth century and, since he
was a Judahite, may well have been shared by Amos. The second is at
least of a very old type. But, though certain scholars have defended
the genuineness of these sayings, or at least the first of them,[11] it is
best to be cautious, for they have no clear parallel elsewhere in the
words of Amos that have been preserved for us. Aside from these
passages Amos offers at best only what has happily been described as
"a fainthearted 'perhaps' " [12] (5:14 f.):

> Amos 5:14   Seek good, and not evil,
> That you may live,
> That Yahweh[13] may be with you
> As you have said he is.
>
> 15   Hate evil, and love good,

---

[10] I am not convinced that these verses belong to a later stratum of the Amos
tradition, as some argue; cf. Wolff, *Amos*, pp. 256–258. On the point, cf. Rudolph,
Joel-Amos-Obadja-Jona, pp. 173–175.

[11] As regards Amos 9:11 f., cf. G. von Rad, *Old Testament Theology*, Vol. II (Eng. tr.,
Edinburgh and London: Oliver & Boyd; New York: Harper & Row, 1965), p. 138; R. E.
Clements, *Prophecy and Covenant* (London: SCM Press, 1965), pp. 111 f. H. Graf
Reventlow has defended the genuineness of vs. 13–15 also; cf. *Das Amt des Propheten
bei Amos* (FRLANT, 80, 1962), pp. 91–104. See also H. D. Preuss, *Jahweglaube und
Zukunftserwartung* (BWANT, 7, 1968), pp. 138–141.

[12] Cf. von Rad, *Old Testament Theology*, Vol. II, p. 134.

[13] MT reads, "Yahweh, God of Hosts" here and in v. 15. But the meter is somewhat
overloaded, and the words "God of Hosts" may be an expansion.

> Establish justice in the courts;[14]
> It may be that Yahweh will be gracious
> To what is left of Joseph.[15]

And it is on this rather hesitant note that we must leave Amos' vision of the farther future.

2. But if the hope that Amos held for the future remains somewhat uncertain, when we turn to Hosea the case is clear. Hosea was steeped in the traditions of the "canonical" events—of exodus, wilderness wandering, and entry into the land—and in the stipulations of Yahweh's covenant, through and through. The theology of Yahweh's eternal covenant with David meant nothing to him (since he was a northern Israelite, naturally it would not have).[16] Indeed, it could be argued from certain texts in his book that he was hostile to the institution of monarchy as such.[17]

Unlike Amos, Hosea spoke to a nation that was dying. Though he began to prophesy in the heyday of Jeroboam's reign (Hos. 1:1; cf. 1:4)—thus only a few years, if at all, after Amos spoke—his career continued into the dark days that followed. This was a time when Israel, inwardly rotten and faced with the Assyrian threat, exploded into anarchy and civil war. King followed king in rapid succession, usually by violence, and the national policy swung this way and that as rival parties snatched at the power. In the course of it all, law and order broke down and neither life nor property was safe (4:1 f.; 7:1; etc.) All this, and worse, we see reflected in the pages of Hosea's book.

Hosea's attack fell primarily upon the apostasy—specifically upon the orgiastic rites of the fertility cult—with which the land was filled. Her departure from Yahweh to run after other gods was to Hosea no less than the sin in which all of Israel's sin consisted; it was both a violation of the cardinal stipulation of Yahweh's covenant and the

---

[14] Lit., "in the gate"; cf. note 5, above.

[15] I see no compelling reason to regard these verses as a later formulation based on v. 4b, as do some; e.g., Wolff, *Amos*, pp. 274, 294 f.

[16] The one allusion to David which his book contains (3:5b) was probably added at a later date when Hosea's words were transmitted in Judah; see the commentaries.

[17] If the sin of Israel "from the days of Gibeah" (9:9; 10:9) and the evil that was theirs "in Gilgal" (9:15) are references to the kingship of Saul (Saul's residence was in Gibeah and he was crowned [I Sam. 11:14 f.] and, according to one tradition, rejected in Gilgal [I Sam. 13:8–15]), then a total rejection of the monarchy would seem clear. But that these allusions have this force is much less than certain; see the commentaries. Hosea, however, was clearly shocked by the manner in which kings in his day were assassinated and replaced by other kings without the slightest pretext of legitimacy (cf. 7:3–7; 8:4; 10:3; etc.).

source of the moral rot that had poisoned the national character. This apostasy is Hosea's central theme and one that he reverts to again and again (e.g., 4:11–14):

> Hos. 4:11   Wine, new wine confuses my people.[18]
> 12   They consult a piece of wood,
> Their staff gives them oracles,
> For a spirit of whoredom has led them astray,
> They have whored away from their God.
> 13   On the tops of the mountains they sacrifice,
> On the hills burn offerings,
> Under oak and poplar and terebinth,
> For pleasant is their shade.
> So your daughters play the whore,
> Your sons' brides commit adultery.
> 14   I'll not punish your daughters when they whore,
> Your sons' brides when they commit adultery;
> For they themselves go aside with the whores,
> With the cult prostitutes they sacrifice.

From top to bottom, young and old alike, Israelite society is rotten; the worship of the gods of the fertility cult has eaten away its moral fiber.

Again and again Hosea taxes Israel with her unfaithfulness to her God; and again and again he throws this faithlessness against the backdrop of Yahweh's grace to her in the exodus and wilderness days. Indeed, he saw Israel's apostasy as beginning the very moment she reached the cultivated land. For example (9:10):

> Hos. 9:10   Like grapes in the desert
> I found Israel,
> Like early figs on the fig tree[19]
> I saw your fathers.
> But they! They came to Baal-peor,[20]
> Devoted themselves to "Lord Shame," [21]
> And became loathesome as their "lover."

Or this (11:1 f.):

> Hos. 11:1   When Israel was a child, I loved him,
> And from Egypt I called my son.

---

[18] Lit., "takes away the heart (i.e., the mind) of my people." We divide the verses following LXX; cf. BH³, BHS.

[19] MT adds, "in its first season" (so RSV), which may be an expansion.

[20] Cf. the story in Num., ch. 25.

[21] MT "shame" (*bōšet*) is a frequent scribal rewriting of *ba'al* ("lord"), the appellation of the chief god of the fertility cult.

> 2 The more I called them,
> The more they went from me,[22]
> Kept sacrificing to the Baals,
> Burning offerings to idols.

Or this (13:4–6):

> Hos. 13:4 I am Yahweh your God
> From the land of Egypt;
> You know[23] no god but me,
> Beside me there is no helper.
> 5 It was I who fed you[24] in the desert,
> In a land of drought;
> 6 When I fed them,[25] they were sated,
> Were sated and then grew proud—
> And so forgot me.

It is clear from passages such as these that Hosea regarded Israel's apostasy from Yahweh as a crime against grace. Israel had been the recipient of the unmerited favor of the God who brought her from bondage, established her in her land and sustained her in it, but, instead of responding to him in grateful obedience, she has completely forgotten him and run after the gods of fertility, and worshiped them as the source of the benefits she has received (cf. 2:2–13; etc.). Moreover, Hosea viewed this ingratitude not as an aberration of recent origin, but as something that reached back through all the generations of the past to the very moment when Israel first took up the sedentary life in the land her God had given her. Israel, in a word, has broken covenant with Yahweh. Though Hosea uses the word "covenant" but rarely (and is the only eighth-century prophet to use it at all), this was clearly his view of the matter. Indeed, in one place (4:1–3) he depicts Yahweh as launching his covenant lawsuit against his people.[26] He has a legal complaint, a case at law (*rîb*, RSV, "controversy") against them (v. 1) because of the total absence among them of the virtues he had

---

[22] So RSV; on the text of the bicolon, cf. BH³, BHS.

[23] On the verb "know" in treaty (covenant) terminology, cf. note 9, above.

[24] So following LXX, which may fit the context better (cf. v. 6). MT has "knew you" (cf. v. 4), which is also attractive. It is difficult to decide.

[25] Cf. BH³, BHS.

[26] The literature on the covenant lawsuit is extensive and cannot be cited here. Cf. J. Harvey, *Le Plaidoyer prophétique contre Israël après la rupture de l'alliance* (Bruges and Paris: Desclée de Brouwer; Montreal: Les Éditions Bellarmin, 1967), where a listing of literature up to date of publication will be found. For an excellent orientation, cf. H. B. Huffmon, "The Covenant Lawsuit in the Prophets" (JBL, 78 [1959], pp. 285–295).

expected of them: "There is no faithfulness, or loyal devotion, or knowledge of God in the land." On the contrary (v. 2), there is nothing but "perjury, lying, murdering, stealing, and adultery, and one crime follows another." One can scarcely fail to be struck by the parallels between this list of crimes and those prohibited in the Decalogue. Hosea seems to presuppose of his hearers a knowledge of Yahweh's covenant stipulations either as embodied in the Decalogue as we know it or in some similar formulation, and he censures them for their flagrant disobedience. And because of this disobedience the land is under the covenant curses (v. 3).

As is well known, Hosea introduced into Old Testament prophecy the figure of marriage to describe the bond between God and people. Whatever may have suggested this figure to Hosea in the first place, it can hardly be doubted that it was shaped in his mind through his own unhappy domestic experience, for, however one interprets the first three chapters of his book, it seems clear that Hosea's wife was unfaithful to him.[27] In his own tragic experience Hosea saw, or came to see, God's experience with Israel symbolically reflected. God had taken Israel to himself and in solemn covenant had "married" her, made her his "bride." And, as any husband would expect of his wife, God expected of Israel absolute faithfulness to him. But in running after other gods, her "lovers," Israel has violated her marriage vows; she has committed "adultery." Since pleading with her had done no good, there is nothing left for God to do but "divorce" her, send her from his presence in disgrace, end her existence as a nation (cf. 2:2-13).

Hosea therefore must announce the divine judgment on Israel, and he does so in terms every bit as strong as those used by Amos. Israel has broken covenant with Yahweh and is no longer his people. In ch. 1 we are told how Hosea's wife bore three children, to each of whom Hosea gave a symbolical name. The youngest of these he called *Lō'-'ammī* ("Not My People"), and explained the name as follows (1:9): "Call his name *Lō'-'ammī*, for you are not my people and I am not your God." [28] If this translation is correct, we have here no less than a reversal of the familiar covenant formula, "I will be your God, and you shall be my people" (cf. Ex. 6:7; Lev. 26:12; Deut. 26:17 ff.;

---

[27] On Hos., chs. 1 to 3, see the commentaries. For an excellent orientation, see H. H. Rowley, "The Marriage of Hosea" (1956; repr. in *Men of God* [London: Thomas Nelson & Sons, 1963], pp. 66–97).

[28] But the text, and its translation, is uncertain. MT has, "and I am not yours," which may be preferable. Cf. the commentaries.

etc.): the covenant is voided, and Israel is no longer God's people. Since Israel has broken covenant, she stands under the covenant curses; and Hosea calls them down with a fury that beggars description (7:12 f.; 9:11–14; 13:7 f.; etc.).[29] He depicts God as saying (9:11 f.):

> Hos. 9:11   Ephraim! Like a bird shall his glory fly away—
> No birth, no pregnancy, no conceiving!
>   12   Even if they rear children,
> I'll bereave them till none is left.
> Ah, woe to them indeed
> When I depart from them!

And to this Hosea responds, as if concurring in the verdict:

> Hos. 9:14   Give them, Yahweh—
> What wilt thou give?
> Give them a womb that miscarries
> And dried-up breasts!

In Hosea's view Israel simply had no future as a nation! Under the curse of her God, nothing could save her—neither her frantic political maneuvers (7:8–13; 8:7–10; 12:1; etc.), nor the gods of fertility to whom she had attributed her well-being (2:2–13; etc.), nor the lavish but empty cultus whereby she has thought to propitiate her God and win his favor (5:15 to 6:6; etc.). All the promised blessings will be taken away; Israel will be torn from her land, sent into exile, destroyed. And when Hosea speaks of the catastrophe he saw coming, he frequently describes it as a new wilderness wandering (2:14; 12:9; etc.)[30] parallel to Israel's experience in the desert before she entered the Promised Land. Indeed, in some texts he seems to speak of it as a new Egyptian bondage: Israel will return to Egypt (8:13; cf. 9:3, 6; 11:5).[31] The patterns of the past, which had been the

[29] On this feature in the prophetic preaching, perhaps more prominent in Hosea than in any other prophet with the exception of Jeremiah, see especially D. R. Hillers, *Treaty-Curses and the Old Testament Prophets* (Rome: Pontifical Biblical Institute, 1964).

[30] On the interpretation of 12:9, see the commentaries. But, however understood, it seems that the future is in some way interpreted as parallel to the desert sojourn of the past.

[31] The interpretation of these texts is disputed; see the commentaries. In some of them, where Assyria stands in parallelism with Egypt (9:3; 11:5), Hosea may be thinking merely of the political realities: Israelites will either have to submit to captivity in Assyria or save themselves by flight to Egypt. (Or it may even be that Hosea was not at the time sure in his own mind which of the two powers would be the agent of Israel's destruction.) But in some of these texts (8:13 and 9:6 [where "Assyria" is not to be read conjecturally into the text]) it seems that he sees exile in Assyria as a type of the ancient bondage in Egypt.

foundation of the national self-understanding and confidence, have become types of the judgment to come. It is back to the beginnings— as if the whole of God's saving history with his people had been stood on its head, reversed!

But, uncompromising as his message of judgment was, it is clear that Hosea held out hope for the still farther future. This was not a hope that Israel would repent and so avert the judgment. If Hosea ever entertained such a hope (and he may well have done so), it appears that he abandoned it as the years went by.[32] Hosea saw, or came to see, his people as incapable of repentance. Such repentance as they offer consists of words only; it is a shallow, insincere repentance, a sham. We see this in 5:15 to 6:6, where Hosea places in the mouth of the people a liturgy of penitence (6:1–3), perhaps a liturgy such as he actually heard them recite in the course of some cultic occasion. It is moving; all the right words are said. But it is rejected (vs. 4–6). It is rejected because it offers words, ritual action, and nothing more.

> Hos. 6:4   What shall I do with you, Ephraim?
> What shall I do with you, Judah?
> Your devotion is like morning mist,
> Like dew that soon disappears.

Then, over against this empty repentance, what God had really wanted of his people is clearly set forth:

> Hos. 6:6   It is loyal devotion that I wished, not sacrifice,
> And knowledge of God rather than burnt offerings.

For Hosea, hope rested not in Israel's repentance, or in any good work that Israel would do, but in the mercy and the character of God who, beyond the judgment, is still *there* (11:8 f.).

> Hos. 11:8   How can I part with you, Ephraim?
> How surrender you, Israel?
> How can I make you like Admah,
> Treat you like Zeboiim?[33]
> My heart recoils within me,
> My compassion grows warm and tender.
> 9   I will not give vent to my fury,

---

[32] G. Fohrer, "Umkehr und Erlösung beim Propheten Hosea" (*Studien zur alttesta-mentlichen Prophetie* [BZAW, 99, 1967], pp. 222–241), sees a development in Hosea's thinking, and believes that at one time he thought repentance possible, but later abandoned the belief.

[33] These were cities allied with Sodom and Gomorrah (Gen. 14:2) and apparently destroyed with them (Gen., ch. 19; cf. Deut. 29:23).

> Nor destroy Ephraim again;
> For I am God, not man . . .

"For I am God, not man." That is plainly to say: If I were a man, I would in my sorely provoked anger let them have it! They deserve nothing else! But I am not a man, nor am I a prisoner to human passions and grudges; I am God—the compassionate, loving, and faithful God, whose purpose is not to destroy, but to forgive and redeem.

So it was that in the farther future, beyond the judgment, Hosea looked for the restoration of Israel in the mercy of God. And to describe this future restoration Hosea once again drew upon patterns derived from the traditions of the past: it will come to pass as a recapitulation of the "canonical" events, the events that made Israel a people in the first place and gave her her land. Through God's judgment Israel will be torn from her land, hurled back, as it were, into the wilderness where she first became God's people. And there, stripped of all that she had, she will find herself once more totally dependent upon her God. There her God will woo her to himself, and she will respond as she once did—in gratitude and obedience. And God will then grant her a new entrance into her land, and a new beginning (2:14 f. [MT, 2:16 f.]).

> Hos. 2:14   Therefore, see! I will allure her,
>   Bring her out into the desert,
>   And speak to her words of comfort.
>   15   There I will give to her vineyards,
>   Make the Valley of Achor a gateway of hope.[34]
>   There she will answer as in the days of her youth,
>   As she did when she came from the land of Egypt.

Then the bond between God and people, so grievously broken, will be restored on a new and profounder level, and the covenant blessings will be showered on Israel in indescribable plenty (2:16–20, 21–23 [MT, vs. 18–22, 23–25]). And this arrangement will endure forever; it will never end.

> Hos. 2:19   I will betroth you to me forever,
>   Will betroth you to me in righteousness,
>   In justice, in devotion, in mercy;
>   20   I will betroth you to me in faithfulness,
>   And you shall know Yahweh.

---

[34] Cf. the story of Achan's theft of the devoted goods, which brought a curse on Israel and which was punished in the Valley of Achor (Josh., ch. 7).

Hosea does not say, "I will make a new covenant . . . ," for he speaks in the metaphor of betrothal and marriage. But that is precisely what is intended. The hope of a new covenant that God would one day make with his people has its beginnings here.

III

Hosea's understanding of the future, then, was shaped by his rootage in the traditions of exodus, wilderness wandering and entrance into the land, and in the obligations imposed by the covenant made in the desert at Sinai. But, as was intimated above, another and somewhat different understanding of the future—both of the immediate future and the farther (eschatological) future—likewise made its appearance in eighth-century prophecy. This found its classical expression in Isaiah of Jerusalem, who prophesied all through the dark days of the Assyrian invasions (from ca. 742 until sometime after 701).

1. Isaiah was rooted in the traditions of Jerusalem and David, and the sure promises that God had made to David.[35] This was, indeed, the theological basis of his lifelong criticism of the national policy; only in the light of it does it even make sense.[36]

At first glance, Isaiah's political advice might well seem to the reader utterly self-contradictory: in his young manhood opposing submission to Assyria through the sending of tribute; later, on more than one occasion, opposing rebellion against Assyria; and, finally, when things seemed darkest of all, counseling defiance of Assyria. One is tempted either to put Isaiah down as a very changeable man, a

---

[35] Isaiah's dependence on the Zion traditions is generally recognized. But it has been denied by some, who argue that the Zion theology was a later development; cf. especially G. Wanke, *Die Zionstheologie der Korachiten* (BZAW, 97, 1966); also Vollmer, *Geschichtliche Rückblicke und Motive in der Prophetie des Amos, Hosea und Jesaja* (reference in note 7), pp. 158–160. I do not find their arguments convincing.

[36] On the message and theology of Isaiah, aside from the commentaries and handbooks, the following articles will be found especially helpful: W. Eichrodt, "Prophet and Covenant: Observations on the Exegesis of Isaiah" (J. I. Durham and J. R. Porter, eds., *Proclamation and Presence: Old Testament Essays in Honour of Gwynne Henton Davies* [London: SCM Press; Richmond: John Knox Press, 1970], pp. 167–188); W. Zimmerli, "Verkündigung und Sprache der Botschaft Jesajas" (1970; repr., *Studien zur alttestamentlichen Theologie und Prophetie: Gesammelte Aufsätze II* [Munich: Chr. Kaiser Verlag, 1974], pp. 73–87); H. Wildberger, "Jesajas Verständnis der Geschichte" (VT, Suppl. Vol. 9, 1963, pp. 83–117); Th. C. Vriezen, "Essentials of the Theology of Isaiah" (B. W. Anderson and W. Harrelson, eds., *Israel's Prophetic Heritage: Essays in Honor of James Muilenburg* [New York: Harper & Brothers, 1962], pp. 128–146); also H. W. Hoffmann, *Die Intention der Verkündigung Jesajas* (BZAW, 136, 1974).

regular weathercock of a man who altered his message with every shift in the political wind, or to seek to bring him into harmony with himself by recourse to massive literary-critical surgery (as some scholars have done!). But these are desperate expedients and, in the final analysis, unnecessary. A single theological line runs through all that Isaiah had to say. His call at all times was to trust in God and his promises—that, and nothing else! He wished his country to orientate its policies upon God and his promises and to place its trust in them rather than in political cleverness and military alliances. In fact, no prophet laid greater stress on the call to faith than did Isaiah.

Isaiah's attitude is abundantly clear from his words and actions during the first political crisis of his career. This was precipitated in the year 735/4, only a few years after Isaiah had begun to preach, and approximately as Ahaz took the throne in Judah.[37] A coalition had been formed to resist Assyria, the leaders of which were Rezin, king of the Aramean state of Damascus, and Pekah ben Remaliah, who had usurped the throne in northern Israel. The confederates, no doubt unwilling to risk the danger of having a neutral and potentially hostile power in their rear, wished Judah to join them. But Judah's leaders wanted no part of such a risky venture, and refused. Thereupon, the members of the coalition moved against Judah with the aim of forcing her into line with their wishes. In fact, it was their intention (Isa. 7:6) to depose Ahaz—quite possibly to execute him—and to replace him with one ben Tab'el, a creature of their own choosing. The continuance of the legitimate royal line was threatened, and the promises of God to David were thrown into question. Ahaz was terrified; "His heart trembled, and the heart of his people, as the trees of the forest tremble before the wind" (v. 2). He saw no way to save himself except to send tribute to the Assyrian king, become his vassal and implore his aid—which shortly he did (II Kings 16:7-9).

Isaiah opposed this course with all the powers at his command. Meeting the king, apparently as the latter was inspecting his water supply in preparation for siege (Isa. 7:1-9), he said to him in effect: Don't do it, your majesty! Get hold of yourself! Keep calm! Don't be afraid of these little kings who attack you! God is in control, and he has not ordained what they propose. Because this is so, "It will not stand, it will not happen" (v. 7b). Then follow the somewhat cryptic words (vs. 8a, 9a):[38]

---

[37] For the details of this crisis, and for the background of Isaiah's career in general, the reader is again referred to my book, *A History of Israel*, pp. 267–286.

[38] V. 8b is best regarded as a later comment (note that RSV places it in parentheses).

Isa. 7:8a   For the head [i.e., the capital] of Aram is Damascus,
             And the head [i.e., the ruler] of Damascus is Rezin.
     9a   And the head [i.e., the capital] of Ephraim is Samaria,
             And the head [i.e., the ruler] of Samaria is ben Remaliah.

It is possible that Isaiah intended the king to complete in his mind the thought of these, in themselves, rather meaningless words by the addition of still a further couplet:

And the head [i.e., the capital] of Judah is Jerusalem,
And the head [i.e., the ruler] of Jerusalem is ben David.

This suggestion has been advanced by various commentators[39] and, while one cannot be certain, it seems best to make sense of lines that are otherwise somewhat pointless and banal. Isaiah meant to say: These two invading kings have their spheres where God has permitted them to rule, but those spheres do not include Judah and Jerusalem, where God has ordained that only a son of David shall rule. Their plans, therefore, to impose their will on Judah will fail. Isaiah then concludes:

Isa. 7:9b   If you will not believe,
             Surely you will not be established.

Or, better to catch the force of the really untranslatable wordplay ('*im lō' ta'ᵃmīnū kī lō' tē'āmēnū*), "If you will not stand firm [i.e., in faith], you will not be stood firm [i.e., confirmed in your position]."

Isaiah labored tirelessly to convince both king and people that the course he advocated was indeed the course that God wished the nation to follow. But without success! [40] Very shortly after the incident described above, Isaiah gave to the king the famous sign of Immanuel (7:10–17), which, however interpreted (and that is one of the most warmly disputed exegetical problems in the entire Isaiah book), was intended to assure him that, if he would only hold fast, the danger would soon be over. But it was also intended as a warning to the king that the policy he was about to embark upon would bring terrible disaster to the nation, a disaster worse than any that had overtaken it since the breakup of the Davidic Empire after Solomon's death (v. 17; cf. vs. 18–25). To the people generally he gave, through the sign of

It breaks the connection between vs. 8a and 9a and, unless the text is emended, is factually difficult as well. See the commentaries

[39] Cf. W. Vischer, *Die Immanuel-Botschaft im Rahmen des königlichen Zionsfestes* (Zurich: Evangelischer Verlag, 1955), pp. 17 f.; recently, Zimmerli, "Verkündigung und Sprache der Botschaft Jesajas" (reference in note 36), p. 78.

[40] All the sayings and incidents in Isa. 7:1 to 8:18 relate to the crisis of 735–33.

Maher-shalal-hash-baz (8:1–4), the same assurance that the danger would soon pass, and the same warning that their want of faith was leading them to catastrophe (vs. 5–8). He begged all who would listen to take a stand against this drift in the national policy (vs. 11–15; note the plural verbs!). When his advice was refused, he apparently wrote down a record of what he had said, and entrusted it to his disciples as a witness for the future that he had indeed spoken as he had (vs. 16–18).[41]

Isaiah's appeal to his king and to his fellow citizens sprang from his own unshakable trust in the sure promises that God had made to David. He certainly did not wish his country to remain inactive and tamely to submit to the coalition's will. But still less did he wish it to attempt to save itself by reliance on Assyrian arms. He wanted it to trust in Yahweh and shape its policy accordingly. In his appeal to Ahaz in 7:1–9 ("If you will not believe . . ."), Isaiah was not merely begging his king to be courageous, or urging him in a general way to credit his assurance that the coalition would do him no lasting harm; rather, he was exhorting the king to put his faith in the very theology that was affirmed in his official cult and to develop policy on the basis of it. The promise of the birth of the royal child Immanuel (7:10–17)[42] likewise was meant to assure the king that the dynastic promises were trustworthy, as well as to warn him of the terrible consequences that failure to trust them would have for the nation. The very name Immanuel ("God is with us") must inevitably have suggested the refrain of the hymn of Zion (Ps. 46:7, 11), "Yahweh of Hosts is with us," which served as a cultic affirmation of God's sure defense of his city and his people. The same refrain occurs in the cultic words quoted in Isa. 8:9 f.:

> Isa. 8:9 Take note,[43] you peoples, and be dismayed!
> Give ear, all you nations from afar!
> Arm yourselves and be dismayed,
> Arm yourselves and be dismayed!
> 10 Form a plan—it will be foiled,
> Speak a word—it will not stand,
> For God is with us (*'immānū 'ēl*).

---

[41] This seems to me, as it does to many others, the best interpretation of these verses. But the point is disputed; see the commentaries.

[42] We cannot undertake to discuss this much-disputed passage here. It has provoked a whole literature in its own right, and even to cite representative selections of it would take pages. The reader must consult the commentaries. I am among those, however, who see the promised child as a son of the royal house.

[43] So with LXX (cf. NEB, JB). MT reads, "be broken" (RSV), or the like.

God has given his promises, and he is his people's sufficient defense. Let them put faith in him and trust in him alone. Such was Isaiah's conviction.

It was precisely this same conviction that, later in his life, caused Isaiah on more than one occasion to oppose rebellion against Assyria. This was the case when, early in Hezekiah's reign (714–712) rebellion broke out in the Philistine city of Ashdod. This rebellion had Egyptian backing; other Philistine cities were drawn in, and Judah, as well as Edom and Moab, was invited to join. Ambassadors both of the Philistines and the Egyptians appeared in Jerusalem seeking to enlist Hezekiah's aid (Isa. 14:28–32; ch. 18). Isaiah was strongly opposed and begged his country's leaders to give the ambassadors a negative answer. Indeed, all the while the rebellion was brewing (ch. 20) he walked about Jerusalem "naked and barefoot"—which probably means that he was clad only in a loincloth, the garb of a prisoner of war—symbolizing the fate that would befall the Egyptians and all who put their trust in them. But this was not merely that Isaiah realized the futility of rebellion (as he almost certainly did), still less was it that he was content to see his country remain a vassal state of Assyria forever. Rather, it moved from his conviction that God, though he might seem to be absent, is nevertheless in control of events and would, in his own good time, give the signal for the overthrow of Assyria (18:1–6); and for this his people must wait. Until then, his word to them was—*trust!*

> Isa. 14:32 What will one answer that nation's envoys?[44]
> "That Yahweh has founded Zion;
> In her his poor people find refuge."

Just what course Judah pursued at this time is not altogether clear. But presumably she did not commit herself, or did not do so irrevocably, for when Sargon's commanding general crushed the revolt (in 712), Judah, so far as we know, was not molested. But whether or not Isaiah's words played any part in shaping his country's policy we have no way of saying.

But later, after Sennacherib (704–681) had come to the Assyrian throne, a rebellion broke out in which Judah played a leading role. A sizable coalition of states in Palestine and Phoenicia had been formed and a treaty with Egypt had been made, assuring the coalition of military aid. Isaiah hotly opposed this whole venture, and his reasons

---

[44] MT, "the envoys of the nation," i.e., the Philistines. But LXX reads plural ("the envoys of the nations"), as though other nations were likewise represented.

for doing so are clear from his words. The nation has placed its trust in Egyptian chariots—and in Egyptian gods (e.g., 28:15)[45]—when it ought to have trusted in Yahweh (30:1 ff.).

> Isa. 30:1   Ah, the rebel sons—Yahweh's word—
> Who carry out a plan—not mine,
> Who conclude an alliance[46] not inspired by me,
> Heaping sin upon sin;
> 2   Who set out to go down to Egypt
> Without asking my counsel,
> To find refuge in Pharaoh's protection,
> To shelter in Egypt's shade. . . .

Can it be only a coincidence that the words translated as "refuge" and "shelter" are of the same roots as those employed at the beginning of the Hymn of Zion, Psalm 46:1 ("God is our refuge and strength")? The king had affirmed this last in his cult, and no doubt had done so piously enough. But when the chips were down his actions say, "Pharaoh is our refuge and strength." And to Isaiah this was sheer hypocrisy.

So Isaiah could predict for the rebellion nothing but disaster (31:1–3):

> Isa. 31:1   Ah, these who go down to Egypt for help,
> Who rely upon horses
> And trust in chariots—for they are many,
> And in horsemen—for they are strong indeed;
> But they look not to the Holy One of Israel,
> Nor seek Yahweh's advice.

One can hardly fail to note the contrast (very possibly intentional) with the sentiments expressed in the Royal Psalm (Ps. 20:7), which the king had perhaps recited, or had heard recited, in the cult:

> Ps. 20:7   Some boast of chariots, some boast of horses,
> But we boast in the name of Yahweh our God.

But now his actions give the lie to his words. When danger arises, it is precisely in horses and chariots, and emphatically not in Yahweh, that he trusts. So Isaiah wheels upon the king and his counselors in anger:

---

[45] The language of this verse (and v. 18) probably conceals an allusion to an oath made, and a treaty concluded, in the name of foreign (Egyptian) gods. See the commentaries, especially W. Eichrodt, *Der Herr der Geschichte* (BAT, 17:II [Stuttgart: Calwer Verlag, 1967]), pp. 128 f.

[46] NEB, "weave schemes." But though the precise force of the words is obscure, it is clear that overtures made to Egypt are referred to.

Isa. 31:3   The Egyptians are men, not God;
             Their horses are flesh, not spirit!

And he warns that, when Yahweh in anger takes action, both the
helper (Egypt) and those who are helped (Judah and its allies) will
stumble and go down together. A little later, when Sennacherib
struck and smashed the rebellion, Isaiah could only regard this as
Yahweh's chastisement of the nation for its rebellious disobedience to
his will (1:4–9; cf. 22:1–14).

This does not mean that Isaiah was in principle opposed to
resistance to Assyria, and certainly not that he was pro-Assyrian in
sentiment. It is difficult to believe that he could have been. But he
was opposed to a resistance that supported itself on armaments and
alliances without reference to Yahweh. He desired his nation to
pursue an independent course in complete trust in Yahweh's faithfulness. This was his call at all times (e.g., 30:15):

Isa. 30:15   In turning and rest you shall be saved;
             In quietness and trust shall be your strength.

So it was that later, when Sennacherib had Jerusalem at his mercy
and all hope of outside aid was gone,[47] Isaiah stood by his king and
calmly counseled him to stand firm in the confidence that Yahweh
would save the city in accordance with his promises. This is most
clearly expressed in 37:33–35, which has been transmitted to us as a
part of a cycle of prophetic narratives ("legends" is the form critic's
word for it) having to do with Isaiah's words and actions during
Sennacherib's blockade of Jerusalem, and which may not preserve the
prophet's precise phraseology. But there is little reason to doubt that
it faithfully reflects his thought, for Isaiah on various occasions
expressed the assurance that Yahweh would never allow Jerusalem
to be taken (cf. 29:5–8; 31:4–9; etc.). Said he:

Isa. 37:33   Therefore this is what Yahweh has said
                  concerning the king of Assyria:
             "He will not come to this city
             Nor shoot an arrow there;
             He will not approach it with a shield,
             Nor throw up a siege-ramp against it.
        34   He will return by the way that he came;
             He will not come to this city—Yahweh's word—

---

[47] The problem of Sennacherib's campaigns cannot be discussed here. In *A History of
Israel*, Excursus I (pp. 296–308), I defended the view that there were two campaigns,
one in 701, the other later. But assurance is impossible. And the point is not of
material importance to the discussion here.

35   I will protect this city and save it
     For my own sake and my servant David's sake."

2. Isaiah's message, then, was rooted in, and shaped by, the traditions of Yahweh's choice of Mt. Zion as his holy abode and his promise to David of a dynasty that would never end. This can hardly be disputed. But we must not be led by this to the conclusion—a conclusion that some have drawn—that Isaiah was ignorant of, or unconcerned with, the older traditions of the Sinaitic covenant, or was unaware of the obligations and the threats which Yahweh's covenant laid before his people. It is true that the first thirty-nine chapters of Isaiah's book contain very few explicit allusions to the exodus and wilderness traditions. Really there are only two that are clear, and both of these are in passages (4:2–6; 10:24–27) that are widely regarded as coming from later hands than Isaiah's. Though I am not myself convinced that this is so, the point cannot be debated here. But the traditions of the exodus and wilderness events, of the old tribal league and of the stipulations of Yahweh's covenant law, were certainly known in Judah, as a reading of Amos or Micah—not to mention the work of the Yahwist—makes clear, and it is difficult to believe that Isaiah was ignorant of them. His attack on the crimes of society (e.g., 5:8–24) is fully parallel to that of Amos and, though he never uses the word "covenant" (as Amos also did not), one senses that it is based in an awareness of the righteous demands and the attendant threats of Yahweh's covenant law. His attack on the lavish cultus whereby the people thought to satisfy the divine demands (1:10–17) is again parallel to that of Amos; and in it one may see that concern for the rights of the helpless—specifically of the orphan and the widow (v. 17)—which is so characteristic of the theology of the ancient covenant law (e.g., Ex. 22: 21–24). Isaiah regarded his people's sin as consisting essentially in a prideful rebellion against the divine Overlord, Yahweh, a willful disregard of his commands, and a want of obedient trust in him. And, like Hosea, on more than one occasion (1:2 f.; 3:13–15) he depicted Yahweh, as the aggrieved party, instituting a lawsuit against his people for their failure to respond to him in grateful obedience, as they were obligated to do. And, once again like Amos, he described the judgment that God would bring upon this proud and rebellious people as the awful day of Yahweh (2:6–21)—a concept surely related to the traditions of the holy wars of the old tribal league.

Corresponding to the pattern of the Sinaitic covenant, Isaiah

understood well that Israel's obligation to her God rested in his
prevenient grace to her, and that it required of her righteous
behavior in accordance with his will under threat of his extreme
displeasure. Nowhere is this clearer than in the matchless Song of
the Vineyard (5:1–7). Here Isaiah steps forward as if to sing a song
about the problem a friend of his had with his vineyard. Behind the
imagery of the vineyard and its owner Isaiah's hearers would readily
have detected overtones of the relationship of a lover with his
beloved, and their interest would have been titillated. The vineyard
was an excellent one, well situated on a sunny, fertile hillside (v. 1).
And its owner had lavished upon it every conceivable care (v. 2); he
had cleared it of stones, turned the soil, and planted the very best
vines. Moreover, he had built a watchtower to guard against thieves
and had hewn out of the rock a wine vat to receive the pressed-out
juice. In short, it was a permanent investment from which he hoped
for a handsome return. But only to be disappointed!

> Isa. 5:2b   He expected it to yield grapes,
>   But it yielded "stinkers." [48]

Isaiah then turns to his hearers (vs. 3 f.) and lays the case before
them. What would you do, said he, if you had a vineyard like that?
Was there anything that I might have done for that vineyard that I
failed to do? Obviously not! (And note how Isaiah now identifies
himself with his "friend"; he has shifted into the first-person style of
divine address and speaks for God, though his hearers are not yet
aware of that fact.) Why, then, did the vineyard turn out so badly?
Isaiah (still speaking in the first person of divine address, though his
hearers would scarcely as yet have gotten the point) proceeds to
answer his own question. What will he do? He will abandon the
vineyard. He will break down its wall and let the cattle trample it; he
will cultivate it no more and will let thorns and briers take possession
of it (vs. 5 f.). Then comes the denouement, as Isaiah drops his mask
and makes his meaning plain:

> Isa. 5:7   For the vineyard of Yahweh of Hosts
>   Is the house of Israel,
>   And the men of Judah
>   His pleasant planting.
>   He looked for justice (mišpāṭ),
>   But see—bloodshed (mišpāh);

---

[48] The Hebrew word may be literally translated so. Of course putrid, inedible grapes
are meant, unfit for use.

> For righteousness ($ṣᵉdāqāh$),
> But see—an outcry ($ṣᵉ'āqāh$).

In a word, Israel has been the recipient of grace and, because of that fact, was obligated to bring forth the fruits of justice and righteousness; because she has not done so, she stands under the judgment of God. However strongly Isaiah may have believed in Yahweh's election of Zion and his sure promises to David, he certainly did not believe that God would protect the nation—no matter what!

One might say, indeed, that in Isaiah the two covenant traditions, the Davidic and the Sinaitic, are in tension and are brought into balance by stress on the possibility of chastisement inherent in the former. This last, of course, is a standard feature in all the classical formulations of the Davidic covenant (cf. II Sam. 7:14–16; Ps. 89: 30–32; etc.); and, in principle, short of the fall of the dynasty, no limits were set on how severe that chastisement might be. In Isaiah chastisement reaches the point of national disaster, so much so that one might gain the impression (wrongly, I believe) that Isaiah expected the total destruction of his country. This seems to have been the case at the time of his call (6:11 f.), and it certainly was the case when Judah rebelled from Assyria at the beginning of Sennacherib's reign (e.g., 30:12–17); and when Sennacherib struck in 701 and left the nation a bloody pulp, Isaiah could only regard this as the expected and well-merited chastisement (cf. 1:4–9, where he likens the nation to a man so fearfully beaten that no sound spot remains on his body from the crown of his head to the soles of his feet).

It is interesting, too, that when Isaiah sought to describe the disaster he saw coming, on occasion he did so in terms of the traditions of great David, which he stood on their head, reversed. This is so in 28:14–22, where, having warned his country's leaders that they have, through the Egyptian alliance, worked the nation into a trap from which it cannot extricate itself (v. 20: "The bed is too short to stretch on/the cover too narrow to wrap in"), and having begged them to come to their senses before it is too late, he says:

> Isa. 28:21 For Yahweh will rise as at Mount Perazim,
> Will rage as in the Vale of Gibeon,
> To do his deed—strange his deed!
> To work his work—alien his work!

Mt. Perazim (Baal-perazim) and Gibeon seem clearly to be allusions to the two battles in which David won definitive victories over the Philistines and drove them from Israelite soil (II Sam. 5:17–25; I

Chron. 14:8–17).[49] Now, says Isaiah, God will act again as he did in David's day, but this time his action will be hostile!

We seem to have another example of this in 29:1–4, where Isaiah speaks of Jerusalem (Ariel) as "the city which David besieged" (so v. 1 can be understood; cf. II Sam. 5:6–10) and declares (if we follow the Septuagint in v. 3) that God will again besiege the city as David did.

> Isa. 29:1   Ah, Ariel, Ariel,
>   City which David besieged!
>   Add year to year,
>   Let the feasts roll round,
>   2   And I will bring Ariel into straits;
>   There will be moaning and groaning,
>   And she will be to me like an Ariel[50]
>   3   I will besiege you as David did,[51]
>   Press hard upon you with towers,
>   Raise siege-works against you.
>   4   Then deep from the earth you will speak,
>   Low from the dust your words will come . . .

If this understanding of the text is correct, the victories of great David have once again become types of the judgment to come.

Isaiah, then, envisioned a terrible catastrophe that would befall the nation because of its sin. Yet one can see no evidence that he looked for the total destruction of the nation, the fall of Jerusalem, the end of the Davidic dynasty, and the carrying of the population into exile. Isaiah nowhere speaks of these things, and one must suppose that he did not reckon with them. In his thinking, Assyria is the instrument of God's judgment, but *only* an instrument. Assyria will never be given the last word in history nor will she, whatever her own estimate of her capabilities might be, ever be allowed to exceed the function God has assigned her; when she has discharged that function—namely, to discipline God's rebellious and godless people—she will for her blasphemous pride be brought low (so classically in 10:5–19).

---

[49] We should probably read "Gibeon" instead of "Geba" in II Sam. 5:25 with the preferable text of I Chron. 14:16. Some see in Gibeon an allusion to Joshua's victory over the Canaanite coalition (Josh., ch. 10); but in the context an allusion to David seems more likely.

[50] There is a wordplay here. "Ariel," which is here used as an appellation for Jerusalem, seems to denote on the one hand the great altar of the temple ("the mountain of God") and, on the other, the underworld, a denizen of the underworld, a ghost; cf. W. F. Albright, *Archaeology and the Religion of Israel* (Baltimore: The Johns Hopkins Press, 3d ed., 1953), pp. 151 f., 218.

[51] Reading the consonants *kdwd* with LXX; so various scholars, and cf. BHS, JB, etc. MT has the consonants *kdwr* ("round about," RSV).

Assyria operates within the framework of God's purpose, and it is his purpose in the end to destroy Assyria, and in such a way that all the world may know that he has done it (14:24–27; 18:1–6; cf. 30:29–33). Mt. Zion is Yahweh's earthly dwelling place (8:18; cf. 31:9), and he will never abandon it to destruction. Its foes may rage against it and threaten it, but (as in the Hymns of Zion) they will be frustrated and driven in confusion (17:12–14; 29:5–8; 31:4–9; 37:22–29).[52] God will humiliate Jerusalem, but in the end will rescue.

Isaiah, then, saw the judgment that was coming as a chastisement —a terrible chastisement, to be sure, but still a chastisement, not a total destruction. It would serve a pedagogical function; it would serve as a purge designed to discipline and refine the people and bring forth a chastened remnant.[53] This concept, which we associate especially with Isaiah, finds classical expression in the first chapter of his book (1:21–26). The piece begins (vs. 21–23) in the form of a lament bewailing the depraved condition of Jerusalem and its rulers. The city before which such a lofty ideal had been held has prostituted itself completely:

> Isa. 1:21   What a whore she has become,
> The once faithful town,
> She that was full of justice,
> Where righteousness used to dwell,
> But now—murderers!
> 22   Your silver has turned into dross,
> Your wine is cut with water.
> 23   Your rulers are rebels,
> Connivers with thieves.
> Every one loves a bribe,
> Runs after graft.
> To the orphan they do not do justice;
> The widow's case—it never gets before them.

Then follows the divine word of judgment (vs. 24–26). It is a fearful judgment, but it is one that will purify and refine, and make Jerusalem once again the city God had intended it to be.

> Isa. 1:24   Therefore, it is the word of the Lord, Yahweh of Hosts,
> the Champion of Israel:
> "Ah, I will have satisfaction from my enemies,

---

[52] Regardless of the problems attaching to various of these passages, it is impossible to deny them as a group to Isaiah. They are perfectly expressive of his theology, which as we have said, was rooted in the traditions of Zion and David.

[53] On this concept, cf. Gerhard F. Hasel, *The Remnant* (Berrien Springs, Mich.: Andrews University Press, 1972).

25   Will get redress from my foes.
      I will turn my hand against you,
      Smelt away your dross in the furnace,[54]
      And remove all your alloy.
26   I will restore your judges as at the first,
      Your counselors as at the beginning.
      Then you will be called
      'City of Righteousness, Faithful Town.' "

The words "as at the first," "as at the beginning," seem clearly to point back to the days of David, when Jerusalem first came under Israelite control. After the judgment the glories and virtues of the Davidic age, now idealized and transfigured in the national memory, will be recovered—and even exceeded!

It is true that the notion of the purified remnant does not dominate the preserved sayings of Isaiah, as one might be led to suppose. In fact, it receives clear expression only in a relatively few passages. Yet the idea seems to have been fundamental to Isaiah's thinking from the beginning, for he gave to his oldest son (7:3) the symbolical name of Shear-yashub ("a remnant will return"). This name can have either a threatening or a promising connotation depending upon which of the two Hebrew words that compose it one lays the stress. It can mean "*a remnant* will return" (i.e., only a remnant will get back), or it can mean "a remnant *will return*" (i.e., at least a few of the people will return to their God in penitence and trust). Both of these connotations are developed in the Isaiah book (cf. 10:20 f., where it is a promise, and vs. 22 f., where it is a threat).[55] It seems that Isaiah cherished the hope that each successive catastrophe that befell his nation would prove to be the needed discipline that would impel at least the best of his people to turn to their God in penitence and trust. This hope, it is true, was repeatedly frustrated, but there is no evidence that until the end of his life Isaiah ever surrendered it. From 22:1–14—a piece that was probably composed when Sennacherib lifted the siege of Jerusalem in 701, thus late in Isaiah's life—we see that even then the prophet had hoped that the Assyrian attack would serve an educative function, driving his people to repentance and dependence upon Yahweh, only to be shocked and grieved to discover that it had taught them nothing.

---

[54] Assuming the transposition of two Hebrew consonants (*bkr* for *kbr*) with various scholars (and cf. JB). MT reads, "as with lye, potash" (cf. RSV, NEB).

[55] The authenticity of these verses is disputed; see the commentaries. We cannot discuss the point here; but both emphases are certainly legitimate developments of the prophet's thought.

3. Isaiah's message in its essential features thus conforms to, and is a consistent development of, those theological traditions associated with Yahweh's election of Jerusalem and his sure promises to the Davidic house. It is therefore scarcely surprising that his vision of the farthest future, his eschatological hope, should develop the same traditions. In Isaiah the "messianic" hope receives its first and classical expression.[56] Two passages stand out in this connection: 9:1-7 (MT, 8:23 to 9:6) and 11:1-9. Both of these passages have been regarded by various critics as later (post-exilic) additions to the Isaiah book (the second perhaps more frequently than the first). Yet neither betrays any knowledge of the destruction of Jerusalem and the deportation of the population, or any yearning for the ingathering of the dispersed of Israel to the homeland. And both fit splendidly within the framework of Isaiah's thought.

The first of these passages (9:1-7), whatever the occasion upon which it was first uttered, is meant to be read (cf. v. 1) against the background of the events of 733/2, when Tiglath-pileser III, in response to Ahaz' plea, fell upon the Aramean-Israelite coalition and crushed it, overrunning all of Galilee, the Coastal Plain, and Transjordan, and turning the area thus seized into three Assyrian provinces (cf., "the way of the sea, the land beyond the Jordan, Galilee of the nations").[57] The piece takes the form of a dynastic hymn, or oracle, such as might have been uttered on the day of the king's coronation. The occasion is described as if it had already taken place; until the very end, all the main verbs are in the perfect tense, and only then (v. 7b, "the zeal of Yahweh of Hosts will do this") is it made clear that the piece is to be read as a promise of future salvation. It is as if the prophet had projected himself ahead into that gladsome day and had witnessed it. Everywhere there is the wildest of joy as a bright light dawns on the beaten and humiliated nation (vs. 2 f.). The oppressor's yoke has been broken in a victory worthy to be compared with the fabled victories of the holy wars of the past,[58] and the gory debris of the battlefield has been disposed of (vs. 4 f.). A

---

[56] As the reader is doubtless aware, the words "Messiah," "messianic," do not appear in their later, technical sense either in Isaiah or elsewhere in the Old Testament. But in the royal redeemer figure depicted by Isaiah we have the first appearance of what was later to become the figure of the hoped-for Messiah. Passages that speak of this figure can therefore with justice be described as "messianic."

[57] Cf. A. Alt, "Jesaja 8, 23-9, 6. Befreiungsnacht und Krönungstag" (1950; repr., *Kleine Schriften zur Geschichte des Volkes Israel*, Vol. II [Munich: C. H. Beck'sche Verlagsbuchhandlung, 1953], pp. 206-225).

[58] "The day of Midian" (v. 4b) is a reference to Gideon's victory over Midian, Judg., chs. 7 to 8.

new king has taken the throne.[59] The great regnal names—"Wonder-
ful Counselor, Godlike Warrior,[60] Father Forever, Prince of Peace"—
have been given to him, and the dominion has been entrusted to him
(v. 6). He will rule in justice and righteousness and his rule,
supported by God himself, will endure forever:

> Isa. 9:7   Great[61] is the dominion,
>   And of peace no end,
>   On David's throne
>   And over his kingdom,
>   To establish it and sustain it,
>   From now on and forevermore.

Against the opinion of many commentators, the second passage
mentioned above (11:1–9) is likewise not to be regarded as post-
exilic.[62] The wording of v. 1 by no means necessarily implies that the
Davidic dynasty has come to an end—i.e., is like a cut-down tree. The
metaphor of the "shoot from the stump [more properly "stem,
root-stock"] of Jesse" seems to be controlled by that of 10:33 f., which
is probably the true beginning of the passage.[63] Yahweh executes
judgment on his foes like a woodman felling trees with his ax, and the
great giants of the forest come crashing down. But a shoot sprouts
from the "stump of Jesse." Jesse, it will be remembered, was David's
father; so the shoot that will sprout from his roots is in the truest
sense a new David. He will be endowed with the divine spirit: "the
spirit of wisdom and understanding, the spirit of counsel and might,
the spirit of the knowledge and the fear of Yahweh" (v. 2)—i.e., all
the charismatic graces will rest upon him, as in theory they rested
upon every Davidic king, but in fact did not. Endowed with these
graces, he will embody the kingly ideal of justice and righteousness,
which all kings were supposed to embody (cf. Ps. 72), but which so
few in fact did. Under his rule oppressors will be struck down and the
helpless vindicated. An era of peace will then ensue in all of creation

----

[59] The words "A child is born to us / A son is given to us" (v. 6a) probably refer to the
coronation, not the birth of the king. On his coronation day the king took the throne as
Yahweh's (adopted) son; cf. Ps. 2:7. See the commentaries for discussion.

[60] "Godlike Warrior" seems to be a more accurate translation of this name (lit.,
"God/Mighty One of a Warrior") than the conventional "Mighty God"; see the
commentaries for discussion.

[61] On the text, cf. BH³, BHS, and the commentaries. Some believe (note the final
mem in the middle of the word) that a fifth regnal name has dropped out here.

[62] The reader will find the commentaries divided on the point. But cf. the excellent
discussion of H. Wildberger, *Jesaja* (BKAT, 10/6, 1972), pp. 436–462.

[63] Cf. O. Kaiser, *Isaiah 1–12* (Eng. tr., OTL, 1972), pp. 156 f.

(vs. 6–9), as if the idyllic felicity of Eden, long ruptured by human sin, had been recaptured. No longer will there be killing and destroying,

Isa. 11:9b   For the earth shall be filled with the knowledge of Yahweh
              As the waters spread over the sea.

Isaiah's vision of the farthest future was clearly no mere "ditto" of the hopes that the populace may have been led to repose in the dynasty through the affirmations of the official cult. Certainly it did not envision a future that was secured by unconditional promises of divine protection. Indeed, it was not a hope for the presently existing order at all, nor was it one that lay in straight-line continuity with the existing order as the goal toward which the national history was in the nature of things inevitably moving. Rather, it stood in discontinuity with the existing order. It lay beyond the judgment that God would bring—indeed, was even then in the act of bringing—upon the faithless and rebellious nation, its rulers and its people, and it would come to pass through a new act of the divine grace beyond the judgment. The divine chastisement allowed for by the official theology was not with Isaiah a theoretical possibility that might conveniently be banished from the mind or, at least, not taken with great seriousness, but rather was expressly announced and affirmed as an imminently impending reality. Moreover, Isaiah's hope of a royal redeemer is no mere recapitulation of the ideal that was laid before every king at the time of his coronation, nor did it direct men's gaze toward a recovery of the lost glories of the past, however much the memory of David's great achievement may have helped to give it shape. Rather, it was the expectation of a king who should come in the future (probably, in Isaiah's mind, in the very near future) who, unlike any actual king that Judah had ever known, would fulfill the kingly ideal, and under whose just and beneficent rule all the dynastic promises would be made actual and the divine rule on earth established. And the blessed state of affairs, thus introduced, would be one that would never end. It would endure forever.

So began that restless longing for Him Who Shall Come, the Anointed One of David's line, the Messiah. It was a longing that would never find fulfillment on its own terms. No such king ever came to sit on David's throne; and at length the nation fell and the eternal dynasty turned out not to be eternal. Yet hope was not surrendered, but rather was projected into the yet farther future. Still it pointed men out ahead, beyond frustration and despair, beyond B.C. and all the possibilities of B.C., until, at the turning point of the years and the end of all B.C., it found (so Christians affirm) a yet greater fulfillment: "To you is born this day in the City of David a Savior, who is Messiah [Christ] the Lord" (Luke 2:11).

4

The Seventh Century: Apostasy and Reform

In the preceding chapter we were concerned with the preaching of the eighth-century prophets and, in particular, with their views regarding what the future—both the immediate future and the farthest, eschatological future—had in store for their people. It will be remembered that we defined eschatology broadly.[1] We did not require that it be understood in suprahistorical terms, as a more or less developed doctrine or complex of ideas regarding the end of the world (the age), the final judgment, resurrection to eternal life beyond the grave, and the like, as it would have been understood in later Jewish or in Christian theology. Rather, we defined it as a vision of God's final provision for his people, the farthest future of his dealings with them within history, the definitive consummation of his purposes for them beyond which no further development was envisioned or expected.

Eschatology in this sense, so it was argued, first made its appearance with the eighth-century prophets. These prophets, although they saw the immediate future as one of terrible judgment, and completely shattered the popular confidence that God would always favor, bless, and protect Israel, nevertheless looked beyond the judgment that loomed to a still farther future in which there would take place a new and definitive divine intervention which would restore the broken relationship between God and people and bring God's purpose in history to a triumphant conclusion. Beyond this new divine act the prophets saw no need to look, and in fact did

---

[1] See above, Ch. 1, pp. 18 f.

not look. It would introduce a state of affairs that would be final and lasting, one beyond which no further development was reckoned with. It was, as far as their thinking was concerned, the "last thing," the *eschaton*.

But we noted that the prophetic vision of the future did not in every case follow the same pattern. Indeed, we saw two distinct patterns emerging, two ways of viewing both God's immediate dealings with his people and his final provision for them. Both of these were to become classical in Old Testament prophecy. Both were related to understandings of God's covenant with his people which had long established themselves in Israel and had become basic to the nation's self-understanding and the ground of its confidence. Let us briefly recapitulate.

1. One of these patterns was given classic expression by Hosea in northern Israel. To Hosea, "covenant" meant the Mosaic-Sinaitic covenant. He was steeped in the traditions of this covenant, and this shaped both his evaluation of his people's present depraved condition and his understanding of what God would do to them and for them in the future. The Sinaitic covenant, it will be recalled, followed the pattern of an international suzerainty treaty; it was a vassal's acceptance of the overlord's terms. The bond that it forged was based in God's unmerited favor to his people in bringing them from bondage and giving them their land, and it obligated the vassal-people absolutely to compliance with the divine Overlord's stipulations: all the future depended on this. If it promised the Overlord's continuing protection and blessing in the event of obedience, it also held out the threat of the covenant curses and the revocation of promise in the event of disobedience.

Hosea evaluated the nation in the light of the stipulations of this covenant, above all in the light of the demand that it should worship no god save Yahweh. He saw its apostasy to the gods of fertility as a crime against grace, the whoring of an adulterous wife, which had irrevocably voided the covenant bond. He therefore saw the nation as under the curse, doomed to total destruction and ejection from its land. Quite consistently, he could view the eschatological future only in terms of a new act of the divine grace beyond the judgment, parallel to the events of exodus and land-giving, which would reestablish the bond between God and people, restore the people to their land, and bring to them the promised covenant blessings.

2. The other pattern for understanding the future was given classical expression by Isaiah of Jerusalem. Isaiah, as we said, was

deeply rooted in the traditions of Yahweh's election of Mt. Zion and of the covenant he had made with David. This last was a promissory covenant through which God had, in effect, bound himself for all the future through his unconditional promises to David. He had chosen Mt. Zion as his eternal abode, and he would dwell there forever among his people, protecting them from their foes; and he had promised to David a dynasty that would never end. True, there was the understanding that a sinful king might bring chastisement—severe chastisement—upon himself and his people. But the promise itself was unconditional and sure: the dynasty would always continue, secure in the faithfulness of God.

Isaiah, to be sure, certainly did not hold to this theology in any rigidly mechanical way. He was well aware of the stipulations of covenant law, and he certainly did not regard the breaking of them as a light and trivial thing; he knew nothing of promises of unconditional divine protection. On the contrary, he saw the nation, precisely because of its crimes against covenant law and its failure to trust the promises, as under God's judgment, and he announced that judgment as one that would amount to national disaster. But that God was faithful to his promises was something that he seems never to have doubted. He viewed the judgment as a divine chastisement, not as one that would involve the final destruction of the nation and the end of the Davidic dynasty. It seems to have been his lifelong hope—though a hope repeatedly frustrated—that each God-sent catastrophe would serve as a discipline to drive his people to penitence and bring from the wreckage of the nation a chastened remnant. Equally consistently, he viewed the eschatological future in terms of God's kingly rule on Mt. Zion and the coming of a king of David's line who would fulfill the dynastic ideal, and under whose just and beneficent rule all the dynastic promises would be made actual.

I

Now it can hardly be denied that a certain tension—or, at least, the possibility of a tension—exists between these two ways of looking at the future. This is not to say that the two are in principle incompatible, or that either of them is illegitimate. Both are legitimate expressions of essential factors in Israel's normative faith, factors that had always been held in delicate balance. The one stressed the sure and unconditional promises of God which nothing could cancel, the other the binding stipulations of his covenant which no one might disregard with impunity. Moreover, both views saw the nation as under God's judgment for its sins, both saw that judgment as one that would be executed at the hands of the imperial power of the day and amounting to national disaster, and both reserved what hope they had to offer for a future beyond the judgment. One might almost say that they differed chiefly with regard to how severe the judgment would be. And here one must remember that they addressed different situations: Hosea's word was to northern Israel, and it turned out to be valid in *that* situation; Isaiah's word was to Judah, and it turned out to be valid in *that* situation.

1. Certainly these two views of the future, whatever *we* may think of them, seem not to have been felt by ancient Israelites to be incompatible. We have an excellent illustration of this in the little book of Micah, the prophet of rural Judah who was Isaiah's contemporary. Here we see the two views juxtaposed in what might appear to be a jarring disharmony. But the very fact that they are so juxtaposed may be taken as evidence that ancient Israelites did not regard them as intrinsically disharmonious.

The Book of Micah develops various themes which we find expressed in the preaching of the other great prophets of the eighth century. Micah's attack on the crimes of society is fully parallel to that of Amos and, like his, seems clearly to presuppose an awareness of the stipulations of covenant law. Indeed, so similar in its expression is Micah's assault on the rapacious rich, and the venal judges who connive in their dastardly schemes, to that of his fellow Judahite, Amos, that were one to hear his words read aloud without indication of source, one might be put to it to decide which of the two prophets was speaking. For example (Micah 2:1 f.):

> Micah 2:1   Ah these who plot mischief,
> Work out evil on their beds!
> When morning dawns they do it,
> For it lies within their power.
> 2   They covet fields and seize them,
> Houses, and take them away.
> They plunder a man and his household,
> A man and his heritage.

Or this (3:1–4):

> Micah 3:1   Listen, you leaders of Jacob,
> You rulers of Israel's house!
> Ought not you to know what is right?—

2   You who hate what is good and love what is bad,[2]
3   Who eat the flesh of my people,
     Strip their skin from off them,
     Break their bones in pieces,
     Chop them up like meat[3] in a kettle,
     Like flesh in a pot. . . .

This note of hot indignation against the powerful for their crimes against the helpless dominates the entire message of Micah, as it did that of Amos. To Micah, as to Amos, these were crimes against Yahweh, gross violations of his righteous demands.

Moreover, like both Amos and Hosea, Micah viewed Israel's derelictions against the backdrop of Yahweh's grace to her in the formative events, the events of exodus, wilderness wandering, and land-giving, and found them doubly heinous. He saw them as crimes against grace, without reason and without excuse. This is made clear in the great covenant lawsuit which we find in 6:1–5. Here Yahweh, as the aggrieved party and accuser, makes his case against his people:

Micah 6:1   Hear now what Yahweh is saying:
             Up! Plead your case before the mountains,
             Let the hills hear your voice!
       2   Listen, you mountains, to Yahweh's case,
             You pillars, enduring, supporting the earth;[4]
             For Yahweh has a case against his people,
             With Israel he will argue it out.
       3   "O my people, what have I done to you?
             Wherein have I wearied you? Answer me!
       4   For I brought you up from Egypt's land,
             From the house of bondage I ransomed you;
             I sent to lead you Moses
             And Aaron and Miriam.
       5   O my people, recall what he plotted,
             Did Balak the king of Moab,
             And how he gave answer to him,
             Did Balaam ben Beor.[5]

---

[2] MT has here, "who tear their skin from off them / their flesh from off their bones." The words seem out of place where they are and perhaps should be read in connection with v. 3; cf. BHS and various commentators.

[3] So with LXX; cf. BH³, BHS, and commentaries. MT transposes two consonants (k'šr for kš'r).

[4] Some commentators (cf. BH³, BHS) with a small emendation read, "Give ear, you pillars (foundations) of the earth."

[5] Cf. the narratives, and especially the ancient poems, in Num., chs. 22 to 24.

[Recall what happened as you moved] [6]
From Shittim to Gilgal,[7]
That you may know the saving deeds of Yahweh."

In Micah's view, Israel owes everything to the grace of Yahweh, who brought her out of bondage to her land, and she is obligated to respond to him in righteous behavior and utter loyalty. Like all the other eighth-century prophets, Micah therefore vigorously attacked the notion that Yahweh's demands could be met by sacrifice and cultic observance alone, no matter how lavish these might be (6:6–8).

Micah 6:6   "Wherewith shall I approach Yahweh,
        Bow down before the God on high?
        Shall I approach him with whole burnt offerings,
        With young yearling bulls?
    7   Will Yahweh be pleased with thousands of rams,
        With ten thousands of rivers of oil?
        Shall I give my first-born for my trespass,
        The fruit of my body for the sin which is mine?" [8]
    8   He has told you, mortal man, what is good.
        And what does Yahweh require of you
        But to act justly, to love with loyal devotion,
        And to walk circumspectly with your God?

Because of his people's forgetfulness of the divine grace, and because of the crimes against justice whereby they had flouted covenant law, Micah pronounced a judgment on Judah every bit as stern as that pronounced by Amos and Hosea on northern Israel. He completely rejected the conceit that Yahweh's election of Mt. Zion and his promises to the Davidic line guaranteed the capital city protection. On the contrary, going far beyond anything Isaiah is recorded as saying, he declared that, because of the crimes of its ruling classes, Jerusalem and its Temple would be laid in ruins (3:9–12):

Micah 3:9   Hear this, you heads of the house of Jacob,
        You rulers of the house of Israel—
        Who abhor justice
        And distort whatever is right,
    10   Who build Zion with bloodshed,
        Jerusalem with wrong.

---

[6] The words are added arbitrarily simply for the sake of the sense. MT has only "from Shittim to Gilgal," and attaches it directly to the preceding colon.

[7] Shittim (cf. Num. 25:1; Josh. 2:1) was remembered as the last encampment before the crossing of the Jordan; Gilgal (cf. Josh. 4:19; ch. 5) was the first stop after entering the Promised Land.

[8] Heb., "the sin of my *nepeš*" (in many EVV, ". . . of my soul"), i.e., "the sin of my self," "my very own sin."

> 11 Its heads pronounce judgment for a bribe,
>   Its priests give instruction for a fee,
>   Its prophets predict the future[9] for pay;
>   Yet they rely upon Yahweh and say,
>   "Is Yahweh not here in our midst?
>   Disaster will not overtake us."
> 12 Therefore—on account of you—
>   Zion shall be a plowed field,
>   Jerusalem shall be a heap of ruins,
>   And the temple mount a wooded ridge.

Micah's theology allowed no room whatever for such complacency as the official theology may have tended to create in the minds of the people.

So far Micah's message, like that of Amos and Hosea, seems to be orientated upon the traditions of Israel's formative period and the stipulations of covenant law, and it seems to presuppose an understanding of the God-people relationship like that observed in the covenant (the Sinaitic) that brought Israel into being as a people. This, as we have said, was a relationship based in the unmerited, prevenient favor of the Deity, which bound the lesser party in the relationship, the people Israel, to full and willing obedience to the divine stipulations under threat of the direst penalties in the event of their failure to comply. In the light of such an understanding of the God-people relationship, and because of his people's egregious violation of covenant law, Micah could pronounce on Jerusalem a judgment of total proportions.

Yet, in spite of this, The Book of Micah contains an abundant promise for the yet farther future. And this promise is articulated all but exclusively in terms of the Zion-David traditions. There are severe critical problems here, involving especially the material of chs. 4 and 5, which can have no place in the present discussion.[10] But it is probably overhasty to relegate the whole of chs. 4 and 5 to a later date, as not a few scholars have done. This is especially so of the

---

[9] Lit., "divine," "make divination." The prophets are here placed on a level with soothsayers and others who practice the mantic arts.

[10] The reader must consult the commentaries. Note how in the present arrangement of the book Micah's message of censure and doom, which reaches its climax in the announcement of the destruction of Jerusalem and the Temple (Micah 3:9–12), is followed immediately (in chs. 4 to 5) by passages telling of Zion's exaltation before all the world, of Yahweh's defense of Zion from foes who attack her, and of a new scion of David's line (5:2–6 [MT, vs. 1–5]) who will deliver his people from Assyria. Many scholars regard chs. 4 to 5, as a whole or in most of its parts, as coming from later hands than Micah's.

"messianic" saying in 5:2–6 (MT, vs. 1–5), which begins:[11]

> Micah 5:2   But you, Bethlehem Ephratah,
>   The least among the clans of Judah,
>   Out of you there will proceed for me
>   The one who will rule over Israel.

This passage represents a theology that seems to have been wide-spread in Judah in the eighth century (note the similar passages in Isaiah discussed in the preceding chapter), and it is by no means inconceivable that Micah himself may have shared it.[12] It may well be that Micah was of a (perhaps sizable) group in rural Judah who had become disgusted with the aristocracy of Jerusalem, both civil and ecclesiastical, and completely alienated from them, and who expected the destruction of that city with its Temple—and perhaps even the end of the presently ruling royal line—but who nevertheless cherished the hope that a new David would come from that king's ancestral city, Bethlehem, to deliver his people from bondage.[13] We cannot pursue the matter here. But, whatever one concludes about the hope that Micah may have held for his country's future, the arrangement of his book in any event shows that its collectors saw no essential disharmony between a judgment by the terms of the Sinaitic covenant and a farther future secure in God's eternal promises to David.

2. Still, the possibility of a tension is there. It was at bottom, as we have hinted, a tension between two ways of viewing Israel's election, her relationship to God and her future under God, which had always been held in a somewhat delicate balance. These could be so articulated that they might—as in course of time they in fact did—give rise to two diametrically opposite ways of viewing the nation's future. There would always be those to whom it would be clear that the nation could be destroyed if it persisted in violating the stipulations of covenant. And there would be those to whom it would become an article of faith that though the nation might be punished for its sins—and punished severely—it could never be destroyed, for

---

[11] On the text, cf. BH³, BHS, and the commentaries.

[12] The passage has probably undergone expansion. Perhaps its original nucleus is to be found in vs. 2, 4a, 5a, 6b (MT, vs. 1, 3a, 4a, 5b), as various scholars have argued. On the traditionary background of Micah's preaching, see especially W. Beyerlin, *Die Kulttraditionen Israels in der Verkündigung des Propheten Micha* (FRLANT, 72, 1959).

[13] On the point, cf. A. Alt, "Micha 2, 1–5, *Gēs Anadasmos* in Juda" (1955; repr., *Kleine Schriften zur Geschichte des Volkes Israel*, Vol. III [Munich: C. H. Beck'sche Verlagsbuchhandlung, 1959], pp. 373–381).

God had assured its continuance through his unconditional election of Mt. Zion and his promises to the Davidic line.

These two views of the matter, we may suppose, developed side by side in Judah. Not only did the theology of God's election of Mt. Zion and of the Davidic line continue to be affirmed in the cult of the Jerusalem Temple; Isaiah's interpretation of events in terms of it enjoyed an enormous prestige. His words were cherished and handed down among his disciples. And in later generations other prophets arose who may be said—in the best sense of the word—to have carried on the Isaiah tradition.

One of these was Zephaniah, who prophesied just prior to Josiah's reform, of which we shall speak in a moment.[14] Zephaniah denounced the abuses, both religious and social, with which the land was then filled (cf. Zeph. 1:2–13; 3:1–4, etc.) and, in Isaiah's tradition, he viewed these as a prideful rebellion against Yahweh and a want of trust in him (cf. 1:12; 3:2, 11, etc.). Zephaniah was assured that God's judgment was imminently coming. And, like Isaiah (and Amos!), he viewed this judgment as the day of Yahweh, a day of indescribable terror and ruin that would shortly break over the peoples of the earth (1:14–18).

> Zeph. 1:14   Near is Yahweh's great day,
>   Near and hurrying fast.
>
> . . . .
>
>   15   A day of wrath is that day,
>   A day of distress and of anguish,
>   A day of wrack and of ruin,
>   A day of murk and of darkness,
>   A day of cloud and of gloom,
>   16   A day of trumpet blast and battle shout . . .

Against the coming of this day, Zephaniah held out no hope save in sincere repentance (2:1–3), for which, one might say, God had offered one last chance:

> Zeph. 2:1   Come together, hold assembly,
>   O nation without shame,

---

[14] Zephaniah's career is placed in Josiah's reign by the superscription of his book (Zeph. 1:1), and the vast majority of scholars accept this as correct. Internal evidence suggests that the bulk of his preaching was done prior to the reform, since many of the abuses he attacked were removed at that time (cf. II Kings, ch. 23). It is not excluded, however, that he may have continued to preach until later in Josiah's reign. A few scholars, to be sure, have questioned this consensus and have sought to place Zephaniah's ministry at a later date; but their views have not carried conviction.

2   Before you are driven away
     Like flying chaff,[15]
     Before there comes upon you
     The heat of Yahweh's wrath,
     Before there comes upon you
     The day of Yahweh's wrath.
3   Seek Yahweh, all you meek of the land,
     Who conform to his way.
     Seek what is right,
     Seek what is humble.
     Perhaps you may be hidden
     In the day of Yahweh's wrath.

But Zephaniah seems to have had little optimism regarding the willingness of his people to repent (3:6 f.), and thus little hope that the day of judgment would be averted. Yet, at the same time, though that day would be fearful beyond description, Zephaniah apparently did not expect the total destruction of the nation. The judgment would come as a chastisement, out of which a purified people would emerge (3:11–13):

Zeph. 3:11   When that day comes
              You will not be shamed by all your deeds
              Through which you have rebelled against me;
              For then I will remove from your midst
              Your proud and boastful ones.
              No more will you flaunt your arrogance
              In my holy mount;
      12   For I will leave in your midst a people
              Humble and lowly. . . .

That words such as these follow in Isaiah's tradition seems evident.

Another prophet who may be said to have stood in the same tradition was Habakkuk, who prophesied near the twilight of the Kingdom of Judah, probably in Jehoiakim's reign (609–598).[16] Habakkuk was moved to question the justice of God's dealings in the world. Crying out at the violence and wrong he observed on every hand (Hab. 1:2–4),[17] he asks, in effect: How long is this to go on? Is God

---

[15] So, roughly, with most EVV. The text and translation of the bicolon is in places uncertain; see the commentaries.

[16] The Book of Habakkuk carries no date, and internal evidence does not allow us to assign one with precision. But Habakkuk seems to have prophesied just as the Babylonians first began to threaten Judah—thus approximately in Jehoiakim's reign. This is the generally held opinion.

[17] Are the perpetrators of this wrong foreign oppressors or powerful men in Judah

going to overlook it? He receives the answer that God is most certainly not going to overlook it. He will use the Babylonians (the Chaldeans), "that bitter and hasty nation," as the instrument of his judgment upon the guilty ones (1:5–11)—the very function, be it noted, that Isaiah had assigned to Assyria a century earlier. Yet Habakkuk could not accept this as final (and no more could Isaiah!): Is Babylon, then, going to be allowed to get away with its ruthless rapacity forever (1:17)? No! Proud Babylon will in its turn be judged. But, meanwhile, God's dealings must have seemed ambiguous, almost wholly opaque. And, in this interim, Habakkuk's word to his people was: Have faith (2:1–4).[18]

> Hab. 2:1   I will stand at my guard-post,
>   Take my place on the tower,
>   And will watch to see what he says to me,
>   What answer he will give[19] to my plaint.
>   2   And Yahweh answered me thus:
>   "Write down the vision,
>   Inscribe it on tablets,
>   So that one may easily read it.[20]
>   3   Still the vision is for its set time,
>   It moves[21] to the end, it does not lie.
>   If it delays, wait for it!
>   It will certainly come, without fail.
>   4   See! [. . . . . . .][22]
>   But the righteous shall live by his faith." [23]

In these last words, later to be taken up in a different context by Paul (Rom. 1:17; Gal. 3:11)—and still later by Martin Luther—we may once again hear the echo of Isaiah's voice.

But if the traditions of Yahweh's election of Mt. Zion and of the

---

who oppress their weaker brethren? The reader will find the commentators divided on the point. It seems to me, however, that the language favors the latter alternative.

[18] The text of this passage is difficult and its meaning at many points obscure. A full discussion cannot be attempted here. The reader must consult the commentaries.

[19] So with BH[3], BHS, and various commentators (and cf. JB). MT has, "I will give. . . ."

[20] Lit., "So that he may run reading it" (or, "who reads it")—which may mean: so that one can read it without trouble as one hurries by; or: so that he who reads it may run (to repeat what he has seen to others), or the like. Cf. the commentaries; e.g., F. Horst, *Die zwölf kleinen Propheten* (HAT, 3d ed., 1964), p. 176.

[21] The word is obscure.

[22] The translation of the colon is quite uncertain. RSV reads, "He whose soul is not upright in him shall fail"; NEB has, "The reckless will be unsure of himself"; JB, "How he flags, he whose soul is not at rights." This illustrates the difficulty.

[23] Or better, "his faithfulness."

Davidic line continued to be affirmed and believed in Judah, the
theology of the Mosaic covenant was likewise not forgotten there. No
doubt it was thrust into the background in the cult of the Jerusalem
Temple, and it may have had little actuality in the minds of large
segments of the people. But the recollection of God's grace to Israel
in the exodus and land-giving, and of the stipulations of his covenant
law, continued alive in Judah, especially no doubt in rural Judah, as
the preaching of both Amos and Micah makes clear. Moreover, there
is every reason to believe that, after the fall of northern Israel, the
sacred traditions of the north (the work of the so-called Elohist, the
laws and traditions that were to form the core of Deuteronomy,
cycles of narratives having to do with prophets such as Elijah and
Elisha, as well as other material), all of which were orientated upon
the old tribal covenant and its institutions, were brought to Jerusalem and transmitted there. It must be remembered that our Hebrew
Bible is essentially a Jerusalem book; traditions at home in northern
Israel were included in it only as they were treasured and handed
down in Judah. Hosea's prophecies were certainly transmitted in
Judah and were known there at least to some.[24] A century later,
Jeremiah was to take up Hosea's metaphor of the adulterous wife and
apply it to Judah; indeed, Jeremiah's early preaching shows various
verbal correspondences to that of Hosea, as we shall see. Jeremiah
also extended hope to northern Israel, now languishing in the
"wilderness" of exile, in Hosea's manner, and declared that she would
one day have a new entry into her land, in the mercy and love of God
(Jer. 31:2–6, 15–22; etc.). We shall say more of this in a later chapter.

    3. It is small wonder that these two understandings of the nation's
relationship to its God, and its future under God, lived on. Not only
did both develop ancient theological traditions; both seemed to have
been vindicated by events.

    Isaiah's words had certainly been vindicated—and dramatically!
He had announced the terrible chastisement that God would visit
upon the nation because of its want of trust in him and the policy it
had adopted in defiance of his proclaimed will; and this had come with
Sennacherib's army, leaving the nation torn and bleeding. But Isaiah
had also declared that Jerusalem would stand, protected by the sure
promises of God, and that the Assyrians would be frustrated in their

---

[24] Various touches in The Book of Hosea illustrate how that prophet's words were
transmitted in Judah and reapplied to the situation there; e.g., 1:7; 3:5b; 5:5c; 6:11a;
etc. See further the commentaries. Of course not every reference to Judah in Hosea's
prophecy is to be explained in this way.

attempt to take it. And, whatever the historical circumstances may have been, that too had happened: the Assyrians did not take Jerusalem. Though we cannot document it in detail, we may safely assume that this not only gave to Isaiah an enormous prestige, but that it also served to bolster confidence in the official theology of God's election of Mt. Zion and his sure promises to David. Not a few must have reasoned within themselves: Is not this understanding of our status and destiny the correct one? Has it not been proven so by events? God may indeed chastise this nation—he has done so, and it is conceivable that he may do so again; but the nation and the dynasty will nevertheless survive, for so God has promised. May we not be assured of this? And may we not, further, look forward with confidence to the downfall of our Assyrian masters and the ultimate vindication of God's kingly rule among us, just as Isaiah has also said? So people, we may imagine, might well have reasoned on the basis of Isaiah's words and the dramatic vindication that they seemed to have received.

But Hosea's words had likewise been vindicated. He had announced the utter destruction of the northern Israelite nation because of its gross violation of its covenant with Yahweh. And it had happened! It can hardly be doubted that there were some in Judah who must have asked themselves: Is it not possible that it might also happen to us if we persist in our disregard of the covenant stipulations? How much such sentiments, harbored perhaps among northern Israelite refugees, as well as among elements in Judah who were sensitive to the essential nature of Yahwistic faith, may have influenced Hezekiah's efforts at reform we have no way of knowing. But Micah's threatening words certainly played a part, and were remembered a century later as having done so (cf. Micah 3:12 and Jer. 26:18 f.). In any event, though again we cannot document it, the theology of the Mosaic covenant was taken seriously by some. Perhaps it was largely forgotten by the clergy of the Jerusalem Temple, and by the populace, or its stipulations externalized and thought to be satisfied by cultic observance alone. But a coterie existed in Judah which saw those stipulations as no less than a threat to the nation's existence: it must conform to them, or perish. The possibility of tension is obvious.

II

The century following Isaiah's lifetime brought to Judah fluctuations of political fortune, together with grave religious crisis and manful efforts at reform. This last may be said to represent no less than the triumph of the theology of Mosaic Yahwism, albeit a triumph that was neither complete nor lasting.

1. We cannot dwell upon the details of Judah's history through the first three quarters of the seventh century B.C. (about which we are not nearly well enough informed in any case).[25] Enough to say that Hezekiah's son, Manasseh (687/6–642), reversed his father's policy at every step and returned to that of his grandfather Ahaz, who had brought the country into submission to Assyria in the first place. Where Hezekiah had tried for independence, Manasseh remained, so far as our certain knowledge goes, a docile subject of Assyria throughout the whole of his lengthy reign.[26] True, Manasseh had little choice in this. Not only had Hezekiah's bid for freedom, in spite of the fact that Jerusalem had been spared, proved costly and futile; Assyria was at this time reaching the zenith of her physical expansion, climaxed by the conquest of Egypt under Esarhaddon (680–669) and Asshurbanapal (668–627). (Asshurbanapal took and sacked the Egyptian capital of Thebes in 663.) Now that the only power was eliminated that could even promise to help him, what could Manasseh do but remain docile?

Nevertheless, the results of Manasseh's policy were disastrous where religion was concerned, as the author of the book of Kings is at pains to make clear (II Kings 21:1–9; cf. 23:4–14). This seems to have followed inevitably. As the policy of Ahaz led to the introduction of all sorts of foreign cults and practices, so did that of Manasseh. Whether or not vassal-kings of the Assyrian Empire were actually compelled to pay homage to their overlord's gods is a subject that has been much debated.[27] But they must have felt it politic to do so. In any event, we read (21:3–5) that altars to astral deities (possibly gods of Mesopotamian origin, though this is not certain) were erected within the Temple enclosure. But it did not stop with that. Perhaps because of the king's own want of religious convictions, perhaps because the nation's shameful position had caused many to lose faith

---

[25] For further details regarding the period covered in this chapter, see my book, *A History of Israel* (Philadelphia: The Westminster Press; London: SCM Press, 2d ed., 1972), pp. 309–323.

[26] II Chron. 33:10–13 reports (II Kings says nothing of it) that Manasseh was on one occasion hauled before the Assyrian king in chains, but was then shown clemency and restored to his throne. This may well suggest that Manasseh's loyalty to Assyria did not go very deep, and that he was at some time in his reign suspected of rebellious activity. But we lack the information to be certain.

[27] Cf. Ch. 3, note 2, and the works of M. Cogan and J. McKay cited there.

in Yahweh, the reforms of Hezekiah were completely repudiated. Local shrines, which Hezekiah had tried to abolish, were restored and pagan cults of all kinds were allowed to flourish (v. 3), as was the practice of divination and magic (v. 6). The fertility cult, with its ritual of sacred prostitution, was carried on within the Temple itself (v. 7; cf. 23:4, 7; Zeph. 1:4 f.). Worse, the barbarous rite of human sacrifice made its appearance (v. 6), with the king himself taking the lead. It was a time of unparalleled religious laxity, and one that represented a grave threat to the integrity of Israel's faith. Indeed, Israel's faith was in danger of slipping into overt polytheism. Instances of violence and injustice seem to have been common (Zeph. 1:9; 3:3 f.). Yet those who ventured to protest apparently met with persecution (cf. II Kings 21:16), and the prophetic voice was silent.[28]

All of this was surely resented by loyal Yahwists of whatever stripe. By those who were nurtured upon the traditions of the Mosaic covenant and its stipulations, manifestly so! Such were those writers who gave us the books of Kings, one of whom brands Manasseh as the worst king ever to sit on David's throne and declares that his sin was alone enough to explain the catastrophe that befell the nation (II Kings 21:10–15; 23:26 f.; cf. Jer. 15:1–4). Said he:

> (II Kings 21:11) "Because Manasseh King of Judah has done these abominations, outdoing in wickedness all that the Amorites did of old,[29] and has led Judah itself into sin with his disgusting idols;[30] (v. 12) therefore this is what Yahweh the God of Israel has said: Believe me, I am going to bring a disaster on Jerusalem and Judah such as will make the ears of every one who hears of it ring. (v. 13) I will stretch over Jerusalem the measuring line of Samaria and the plumb bob of the house of Ahab,[31] and I will wipe Jerusalem as one wipes a dish, wiping it and turning it upside down. . . .

And so on he goes.[32] But those who were orientated upon the Davidic

---

[28] At least we know of no prophet who functioned between the time of Isaiah's death early in the century and the years immediately prior to Josiah's reform (completed in 622/21).

[29] Lit., "before him." But "Amorite" is of course a blanket term for the fabulously wicked pre-Israelite people of Palestine who, according to the tradition, were destroyed many centuries previously.

[30] The word is a derogatory epithet for idols, apparently literally "pellets of dung."

[31] I.e., God will measure Jerusalem by the same standards as those by which northern Israel, and especially the Omride house, was measured.

[32] It is probable that these words come from the final (exilic) edition of the Deuteronomic historical corpus, after Jerusalem had fallen to the Babylonians. (On the composition of the Deuteronomic History, see below, note 44.) But none of the contributors to this work had any good word to say of Manasseh.

traditions (Zephaniah was such!) resented Manasseh's policy no less. No doubt they found it as offensive as Ahaz' policy had seemed to Isaiah two generations previously: Yahweh forced to give place to other gods in his very own house! The nation fawning upon Assyria instead of trusting in him! We are therefore not surprised to find that there were those in Judah who were biding their time, waiting for a chance to make a change.

The chance came under Manasseh's grandson, Josiah, who (ca. 640) had been placed on the throne as an eight-year-old boy (II Kings 22:1) upon the assassination of his father, Amon. The immediate occasion for the change was the sudden and dramatic crack-up of the Assyrian Empire. When Josiah came to the throne Assyria was ruled by Asshurbanapal, the last of its great warrior kings. Though faced with troubles both internal and external, Asshurbanapal had been able (save that Egypt was lost) to hold the empire fundamentally intact. But ca. 627, just as Josiah was coming to manhood, Asshurbanapal died and Assyria was plunged into civil strife, in the course of which she lost hold of her empire and was soon fighting for her life against the Babylonians and the Medes. (Nineveh at last fell in 612; and the exultant joy that this event awakened in Judahite hearts— and not, we may suppose, in theirs only—is reflected in the little book of Nahum.)[33] The weakening of Assyria meant that Judah, after a hundred years of servitude to her imperial master, was once again a free country. We do not know just how, or just when, this came about. Presumably it came about by simple default as Assyria, in the troubled years after Asshurbanapal's death, was obliged progressively to concentrate all her forces for the defense of the homeland. But not only was Judah free; Josiah proceeded—though again we know none of the details—to annex large portions of northern Israel, now abandoned by the Assyrians.[34] At the same time he launched the

---

[33] On the date of Nahum and the problems relating to that book, see the Introductions and commentaries. The prophecy is usually placed shortly before the fall of Nineveh. It was certainly uttered after Asshurbanapal's sack of Thebes (No-Amon) in 663 (cf. Nahum 3:8). D. L. Christensen (ZAW, 87 [1975], pp. 11–30) argues for a relatively early date within this period.

[34] The extent of Josiah's annexations is not clear. He certainly took possession of the province of Samaria, for his reforming activity was extended into that area (II Kings 23:15–20). Apparently, he took parts of Galilee as well; according to II Chron. 34:6 f. his reforms were put into effect there, and (II Kings 23:29 f.) he died defending Megiddo, which presumably means that he regarded it as part of his territory. At least for a while, too, his control reached to the Mediterranean coast, as archaeological discoveries indicate; cf. Bright, A History of Israel, p. 316, n. 21, for references. Whether, or to what degree, his control reached into Transjordan we do not know.

most sweeping reform in all of Judah's history. This reform—if we
follow the account of the Chronicler (cf. II Chron., ch. 34), which
seems at this point to be preferable—was carried out in stages,
beginning apparently even before Asshurbanapal's death and reaching its climax in the eighteenth year of Josiah's reign (622/21).

2. Josiah's reform represented a consistent effort to return to the
purity of Mosaic Yahwism. What it sought to do is clear from II
Kings, ch. 23: it was a thoroughgoing purge of all foreign cults and
practices. Such cults as may have been of Assyrian origin, being
hated symbols of the national humiliation, were doubtless the first to
go. But other pagan cults, some introduced by Manasseh, some of
long standing, were likewise ruthlessly extirpated. Their personnel,
including eunuch priests and sacred prostitutes, were executed.[35] The
practice of the occult arts, divination and magic, was suppressed (v.
24). Nor did the reform stop at the frontiers of Judah. As Josiah
extended his control into northern Israel, his reforming measures
were carried out there also; the shrines of Samaria (of Galilee also,
according to II Chron. 34:6 f.), particularly that of Bethel, since they
were from Josiah's point of view uniformly idolatrous, were dese-
crated and destroyed and their priests put to death (II Kings
23:15–20). As his crowning measure Josiah did what Hezekiah had
attempted to do, but without permanent success: closing all shrines of
Yahweh in the outlying towns of Judah, he centralized all worship of
Yahweh in Jerusalem.[36] Priests of these shrines were invited to come
and take their place among the Temple clergy—which, so we are told
incidentally, many of them refused to do (vs. 8 f.).

A reform so sweeping cannot be explained by any single factor.
Nationalistic sentiment alone would have made some sort of reform
inevitable at this time. Independence and reform always went hand
in hand in Judah. It is certainly not a coincidence that Ahaz, who first
brought the country into submission to Assyria, should have been
remembered as a great apostate; that Hezekiah, who struggled
manfully for independence, should have been remembered as a

[35] The verb in v. 5, rendered "deposed" (RSV) or "suppressed" (NEB), is literally
"caused to cease"; execution is implied (and cf. II Chron. 34:4 f.). The "idolatrous
priests" (RSV; Heb., kᵉmārîm) are probably best understood as eunuch priests; cf. W.
F. Albright, *From the Stone Age to Christianity*, 2d ed. (Doubleday Anchor Book, 1957),
pp. 234 f.

[36] Archaeology may have given us a graphic illustration of this measure of Josiah's.
At Arad, in the Negeb, a shrine to Yahweh had existed since the tenth century; but in
the seventh century the sanctuary was destroyed and abandoned (a casemate wall was
laid through it). Cf. Y. Aharoni, BA, 31 (1968), pp. 18–27; *Archaeology and Old
Testament Study*, D. Winton Thomas, ed. (Oxford: Clarendon Press, 1967), pp. 395–397.

reformer; that Manasseh, the obedient vassal, should have been branded as the most despicable of apostates; and that Josiah, king of independent Judah, should have been praised as the greatest reformer of them all. Reform was a facet of independence and nationalism. These were heady times in Judah: Assyria, the hated master, gone at last, Judah free again after a hundred years of humiliating servitude, and all Israel on its way to being reunited under David's throne! It was a time of nationalistic self-consciousness. Men must have said to themselves: Now that we can be ourselves politically again, let us be ourselves religiously also! Out with everything foreign! Indeed, the very fact that the nation no longer had to bow to the Assyrian king and acknowledge the supremacy of his gods may have impelled men more readily to turn once more to Yahweh as the nation's proper Overlord and to enter into a treaty-covenant arrangement with him to serve him alone.[37]

But other factors than nationalism entered in, not the least of which was the preaching of certain of the prophets. One of these was the young Jeremiah, who began his career in 627, just as Asshurbanapal died and Judah regained its independence. We shall say more of him later. Another was Zephaniah, of whom we have already spoken. Both of these men, albeit in different ways, assailed the paganism with which the land was then filled, warned of judgment to come, and urgently called for repentance. We can hardly doubt—though we have no way of measuring it—that their words found a hearing among sensitive people and at least helped to prepare the climate for reform.

But what gave the reform direction and drove it to its conclusion was "the book of the law" which was found in the Temple in the year 622/21 (cf. II Kings, ch. 22). This book did not institute the reform, for it was found in the course of repairs to the Temple; and these undoubtedly represented, at least in part, a purification of that structure after Manasseh's abominations. In other words, the reform was already under way when the lawbook was found. But the lawbook gave the reform direction and a heightened urgency, and imparted to it its distinctive character. When it was brought to the king's attention, the king tore his clothing in dismay. Apparently he took the lawbook and its demands seriously, and reacted to it

---

[37] Cf. R. Frankena, "The Vassal-Treaties of Esarhaddon and the Dating of Deuteronomy" (*Oudtestamentische Studiën*, 14, 1965, pp. 122–154; cf. pp. 150–154). This does not, however, involve one in the conclusion that Israel learned of the treaty-covenant form for the first time from Assyrian treaties of the seventh century.

instinctively and with deep emotion: If this be Yahweh's law, then God help the country, for we have flagrantly disobeyed it! Assured by a prophetic oracle that it was indeed Yahweh's law, he summoned the elders and notables of the people to the Temple and entered into solemn covenant with them to put it into practice (23:1–3).

3. As is generally agreed, this lawbook was some form of the book of Deuteronomy.[38] And Deuteronomy is the classic expression of the theology of the ancient Mosaic covenant. Deuteronomy was no new law; still less was it a document piously concocted for the occasion by well-meaning men who sought to claim the authority of Moses for the reforms they wished to introduce, then hidden away and later conveniently "found." Rather, Deuteronomy is a homiletical collection of laws, mostly of ancient origin, which derived ultimately from the legal tradition of a very early period of Israel's life as a people. Apparently it had been handed down in northern Israel and, after the fall of Samaria, had been brought to Jerusalem and there, at some time between Hezekiah's reign and the early part of Josiah's, had been reworked and made into an instrument of reform.[39] Its laws, therefore, could not have been for the most part so very novel. What *was* novel was the picture Deuteronomy gives of the Mosaic covenant and its stringent demands, demands that the official religion had forgotten, failed to stress, or externalized.

Deuteronomy places the nation's very existence under the stipulations of covenant. It knows nothing of unconditional promises! Even the promise of the land is laid under a warning and a threat. In positively classical fashion it addresses Israel as if she stood perpetually antecedent to the giving of the land—as if the promise of land, long ago fulfilled, was yet an open question and subject to conditions.[40] It addresses each generation of Israelites as if they had themselves stood with their ancestors at Sinai (Horeb) and had

[38] First suggested by certain of the church fathers (e.g., Jerome), this has become in modern times the generally accepted view. For a review of the discussion, with bibliography, cf. H. H. Rowley, "The Prophet Jeremiah and the Book of Deuteronomy" (1950; repr. in *From Moses to Qumran* [London: Lutterworth Press, 1963], pp. 187–208).

[39] On the northern origin of the tradition behind Deuteronomy, cf. *inter alia* G. von Rad, *Studies in Deuteronomy* (Eng. tr., London: SCM Press, 1953); G. E. Wright, IB, Vol. II (1953), pp. 311–329; A. Alt, "Die Heimat des Deuteronomiums" (*Kleine Schriften zur Geschichte des Volkes Israel*, Vol. II [Munich: C. H. Beck'sche Verlagsbuchhandlung, 1953], pp. 250–275). For an excellent review of the question, cf. E. W. Nicholson, *Deuteronomy and Tradition* (Oxford: Basil Blackwell, 1967).

[40] "Through such a fictitious temporal future the existential future is to be made clear"; H. H. Schmid, ZThK, 64 (1967), p. 13, quoted by W. Zimmerli, *Man and His Hope in the Old Testament* (Eng. tr., London: SCM Press, 1968), p. 76.

personally bound themselves to the terms of the covenant. So, for
example, in the speech of Moses prefacing the Decalogue in Deuteronomy, ch. 5:

> (Deut. 5:1) Hear, O Israel, the statutes and the ordinances which I speak in
> your hearing this day. You shall learn them and shall be careful to do
> them. (v. 2) Yahweh our God made a covenant with us at Horeb. (v. 3) It
> was not with our ancestors that Yahweh made this covenant, but with us,
> all of us who are here and alive this day. (v. 4) Yahweh spoke with you
> face to face on the mountain out of the fire, (v. 5) while I stood all the
> while between Yahweh and yourselves to make known to you Yahweh's
> words[41]. . . .

Since in its view all Israelites of whatever generation have committed
themselves to Yahweh's covenant, Deuteronomy calls them to absolute obedience to the covenant stipulations and warns them that, if
they do not obey, all the promised blessings will be taken away.

This note dominates the homiletical framework of Deuteronomy
and could be illustrated almost at will. For example, 11:26–28:

> (Deut. 11:26) Look, I set before you today a blessing and a curse—(v. 27)
> the blessing if you obey the commandments of Yahweh your God which I
> enjoin upon you today, (v. 28) and the curse if you do not obey the
> commandments of Yahweh your God, but turn aside from the way which I
> enjoin upon you today, to go after other gods whom you have not known.

Or this (30:15–20):

> (Deut. 30:15) See, I have set before you today life and good, death and
> disaster. (v. 16) If you obey the commandments of Yahweh your God [42]
> which I enjoin upon you today, namely, to love Yahweh your God, to walk
> in his ways, and to keep his commandments, his statutes, and his
> ordinances, then you shall live and increase in number, and Yahweh your
> God will bless you in the land which you are entering to make it your own.
> (v. 17) But if your heart turns away, if you will not listen, if you are
> beguiled into worshiping other gods and serving them, (v. 18) then I
> declare to you today that you will surely perish. . . . (v. 19) I call heaven
> and earth to witness against you today that it is life or death that I have
> set before you, the blessing or the curse; so choose life that you and your
> descendants may live, (v. 20) . . . that you may dwell in the land which
> Yahweh swore to your ancestors, Abraham, Isaac, and Jacob, that he
> would give them.

Or see such passages as 6:10–15, or ch. 8 (we cannot quote them here).

---

[41] So with various Vrs.; MT reads singular.
[42] This clause is lacking in MT; it is added with LXX (and so most EVV).

Or see the long catalog of blessings and hair-raising curses (the curses far outweighing the blessings) that are laid before Israel in ch. 28. Deuteronomy by no means closes the door to the future, for it repeatedly and with utmost clarity promises to the nation continued existence and every blessing if it is obedient to the commands of Yahweh. But again and again, and with equal clarity, it places before the nation the threat that if it fails in this regard, it faces total destruction.

No wonder the godly Josiah tore his clothing in dismay! It must have seemed to him that, because of its derelictions, the curse was already hovering over the nation, and must soon bear it down to its ruin. The thought must have occurred to him that the nation had been living in a fool's paradise in assuming that Yahweh was irrevocably committed to its defense through his covenant with David. Deuteronomy offered the nation no unconditional promises of whatever sort. Here there is no assurance of the protection of the nation, of continued possession of the land, of God's defense of Mt. Zion, of the eternity of the Davidic line—or of anything else! Here everything is "either-or"; here all the future is laid under the little word "if." In committing the nation to the observance of the Deuteronomic law, Josiah called it back behind the official theology of the Davidic covenant to an older notion of covenant, and he sought to bring the nation and all its institutions into obedience to the terms of that covenant.

4. One might, indeed, go so far as to say that Deuteronomy undermines the Davidic covenant altogether. It renders the position of the monarchy insecure by placing it under conditions. This is not to say that Deuteronomy is in principle hostile to the monarchy, or that it actively anticipates its downfall. But it does show a remarkable reserve toward the monarchy; it does not regard monarchy as a necessary institution, but as an almost optional one, one that represents, one might say, a concession on the part of God and one that exists through divine sufferance, subject to divinely imposed conditions. It says nothing of the inalienable right of any royal line to rule in perpetuity. Deuteronomy's view of kingship is expressed in 17:14–20. Here the people are told that, when they reach the Promised Land, they will doubtless ask to have a king. Though this request will arise out of a desire to imitate the surrounding nations (v. 14), Yahweh will allow it: They may have a king if they insist (v. 15). But this king must be one who rules by divine election, and he must be a native Israelite. Then it adds (vs. 16 f.):

(Deut. 17:16) Only he shall not accumulate for himself great numbers of
horses, nor force the people to return to Egypt to accumulate horses . . . ,
(v. 17) nor shall he accumulate for himself large numbers of wives, lest his
heart go astray, nor shall he accumulate for himself large amounts of
silver and gold.

The northern-Israelite bias of the tradition behind this passage is
evident. It seems to be saying as clearly as words could say: A king, if
you insist—yes; but let him be as little like Solomon as possible.[43] The
passage then goes on to say (vs. 18–20) that the king must, in any
event, keep a copy of the law beside him, and must read from it daily,
that he may learn to fear Yahweh and not to imagine that he is in
some way elevated above his fellow Israelites, or that he stands
superior to the divine commands. And this he must do "in order that
he may continue long on his throne, he and his descendants, in Israel"
(v. 20b). The ruling dynasty is by no means rejected; but its
continuance is not unconditionally guaranteed.

This reserve toward the monarchy is even clearer in the so-called
Deuteronomic historical corpus, which was composed in the wake of
the reform and in its spirit.[44] This work, which comprises the books
Joshua through II Kings (except Ruth) and also, in all probability, the
narrative framework of Deuteronomy, traces the history of Israel
from the last years of Moses' life to the writer's own day.[45] But
though we rightly speak of it as a history, its aim is not merely to
record historical events; rather, it records events and preaches from
them. It relates every vicissitude of Israel's history, both good
fortune and bad, to the nation's obedience or disobedience to the
stipulations of the Mosaic covenant. It seeks to show that at every
step of the way history itself has shown the theology of the covenant,
as expressed in Deuteronomy, to be true.[46] And it begs the people to

---

[43] That the passage is a polemic against the policies of Solomon (and by inference also
against the exclusive claims of the Davidic house) seems evident; cf. the commentaries,
e.g., G. E. Wright, IB, Vol. II (1953), p. 441; R. E. Clements, *God's Chosen People*
(London: SCM Press, 1968), pp. 40–42.

[44] The question of the date of the composition of this work cannot be discussed here.
Scholars divide themselves broadly into two camps. Some believe that it was composed
during the Babylonian exile (the last event recorded, II Kings 25:27–30, carries us down
to about 562). Others believe that it was originally composed before the fall of
Jerusalem, very possibly in Josiah's reign, and was later re-edited and brought down to
date during the exile. I feel strongly that the latter position is correct.

[45] On the structure of this work, see especially the fundamental treatment of M.
Noth, *Überlieferungsgeschichtliche Studien I* (Halle: M. Niemeyer, 1943). Whether it is
to be regarded as basically the work of a single historian, as Noth believes, or was
produced by a school of like-minded men, is a question to which no certain answer can
be given. But the question is not of material concern to us here.

[46] On the theological concern of the Deuteronomic History, and the question of what
hope, if any, it held out for the future, there is a considerable literature. Aside from

heed the lessons of history before the midnight hour strikes.

Though the Deuteronomic Historian (we use the singular for convenience) is anything but hostile toward the monarchy—indeed, sets great store by the promises that God has extended to David—he by no means takes the monarchy or the dynasty for granted. Not only does he evaluate each king in the light of his loyalty or disloyalty to the pure worship of Yahweh as specified in Deuteronomy ("he did that which was right/evil in the sight of Yahweh"); he places the very existence of the institution of kingship under the terms of the Mosaic covenant. This is perhaps clearest of all in the farewell speech said to have been uttered by Samuel on the occasion of Saul's election as king (I Sam. 12:1–15). Here the old prophet, having justified his administration of affairs and absolved himself of all charges of dishonesty or self-seeking, reviews the whole history of God's gracious and saving acts toward Israel beginning with the deliverance from Egypt and continuing through the giving of the land and through God's continual defense of his people during the period of the Judges, right on down to his own day. He then (v. 12) alludes to the people's demand for a king. And he does so with bitterness, for he regards this as nothing less than a rejection of Yahweh's own rule over them. Then he says:

> (I Sam. 12:13) Now see the king whom you have chosen, and for whom you have asked. See, Yahweh has placed a king over you. (v. 14) If you will fear Yahweh and serve him and obey his voice, and do not rebel against Yahweh's orders, and if both you and the king who rules over you will follow Yahweh your God, it will be well. (v. 15) But if you do not obey the voice of Yahweh, but rebel against Yahweh's orders, the hand of Yahweh will be against you and your king.[47]

Such a view of kingship must inevitably have stood in a certain tension with the theology of God's unconditional promises to David, as these were popularly understood. As we have said, the Deuteronomic Historian is in no sense hostile to the Davidic dynasty, nor does

---

the work of Noth (see preceding note), cf. especially G. von Rad, *Old Testament Theology*, Vol. I (Edinburgh and London: Oliver & Boyd; New York: Harper & Brothers, 1962), esp. pp. 334–347; *idem*, "Die deuteronomistische Geschichtstheologie in den Königsbüchern" (1947; repr., *Gesammelte Studien zum Alten Testament* [Munich: Chr. Kaiser Verlag, 1958], pp. 189–204); H. W. Wolff, "The Kerygma of the Deuteronomic Historical Work" (1961; Eng. tr., in W. Brueggemann and H. W. Wolff, *The Vitality of the Old Testament Traditions* [Atlanta: John Knox Press, 1975], pp. 83–100); F. M. Cross, "The Structure of the Deuteronomic History" (*Perspectives in Jewish Learning*, III, pp. 9–24).

[47] So following LXX; MT, "and your fathers."

he in any way wish for its downfall. On the contrary, he regarded David as the ideal king, and no higher praise could he bestow on any later king than to say that his conduct in every respect measured up to that of David (II Kings 18:3; 22:2). And he was able to explain the fact that the Davidic dynasty continued to rule in Judah, even when the northern tribes fell away, in terms of Yahweh's gracious favor in accordance with his promises to David (I Kings 11:32, 34–36). But he could not allow that these promises should be understood as being without qualification. Again and again through the books of Kings we find him introducing a conditional element. To be sure, some allusions of this sort are doubtless to be attributed to the exilic edition of the historical corpus, which was written at a time when the Davidic dynasty had already fallen, and when it was evident to all that the official theology needed correction.[48] But not all such passages can be explained in this way. In some passages that betray no awareness of the fall of Jerusalem and the end of the dynasty, a conditional element is already present. I Kings 2:1–4 is an example. Here the aged David, while lying on his deathbed, calls Solomon to his side and speaks to him:

> (I Kings 2:2) I am about to go the way of all the earth. Be strong. Act like a man. (v. 3) Keep the charge of Yahweh your God, walking in his ways, keeping his statutes, his commandments, his ordinances, and his decrees, as written in the law of Moses, that you may be successful in all that you do and wherever you turn—(v. 4) *so that* Yahweh *may* fulfill his word which he spoke concerning me, "*If* your sons take heed to their ways, and walk before me in faithfulness and with all their heart and soul, you shall never lack a man [to sit] on the throne of Israel."

"If" is a small word, but it introduces a not inconsiderable difference: the continuance of the dynasty is not flatly and unconditionally assured. We find a similar note in the word that Solomon received as he was building the Temple (I Kings 6:12 f.):

> (I Kings 6:12) As to this house which you are building, *if* you will walk in my statutes, obey my ordinances, keep all my commandments and follow them, then I will fulfill my word about you, which I spoke to your father, David, (v. 13) and I will dwell among the Israelites and I will not forsake my people Israel.

---

[48] I Kings 9:6–9 probably falls in this class. But even in vs. 1–5, which are probably pre-exilic, a conditional element has already been introduced. There is little agreement in detail as to which touches in the Deuteronomic History must be assigned to the exilic edition; for a representative opinion, cf. Cross, "The Structure of the Deuteronomic History" (reference in note 46), pp. 18 f.

Again the word "if" is introduced. In none of these passages—and still others of the sort can be found—is the validity of the promises to David denied, nor is the continued existence of the dynasty positively threatened; still less, is it actually desired. But the promises are somewhat muted by the introduction of a conditional element not to be found in the classical formulations of the Davidic covenant (cf. II Sam. 7:12–16; Ps. 89).

III

Josiah's reform, then, laid the nation under the stipulations of the Mosaic covenant as these are set forth in Deuteronomy, and committed it to the observance of covenant law. One might call this the victory of the Mosaic covenant over the Davidic. But, if such it was, the victory was neither complete nor lasting.

1. We know too little of the later years of Josiah's reign to say how the reform actually worked out in detail. True, we may be sure that as long as Josiah lived it was officially maintained. After all, Josiah was zealous for it; it was his official royal policy, and there is no reason to believe that he ever retreated from it (the Deuteronomic Historian certainly does not suggest that he did, but rather the contrary). We may also believe that the removal of pagan cults with their nameless, immoral rites proved to be a profound benefit to the nation, morally and spiritually. Moreover, since Josiah had committed the nation to the observance of covenant law, and since he was himself a just man (even Jeremiah could give him unstinted praise in this regard; Jer. 22:15 f.), it is all but certain that a marked improvement in public morality resulted. Of course, the reform, while solving problems, created yet others in their place. At least, so it would seem to us—though whether or not Josiah and those about him sensed these as problems and, if so, what steps they contemplated to deal with them, we have no way of saying. In particular, the closing of the outlying shrines in Judah must have created somewhat of a spiritual vacuum, since it meant that citizens living far from Jerusalem would no longer be able to participate in religious occasions with regularity. The reform certainly had its opponents, not least among the rural clergy, many of whom (II Kings 23:9) refused meekly to surrender their ancient prerogatives, transfer to Jerusalem, and integrate themselves with the clergy there (in a status of inferiority, no doubt). But, though there were always those who opposed the reform, and though its results were not all of them

unqualified gain, we can hardly doubt that its good results far outweighed the bad. In a word, the reform was far from a failure.

Nevertheless, it also fell far short of effecting a radical purification of the national character. This is in no way surprising. One might ask how it could possibly have been expected to accomplish such a thing. It was the official policy of the state; but no official state policy can work such magic. A state can by its official policies force external reforms, and thereby exert a beneficial influence upon public morality; but it cannot fundamentally change character. There is reason, indeed, to suspect that the reform, for all its thoroughness and the zeal with which it was carried out, never cut deeply into the attitudes and conduct of the populace but, like other reforms at other times and places, tended to stop with externals. It seems to have resulted in the forced suppression of pagan cults and practices, and in heightened religious activity, but in no general return to godliness and righteousness in obedience to the stipulations of Yahweh's covenant. At least, so Jeremiah complained repeatedly, as we shall see.

It is probable, indeed, that the very fact of reform only served in the minds of many to bolster a false sense of security. Many people must have reasoned within themselves: Since the Deuteronomic law demanded reforms as the price of the national existence, and since through Josiah's measures these reforms have been made, the demands of the law have satisfactorily been complied with and the stipulations of the covenant met, and God's favor thereby secured; since this is so, the nation may rest secure in God's promises to David and his presence in his temple-palace on Mt. Zion. If we read Jeremiah correctly, this is what certain of the clergy were telling the people. It seemed to Jeremiah that they were simply salving the national cancer with skin balm. Said he (Jer. 6:14; cf. 8:11):

> Jer. 6:14 They treat my people's fracture
> With nostrums,[49] and cry,
> "It is well! It is well!" [50]

To Jeremiah, this was a bald-faced, unmitigated lie. He could only cry, "But there is no peace" (i.e., it is *not* well). One gains the impression that, as a result of the reforms that had been made, the theology of the Mosaic covenant had been turned into a handmaid of

---

[49] Lit., "lightly," "superficially."

[50] Lit., "Peace! Peace!" But one must realize that the word šālōm does not signify merely the absence of conflict, but embraces "wholeness," "well-being" in its broadest connotations. The priests assure the people that peace with God is theirs, and that the national well-being is therefore secure.

the national complacency: security bought at the price of external compliance. Armed with such a complacency, the nation was ill fitted to meet the troubles that were soon to come.

2. In any event, whatever its immediate results may have been, the reform did not survive Josiah's death intact. This last was a great tragedy. Let us briefly sketch the events. It will be recalled that Judah had regained her independence when, after the death of Asshurbanapal (ca. 627), Assyria had entered a period of internal disturbance and had been unable to maintain her hold upon her empire. From this point onward Assyria's fortunes ran steadily downhill. Soon she was fighting for her life against the Babylonians —now independent and resurgent under Nabopolassar, the father of Nebuchadnezzar—and the Medes, an Indo-Aryan people from the highlands of Iran. Though Assyria found an ally in the Egyptians— who doubtless wished to keep a weakened Assyria in existence as a buffer against a potentially more dangerous Medo-Babylonian axis and, at the same time, to gain for themselves a free hand in their ancient sphere of influence in Palestine and Syria—the impending collapse could not be forestalled. In 614 the ancient capital of Asshur fell to the Medes, and in 612 the Medes and the Babylonians took Nineveh itself and utterly destroyed it. The wreckage of the Assyrian army then fell back westward to the city of Harran, in northwestern Mesopotamia, and endeavored to keep resistance alive. But in 610 the Babylonians and their allies stormed Harran and drove the Assyrians back across the Euphrates into the arms of the Egyptians. So it was that in 609 the Egyptian pharaoh, Necho II, led an army northward through Palestine toward the Euphrates to assist the Assyrians in a last attempt to retake Harran and regain a foothold in the homeland. Josiah, doubtless regarding this as an infringement on his (now expanded) territory, and certainly not wishing an Egypto-Assyrian victory, tried to stop him near Megiddo. But he was killed and brought dead in his chariot to Jerusalem (II Kings 23:29 f.). This marked the end of Judah's brief independence (vs. 30–35). Though the people immediately crowned Josiah's son, Jehoahaz, as their king, within three months the pharaoh had summoned him to his headquarters in central Syria, deposed him, and exiled him to Egypt. His brother, Jehoiakim, was then placed on the throne as an Egyptian vassal, and the land laid under heavy tribute.

Under Jehoiakim the reform may be said to have lapsed. There is no evidence that it was officially canceled; it was just not pushed. While there was no return to the officially sponsored paganism of

Manasseh's reign, if Jeremiah and Ezekiel are to be believed (and there is no reason why they may not), pagan practices crept back and public morality deteriorated. The reasons for this were no doubt complex and various. Perhaps it was in part simply that Jehoiakim, who seems to have been a man without religious sensitivity or depth of character (or so we may judge from what Jeremiah has to say about him), had little sympathy for the aims of the reform and so did not strive to keep it alive. But it is not improbable that, in the minds of many, the tragedy of 609 had discredited the very Deuteronomic theology upon which the reform was based, and had caused a widespread loss of interest in maintaining its ideals. We can imagine men saying to themselves: The law demanded reform, and we *did* reform. But we got for it not the promised blessings, but disaster! And the king who sponsored the reform, and who had been promised by the prophetic oracle that he would be gathered to his fathers in peace (II Kings 22:18–20), cut down in the prime of his life in battle! How is this to be explained in the light of the Deuteronomic theology? What truth can there be in such a theology? Why should anyone take it seriously? This is admittedly surmise. But we know that, years later (cf. Jer. 44:15–18), there were people who viewed the reform as a great mistake, and even blamed the disaster that had overtaken the nation on their failure to continue propitiating other gods than Yahweh.

From all we can tell, and regardless of what the reasons may have been, the nation as a whole banished from its mind any thought of its possible destruction, and entrusted its future to the sure promises of God as affirmed in the cult. That is certainly the impression that one gains from The Book of Jeremiah. Jeremiah continually clashed with prophets who were telling the people, "You shall not see the sword, nor shall you have famine, but I will give you assured peace in this place" (Jer. 14:13; cf. 5:12; 23:17; etc.). He also heard the people parroting: "Yahweh's temple, Yahweh's temple, Yahweh's temple is this" (7:4)—i.e., they found security in the physical presence of the Temple in their midst, which, they believed, was Yahweh's chosen earthly dwelling; since they could not believe that he would ever allow it to be destroyed, they felt equally confident that the city in which it stood was safe. Certainly the nation faced what turned out to be its destruction with an amazing confidence, as we shall see. It was a foolhardy confidence, and it drove the nation to suicide. But we can only suppose that the nation's leaders would not have dared to take the course they did had they not felt assured that God would come to their aid.

One might easily be moved to amazement by what can only seem to have been a blind complacency. But perhaps it would be unfair to call this complacency: the times did not really leave room for complacency. In the popular mind there was simply nowhere else to go! The notion that the nation might be threatened with destruction was simply too terrible to be entertained. And the official theology must have seemed to many to have stood the test of history remarkably well. Had not Isaiah announced the Assyrians as the rod of God's anger to chasten his people? But had he not also declared that the nation would survive, that Jerusalem would stand, and that Assyria would itself at length be brought down? And has it not been exactly so? Well, then (so men might tell themselves), God saw us through *that*, and he will see us through *this*. Discipline us he may, but he will never abandon his sure promises to David.

Indeed, it is probable that, a century after his time, Isaiah had disciples in Jerusalem whom that great prophet would have flatly repudiated, had he been present to hear them. There seems to have been a tendency to generalize from Isaiah's word to Hezekiah, spoken when Sennacherib threatened the city ("I will defend this city and save it, for my own sake and my servant David's sake," Isa. 37:35), and to turn it into a dogma of absolute validity for all time to come: Yahweh, who dwells on Mt. Zion, is committed through his promises to David to the defense of this nation—at all times, through thick and thin, no matter what! Any suggestion that he might allow Jerusalem to be taken and destroyed could only be regarded as treason and blasphemy! Is this not tantamount to accusing God of unfaithfulness to his covenant with David?

Against this background the tragedy of Jeremiah became inevitable. It was into this situation of reform and its aftermath, of national independence and the loss of it, that the young Jeremiah stepped. Jeremiah being Jeremiah, there was bound to be a collision. And to that we must now turn.

5

Jeremiah: The Prophet
Contra Mundum

1. We have seen how the Kingdom of Judah had throughout its entire history been supported by a theology that was fundamentally optimistic, one that engendered an enormous confidence in the future. This is not to say that, rightly understood, it allowed for *complacency* regarding the future. Indeed, it is hard to see how anyone in Judah in the late seventh century could possibly have been complacent about the future. The nation had by this time lived through a century of Assyrian rule. It had experienced the horrors of war, death, destruction, and brutal suffering; it had known shameful servitude and ruinous taxation—enough, one would think, to put an end to whatever complacency there may have been. And even though Assyria's decline and ultimate collapse had allowed Judah once more to regain her independence, rival powers (Egypt, Babylon, the Medes) were quarreling over the corpse of the empire. Who could tell what the future would bring? The situation was packed with danger. No one in Jerusalem with a brain in his head could possibly have been complacent about the *immediate* future.

But where the *farther* future was concerned, the ultimate future, one could always be optimistic. Men could tell themselves that, regardless of what the future might hold, no reason existed to worry about the nation's continued survival. Has not God promised to David a dynasty that will never end? Is not his temple-palace here in our midst on Mt. Zion? Is it conceivable that he would ever abandon it, and the city in which it stands, to destruction? Perhaps the future will bring crisis after crisis—who knows? But one thing is sure: this nation will always survive. God has so promised, and he does not alter the word that passed from his lips or lie to David (Ps. 89:33–37).

Perhaps some could feel confident of even more than this. Perhaps some at least could assure themselves not only that the nation would always survive but that its future would ultimately be one of unimagined greatness and glory. Have we not been told, has it not consistently been affirmed by our religion, that God will one day establish Mt. Zion as the center of his triumphant kingly rule on earth? Have we not been assured that one day there will come (and may it be soon!) an ideal king of David's line under whose just and beneficent rule all the promises will be made actual, and peace and felicity will endlessly reign? At least, so the great Isaiah said; and his words in every other respect have been dramatically vindicated by events. May we not trust them also in this? Let us then cling to these promises and face the future, if not without fear, at least with confidence. So we may imagine that men may have reassured themselves in the dangerous days of the late seventh century B.C.

2. Of course not everyone in Jerusalem shared this optimism. In the preceding chapter we saw how in the last half century of Assyrian rule, under the notorious Manasseh, Judah lapsed into unparalleled syncretism, with pagan cults tolerated—indeed fostered —within the precincts of the Temple itself. We also saw how, as Assyria's power weakened and Judah regained independence, Manasseh's grandson, Josiah, launched the most sweeping reform in Judah's history, removing every vestige of paganism from the land and centralizing all worship of Yahweh in Jerusalem.

Josiah's reform, as we said, was given direction by a copy of some form of the Deuteronomic law which had been found in the Temple. And, as we also said, Deuteronomy is the classical articulation of quite a different understanding of the nation's relationship to its God, namely, that of the Mosaic covenant. Here the future is not necessarily one of optimism at all. Rather, the future is problematical: it is life *or* death, blessing *or* curse. The well-being of the nation—even its survival—is not unconditionally assured. All depends upon its obedience to the stipulations of Yahweh's covenant; if it fails to obey, it can and will be destroyed.

It is impossible to understand Josiah's reforming zeal, or his dismay when the lawbook was brought to his attention, except under the assumption that Deuteronomy came to him as the veritable thunderclap of conscience, like the trumpet announcing the Last Day, as it were. What is this? What do I read here? God, then, is after all *not* irrevocably committed to the defense of this nation through his election of David? In allowing the worship of other gods, this nation has been guilty of violating the cardinal stipulation of his covenant! It has therefore fallen under the curse and is doomed to destruction unless it reforms its conduct, radically and at once! So reform was made and all foreign gods were put away.

3. The reform thus represented, one might say, the triumph of Mosaic Yahwism. But the triumph, as we said, did not last. Whether this was because Josiah's tragic death undermined confidence in the truth of the Deuteronomic theology upon which the reform was based, or whether the people imagined that with the removal of pagan cults the demands of covenant had been met and the matter therefore closed, or whether it was simply that after three hundred years the official theology had so firmly entrenched itself in the popular mind that it could not be dislodged, we do not know. But whatever the reasons, the nation as a whole, its leaders and people alike, seems to have entrusted its future to the sure promises of God as affirmed in the cult. The thought that the nation might be marching to its destruction seems not to have been entertained. Any suggestion to that effect would be regarded as both treason and blasphemy. Not only is it bad for morale; it is tantamount to accusing God of going back on his covenant with David. And that is unthinkable—indeed, "unspeakable" (in the sense that it was decidedly unsafe to speak of it!).

With that we come to the prophet Jeremiah. We also come back to the question with which we began these chapters, for it was with this mind-set that Jeremiah collided all the days of his life, and without any noticeable success; this mind-set was the chief external source of the tragedy that befell him.

I

We are told (1:2; cf. 25:3)[1] that Jeremiah began his career as a prophet in the thirteenth year of Josiah's reign (627 B.C.), thus some five years before that king's reform was brought to its climax.[2] The

---

[1] Scripture references in this chapter and the next are to The Book of Jeremiah unless otherwise indicated.

[2] With the vast majority of scholars, this date is accepted as correct. It is true that a number of scholars (in English, cf. J. P. Hyatt, IB, Vol. 5, 1956, pp. 779 f.; W. L.

land was then still encumbered with the evil legacy of Manasseh's reign; pagan practices flourished everywhere.

1. What Jeremiah thought of Josiah's reform, and of the Deuteronomic law that undergirded it, is a question that has always provoked the widest difference of opinion. It is a question to which the book itself gives no unambiguously clear answer. Some scholars believe that Jeremiah enthusiastically supported the reform and even played an active part in its implementation—indeed, that he went up and down the country as a peripatetic evangelist preaching in its interests.[3] This seems unlikely. Not only does it rest too largely on a questionable interpretation of 11:1–17 (especially v. 6);[4] we must remember that the reform was carried out on the king's initiative, and in solemn covenant with Judah's elders and notables (II Kings 23:1–3), and it scarcely needed the evangelizing efforts of a still relatively unknown young prophet to ensure its adoption. Jeremiah's preaching may well have helped to prepare the climate for reform, but it is highly unlikely that he played any active part in bringing it to pass.

On the other hand, it is doubly difficult to believe—indeed, well-nigh unbelievable—that Jeremiah was opposed to the essential aims of the reform. His early preaching, as we shall see in a moment, was primarily a vigorous attack upon the pagan practices with which the land was then filled, the very practices that the reform aimed to remove. It is unthinkable that Jeremiah should have disapproved of this, or should have wished that pre-reformation conditions should continue. What is more, we know that at least on one occasion Jeremiah (who is not remembered as one who indulged in flattery!) expressed unbounded admiration for Josiah (22:15 f.)—something he would scarcely have done had he regarded that king's major official action as a deplorable error, if not a sin. In addition to this, we know of more than one occasion, some of which will be mentioned as we proceed, on which the sons of the reformers took Jeremiah's part, and even were instrumental in saving his life. This, to be sure, tells us

Holladay, *Jeremiah: Spokesman Out of Time* [Philadelphia: United Church Press, 1974], pp. 16–24) have argued that Jeremiah did not begin to prophesy until the beginning of Jehoiakim's reign in 609, or shortly before (the scholars just mentioned regard 627 as the date of Jeremiah's birth). The point cannot be debated here. But for reasons developed elsewhere (cf. *Jeremiah* [AB, 1965], pp. lxxx–lxxxv) it seems to me that the evidence strongly favors the traditional view.

[3] E.g., G. A. Smith, *Jeremiah* (New York and London: Harper & Brothers, 4th ed., 1929), pp. 141–146; cf. J. Skinner, *Prophecy and Religion: Studies in the Life of Jeremiah* (London: Cambridge University Press, 1922; repr. 1955), pp. 96–103.

[4] Cf. my remarks in AB, pp. 88 f.

nothing directly of Jeremiah's attitude toward the reform, but it tells a great deal regarding the reformers' attitude toward Jeremiah! Far from regarding him as an enemy of the country, they had at least a measure of sympathy with what he had to say. Whatever Jeremiah's opinion of the reform and its results came in retrospect to be, he must initially have approved of its essential aims.

In any event, there certainly can have been no fundamental conflict between Jeremiah's theology and that of Deuteronomy. Jeremiah's entire thinking was rooted in the recollection of Yahweh's grace to Israel in exodus and land-giving, and of the stern stipulations of his covenant, just as was the theology of Deuteronomy. Indeed, no prophet, with the possible exception of Hosea, stands more clearly in this tradition than does he.[5] The whole complex of ideas associated with the traditions of Zion and David is really alien to him; it plays virtually no role in his thinking, save in a negative way. Indeed, as we shall see, Jeremiah explicitly subordinated the assurance of Yahweh's election of the Davidic line, and the promise of his continued presence in the temple on Mt. Zion, to the stipulations of the Mosaic covenant. He saw the nation's very existence as based in Yahweh's grace to it in the past and as subject to the stipulations of his covenant, and he viewed its future in terms of its obedience or disobedience to those stipulations. In his entire orientation Jeremiah is closely akin to Hosea, whose prophecies he certainly knew; his early preaching, in particular, clearly shows Hosea's influence.

Jeremiah's distance from the traditions of the official theology is perhaps not surprising, for his background was not Jerusalem. We are told (1:1) that he came of a priestly family from the village of Anathoth in the land of Benjamin. This statement tempts us to speculations which, though quite incapable of substantiation, are nevertheless interesting and by no means implausible. Since it is unlikely that so small a village as Anathoth contained several unrelated priestly families, it is quite reasonable to suppose, as a number of scholars have done, that Jeremiah may have been descended from David's priest, Abiathar, who had been dismissed from office by Solomon and banished to his home in Anathoth because of his complicity in Adonijah's abortive attempt to usurp the throne (I

---

[5] Jeremiah's rootage in this tradition is all but universally recognized. It is perhaps not uninteresting that the covenant curses, a feature at home in the Mosaic covenant form, play a far more prominent role in Jeremiah's preaching than in that of any other prophet, with Hosea as his closest rival in this regard. Cf. D. R. Hillers, *Treaty-Curses and the Old Testament Prophets* (Rome: Pontifical Biblical Institute, 1964), esp. p. 77.

Kings 2:26 f.). If this was so, Jeremiah could boast of one of the proudest pedigrees in all of Israel, for he could, through Abiathar, claim descent from none other than the house of Eli (cf. I Sam. 14:3; 22:20; I Kings 2:27), which had served as custodians of the Ark at Shiloh in the days of the old tribal league and, beyond that—for so tradition would have had it—from the family of Moses himself. True, we cannot prove that this was so; but it is by no means improbable. It would do much to explain why Jeremiah was orientated, not upon the traditions of Jerusalem and David, but upon those of a more ancient order. It would also help to explain his deep and sympathetic concern for the people of northern Israel, as well as his spiritual kinship to North Israel's great prophet, Hosea.

2. Jeremiah seems to have begun his career already haunted by that premonition of judgment which was later to become well-nigh his entire burden. His earliest preaching was a slashing attack, fully in the tradition of Hosea, upon the paganism with which the land was then filled. We find samples of this in chs. 2 and 3, and elsewhere.[6] Here Jeremiah scores the nation's apostasy in a series of vivid, rapidly changing figures, as something that is unexampled, unnatural—and stupid. Israel, says he, is like a farm animal that refuses to pull in the traces; she is a choice vine that bears strange, putrid fruit; she is stained with a stain that will not wash (2:20–22); she has run after false gods with the unrestrained passion of an animal in heat (vs. 23–25)! Like Hosea before him, Jeremiah throws this unfaithfulness against the backdrop of God's grace to his people in bringing them from bondage and giving them their land and, on the basis of this, he depicts God as launching his lawsuit (*rīb*) against them (2:4–8):[7]

> Jer. 2:4 Hear the word of Yahweh, O house of Jacob,
> All you clans of Israel's stock!
> 5 This is what Yahweh has said:
> "What was it your fathers found wrong in me
> That they departed from me so far
> And, following 'Lord Delusion,'
> Deluded became?[8]

---

[6] To locate the undated sayings of Jeremiah in their historical setting is often a difficult task, and one that allows for a considerable difference of opinion. But, in common with many others, I believe that the material of chs. 2 and 3 relates basically to the period prior to the completion of Josiah's reform; cf. AB, pp. 9–27.

[7] Translation of passages from Jeremiah will follow in general those given in the AB volume (reference in note 2). The reader is referred to that volume for further comments and text-critical notes.

[8] Lit., "They followed the *hebel* and became *hebel*"; *hahebel* ("wind," "emptiness,"

> 6   They never said, 'Where is Yahweh,
> Who brought us up from Egypt's land,
> Who guided us through the desert,
> Land of steppe and ravine,
> Land of drought and of danger,
> Land through which nobody passes,
> Where no human being dwells?'
> 7   To a land like a garden I brought you,
> To eat of its bountiful fruit.
> But you entered and fouled my land,
> And made my heritage loathsome.
> 8   The priests never said, 'Where is Yahweh?'
> Those skilled in the law did not know me;
> And the prophets—by Baal they prophesied,
> And followed the useless ones." [9]

Because of their forgetfulness of his grace and his claims, Yahweh announces that he must bring suit against his people, and will continue to do so through all the generations of the future (2:9–13). Their conduct has been without parallel, without excuse, and utterly senseless. In forsaking her God, Israel is like one who exchanges a spring of fresh, life-giving water for cisterns whose water is flat and stale—and cracked cisterns at that, which allow even this to seep away.

> Jer. 2:9   "So—still I must state my case
> against you—Yahweh's word—
> Against your children's children I'll state it.
> 10   For cross to the western isles, and look!
> Send out to Kedar and closely observe!
> And see—has the like ever been?
> 11   Has ever a nation changed gods
> (Though these, to be sure, are not gods)?
> But my people! They've traded my Presence[10]
> For—'Lord Useless!' [11]
> 12   Be appalled, O heavens, at this!
> Shudder and shudder again! [12]—Yahweh's word.

"vacuity") seems to be a pun on *habba'al* ("the lord"), i.e., Baal, an appellation for the god of fertility.

[9] Heb. *lō' yō'îlū* ("things that do not profit") seems again to be a pun on Baal (or, the Baals; cf. v. 23).

[10] Lit., "my glory"; MT, "its (their) glory" is a scribal correction. Reference is to the Glory of Yahweh, the shining effulgence of the divine presence conceived of as dwelling in the Temple.

[11] Heb. *bᵉlō' yō'îl* ("for what does not profit") seems again to be a pun on Baal.

[12] The text is corrupt; cf. AB, p. 15. I have chosen to follow the reading of LXX, since this involves a minimum of emendation.

13   For it's a twofold wrong
          my people have done:
      Me they have forsaken,
      The fount of living water,
      To hew themselves cisterns,
      Cisterns that crack
      And cannot hold water."

With this expression of outraged hurt the lawsuit ends. No judgment is pronounced; but a warning and a threat are clearly implied.

To describe the nation's apostasy, Jeremiah borrows Hosea's metaphor of the unfaithful wife. He likened the covenant bond between God and people to a marriage consummated in the wilderness, and he depicts Yahweh as fondly remembering Israel as his once-faithful bride whom he lovingly guided and protected (2:2 f.):

Jer. 2:2   I remember your youthful devotion,
            Your bridal love,
            How you followed me through the desert,
            The untilled land.

But now Israel has long forgotten Yahweh's grace and loving care and has gone running after other gods. How can this be?

Jer. 2:32   Will a maid forget her jewels,
            Or a bride her sash?
            But my people! They've forgotten me
            Days beyond count.

To point up his people's untenable position, Jeremiah on one occasion appealed to the law regarding the remarriage of divorced persons (3:1–5). He says:

Jer. 3:1   If a man should divorce his wife,
            And she should leave him
            And become the wife of another,
            Can he take her back again? [13]
            That would bring great pollution, would it not,
            Upon that land?
            Yet *you*, who have whored with hosts of lovers,
            You would return to me?—Yahweh's word.

The law referred to is the one found in Deut. 24:1–4.[14] Here it is

---

[13] Lit., "Can he go back to her again?" LXX has, "Can she go back to him . . ." The reading of MT is preferred here and elsewhere in this verse; cf. AB, p. 23.

[14] It has been denied that Jer. 3:1 depends on Deut. 24:1–4; cf. T. R. Hobbs, ZAW, 86 (1974), pp. 23–29. Whether or not there is literary dependence may well be debated (it

stated that if a man should for any reason divorce his wife, and if she should then remarry, if the second husband should subsequently die, or should in turn divorce her, it is forbidden that her first husband should take her back as his wife. But, says Jeremiah, if the law forbids remarriage under such circumstances, how can Judah, who has left her divine "husband" to lead the life of a common whore with false gods (3:1b–2), hope to come wheedling back to him and expect him to overlook her conduct as though nothing had happened (vs. 4 f.)? No! Under the law this "marriage" is broken; it cannot possibly be patched up. Judah has forsaken her God-husband to "whore" with a host of false gods, and has lost all claim to his mercy and care.

In a word, the covenant has been broken and the bond between God and people voided. So there was nothing for Jeremiah to do but to warn of the judgment that must inevitably come. He saw this judgment as one that was to be executed by the terrible "foe from the North." The identity of this foe, who is described in a series of vivid and moving poems scattered for the most part through chs. 4 to 6 (cf. 4:5–8, 11–17; 5:15–17; 6:22–26; etc.), is a subject that has provoked endless discussion—a discussion into which we cannot enter here.[15] Certainly Jeremiah eventually came to see that this destroying foe would be the Babylonians; but a premonition of coming disaster seems to have haunted him long before the Babylonians became a threat (Babylon became a power to be reckoned with on the world scene late in the reign of Josiah; its advance into the west did not begin until 605). Indeed, Jeremiah seems to have had such a premonition since the very beginning of his career,[16] though it is impossible to say what enemy nation he originally had in mind. The language used to describe this foe is in good part conventional, and may suggest that Jeremiah at first had no specific foe in mind, but only the moral certainty of judgment to come. Whatever the truth may be, Jeremiah was from the beginning oppressed by the certainty that the land lay under God's judgment. The "foe from the North" would come as the agent of that judgment, would fall upon the nation

---

is quite possible that the Deuteronomic law had not yet been published at the time Jeremiah spoke). But it is most unlikely that the law found in Deuteronomy represents a new enactment. Jeremiah may well have appealed to an older and well-known form of the same law.

[15] See further my summary remarks in AB, pp. lxxx–lxxxv.

[16] But be it noted that mention of the "foe from the north" in 1:13–16 does not necessarily imply that he had such a foe in mind when he received his call. Ch. 1 is not an original unit; the two visions of 1:11–16 may have come to him somewhat later—though in all probability not a great deal later. On the structure of ch. 1, cf. AB, pp. 6–8.

without pity, rip it apart and destroy it, because of its violation of Yahweh's covenant.

It was no doubt in good part because of this premonition of disaster that Jeremiah never married. To be sure, the passage that tells us of this (16:1–9) was in all probability written down in its present form at a much later date. But the very fact that Jeremiah did not marry suggests that he must have felt a compulsion against taking such a step ever since his youth; in ancient Israel men were normally married at a very early age, while bachelorhood was all but unheard of. Jeremiah felt that God had commanded him not to marry and that, in taking this course, he was to serve, proleptically, as a memorial to the death of his country. In his loneliness and childlessness he was to be a living symbol of the bereavement of his people.

3. Jeremiah offered his people no hope whatever save in sincere repentance and return to Yahweh. He pleaded with them to return before it was too late (and frequently in language reminiscent of Hosea). He warned them that, having forsaken Yahweh, they could never save themselves by political cleverness (2:17–19, 33–37; etc.), and that their handmade gods would be of no help to them whatever in the time of trouble that was coming (vs. 26–28). He portrays God as puzzled, wondering how he can treat such a faithless people as his children and give them the promised blessings (3:19); and he imagines God as concluding that he can do so only if they both address him as "Father" (as they so unctiously do; cf. v. 4) and at the same time show him the loyal obedience that sons ought to show (as they so emphatically do not; cf. v. 5). He depicts God as pleading with his people to repent (v. 22a; cf. Hos. 14:1, 4 [MT, vs. 2, 5]):

Jer. 3:22a   Turn back, backsliding sons,
              I would heal your backslidings!

And he places in the people's mouth the words with which they *must* reply: a liturgy of penitence (vs. 22b–25).[17]

Jer. 3:22b   See! we come to thee,
              For thou art Yahweh our God.
      23   Truly the hills are a swindle,
              The hubbub on the heights.[18]
              Truly in Yahweh our God
              Is Israel's help.

---

[17] On the text, cf. AB, pp. 19–23. In vs. 24 f. the original metrical form seems to have been somewhat expanded in transmission.

[18] Reference is to the cult of fertility, which was practiced in open-air shrines on the hilltops (cf. 2:20; 3:13; etc.).

    24   But the Shame,[19] it has devoured
            All our fathers e'er acquired from our youth,
            Their flocks and herds,
            Their sons and daughters.
    25   Our shame, be it our bed;
            Our disgrace, be it our cover!
            For against Yahweh our God we have sinned,
            We and our fathers,
            From our youth until this day.
            We have not obeyed the voice of Yahweh our God.

This is how it *must* be; there is no other way! No excuses offered, no merit or good works claimed—just abject confession of sin: *Peccavimus!* Under the law Israel has lost all claim upon her God; she can only receive his grace, and respond in penitence and trust.

But did Jeremiah actually expect that Josiah's reform would produce such repentance? We do not know. Certainly he was not without hope that his own preaching would have a constructive effect. At his call (1:10) he understood his mission to be "to uproot and tear down," but also "to build and to plant." And he must have rejoiced when idolatrous practices were put away and Judah's elders and princes entered into solemn covenant before Yahweh to obey his commandments (II Kings 23:1–3). There is even evidence that as Josiah moved to take possession of large parts of northern Israel, Jeremiah entertained a lively hope that the people of the north would once again be united with Judah in the worship of Yahweh (31:2–6).[20]

    Jer. 31:6   For soon comes the day when
                the watchmen will shout
            On Ephraim's hills,
            "Up, let us go to Zion,
            To Yahweh our God."

He depicts God as moved to compassion over Ephraim's (northern Israel's) plight and deeply felt remorse (31:15–20), and pleading with his long-lost children to return (vs. 21 f.; 3:12 f.). It is interesting, too, that Jeremiah in his early preaching, though showing nothing remotely resembling optimism, does not announce the judgment as inevitable, as he was later to do. He warns of it, but he does not announce it; sincere repentance can avert it. Like Deuteronomy

---

    [19] "Shame" (*bōšet*) frequently occurs in the Bible as an intentional alteration of "Baal." Here it is used for the sake of the wordplay with "shame" in v. 25.

    [20] In common with many scholars, I should assign 31:2–6, 15–22, as well as 3:6–13(14), to Jeremiah's earliest period, in Josiah's reign.

itself, he leaves the future open; it depends upon an "if" (e.g., "If you return to me . . . ," 4:1 f.).

But actually what Jeremiah wanted was far more than Josiah's reform—or any officially sponsored reform, for that matter—could possibly produce. The repentance he called for involved far more than the formal abolishment of pagan cults, external compliance with the law, lavish sacrifice and cultic busyness, ever larger throngs in the Temple on feast days, and the like. He called for a genuine return to the "ancient ways" (6:16) of life in covenant with Yahweh, for an inner commitment to Yahweh's covenant stipulations, a reform of the whole manner of living—in a word, repentance from "the heart." [21] He summoned his fellow citizens to signify their membership in Yahweh's community not merely by their physical circumcision, but by circumcision of "the heart" (4:3 f.; cf. Deut. 10:16). This must be done or the judgment will become inevitable.

Jer. 4:3 Plow up your unplowed ground!
Do not sow among thorns! [22]
 4 To your God circumcise you;
Remove your heart's foreskin,
O men of Judah, O Jerusalem's citizens;
Lest my wrath break out like fire,
And burn so that none can quench it,
So wicked have been your deeds.

Readers of the New Testament will recall how Paul later took up this thought of the circumcision of the heart and developed it in another context (Rom. 2:25–29).

Jeremiah asked a great deal of his people. Realistically, one might feel that he asked too much. Certainly it was far more than any reform sponsored by the state, such as Josiah's was, could reasonably be expected to produce. A state can, through wise measures, remove abuses and so exert a beneficent effect on public morality, but it cannot by its best efforts produce a radical inner change of attitude and character—and that was just what Jeremiah called for. Could it be that in his youthful enthusiasm Jeremiah had hoped that the reform would have such an effect? It is not impossible that he did. But we have no real evidence for saying so, and we have to admit that we do not know.

---

[21] This note is frequently sounded in Jeremiah and is characteristic of him. But we must be careful not to sentimentalize it. To the ancient Israelite the "heart" connoted not so much the seat of the emotions, as it does with us, as the mind and will.

[22] Cf. Hos. 10:12 for similar words. One is reminded of our Lord's parable of "the sower"; Mark 4:1–9 and parallels.

II

Whatever Jeremiah may have expected of the reform in the first place—and we have just said that we do not know what he expected—he ultimately became keenly aware of its shallowness. It had produced no radical change in the national character, no sincere repentance or return to life in covenant with Yahweh.

1. How long Jeremiah was in reaching this evaluation of the situation we cannot say. We know too little of affairs in Judah, and of Jeremiah's own life, in the years just after the reform to allow us to be sure. Some believe that Jeremiah was for a time so completely satisfied with the reform, and so pleased with its positive accomplishments, that he saw no further need to speak, and therefore remained silent through most of the rest of Josiah's reign.[23] One finds this difficult to believe.[24] Perhaps he did remain silent for a while; but so long a silence is difficult to credit and seems highly unlikely. It is difficult to believe that so perceptive a person as Jeremiah would have required ten years or more to have had misgivings about the reform and doubly difficult to believe that, having had them, one so outspoken would have been content to remain silent. It is true that no saying of Jeremiah can be *proved* to have been uttered in the years immediately following the reform. But there are a number that fit well in that context, and they may cautiously be advanced as evidence that it need not have been long before Jeremiah began to have serious misgivings about what had taken place—though once again let it be said that full assurance is impossible.

In any event, it is certain that Jeremiah ultimately became completely disillusioned with what the reform had accomplished. It had not produced the needed repentance. It had produced only a great cloud of incense smoke and throngs of people in the Temple, but no return to a life of righteousness in obedience to God's commands. Jeremiah saw his people as spiritually blind and deaf, in full rebellion against Yahweh's rule (5:20–25).[25] In this passage the prophet

[23] We have already (see note 2 above) registered our disagreement with those who argue that Jeremiah did not begin his career as a prophet until the end of Josiah's reign or the beginning of Jehoiakim's.

[24] I have expressed my own views at greater length in AB, pp. xcii–xcvi.

[25] This piece and others cited here, though none can be exactly dated, give us samples of Jeremiah's post-reform preaching. It will be noted that the gravamen of his complaint in these passages no longer falls on idolatrous practices, but on the crimes of the powerful against the weak, a complacent assurance of rightness with God, together with a stubborn refusal to return to him.

borrows imagery from the world of myth. As in the mythology of various ancient peoples the god is said to have slain the chaos monster in order to establish the dry land, so here Yahweh, the Creator God, has set bounds to the watery chaos of Sea (personified!) so that, try though it may, it can never break free. But what Sea cannot do, Israel can do and has done: she has rebelled against her God, and gone!

Jer. 5:21	Hear this now
	You people stupid and senseless,
	Who have eyes, indeed, but see not,
	Ears, but cannot hear.
22	You do not fear *me?*—Yahweh's word—
	Or tremble before me?
	Who have set the sand as Sea's frontier,
	An eternal decree which it
	may not transgress;
	Toss it may, but it cannot prevail,[26]
	Its billows may roar, but they cannot
	get through.
23	But this people! Theirs has been
	A will contumacious and rebel;
	They have turned, they have gone. . . .

All about him the prophet saw scoundrels who had unscrupulously taken advantage of the helpless and who had grown rich and fat from their ill-gotten gains (5:26–29). He heard the clergy lulling the people into a false sense of security by telling them that all was right between them and God and that no trouble would ever befall them (5:12, 30 f.; 6:13 f.; 8:10 f.; etc). It seemed to him that the people had refused either to return to the ancient ways *or* to heed the prophetic warning of judgment for failure to do so (6:16 f.).

Jer. 6:16	This is what Yahweh has said:
	"Stand at the crossroads, and look;[27]
	Ask for the ancient paths
	Where the good way lies. That take,
	And find for yourselves repose.
	But they said, 'We will not!'
17	So I stationed over them[28] watchmen:[29]

---

[26] The reading here follows LXX and other Vrs.; cf. AB, p. 38.

[27] Lit., "Stand by the roads, and look." The meaning could be as suggested in the translation, or simply, "Stop where you are . . ."

[28] This is a logical correction; Heb. has, "over you."

[29] I.e., prophets who warn of danger (cf. Ezek. 3:16–21, etc.).

'Give heed to the blast of the horn!'
But they said, 'We will not!' "

Jeremiah seems to be saying as clearly as words could say that they
have refused both sides of the Deuteronomic alternative (cf. Deut.
11:26–28; 30:15–20; etc.); they have refused to follow the way of life
and of blessing by walking in obedience to Yahweh's covenant, and
they have refused to take seriously the possibility of death and the
curse. Since this is so, the lavish cultus by which they had thought to
satisfy the divine demands is simply unacceptable (vs. 19–21): God
will not have it, and it will not save them from the disaster that he
will bring upon them.

Jeremiah was increasingly driven to the conviction that his people
were incorrigible in their backsliding. He seems to have asked
himself the question: Is it possible that a people should apostatize and
never repent? And he was forced to return the sorrowful answer:
Yes, it is possible; it has happened! This we see in 8:4–7 which, in
spite of the editorial heading in v. 4a linking the passage to the
preceding section, is not a word from Yahweh, but a soliloquy of
Jeremiah.[30] The piece begins:

> Jer. 8:4a   Do men fall down, and not get up
>   Or miss the way, and not turn back? [31]

The questions are rhetorical, and the answers obvious. If a man
stumbles and falls, he instinctively scrambles to his feet. And if he
finds that he has taken the wrong path and is lost, he of course
retraces his steps and tries to find his way again. But these questions
only serve to lead into the question that follows—which is not
rhetorical, and which underscores the enormity of the people's
conduct as Jeremiah has come to see it:

> Jer. 8:5   Why, then, has this people slid back
>   In backsliding perpetual?
>   They cling to deceit,
>   Refuse to return.

Jeremiah then goes on to say (v. 6) that, though he has listened
attentively, he has heard from his people no word of repentance or
remorse; on the contrary, they are rushing headlong to their ruin like
a cavalry charge which, once unleashed, cannot be halted. Indeed, he

---

[30] On the problems of translation, cf. AB, pp. 60–65.

[31] Lit., "Does one turn (away) and not turn (back)?" As frequently in Jeremiah, there
is a play on the verb *šûb*.

declares (v. 7) that his people do not display the sense of wild
creatures. Wild birds instinctively know the order of nature that
governs their migrations, and they obey it; but Israel does not know
the rule, or ordinance, of Yahweh that governs its existence.

Following upon this piece and closely related to it in thought,
though formally separate, is another (vs. 8 f.) in which Jeremiah
engages in disputation with the spiritual leaders of the people, who
boast of their wisdom in all matters pertaining to God and his
demands. This links closely to v. 7 and carries forward its thought
beautifully. There Jeremiah has declared that the people do not have
the sense of wild creatures, because they do not know the "ordinance"
of Yahweh. To this we may imagine the clergy replying indignantly:
What do you mean—we do not know the ordinance of Yahweh? We
know it very well! We have it written in the law! Jeremiah hotly
rejects this conceit. Says he:

> Jer. 8:8 How can you say, "Why, we are wise,
>   For we have the law of Yahweh"?
>   Now do but see—the deception it has wrought,
>   The deceiving pen of the scribes! [32]
>   9   Shamed are the wise,
>   Stunned and trapped!
>   Look! They have spurned the word of Yahweh,
>   So what manner of wisdom have they?

The passage is one of the most disputed in the Jeremiah book. The
law in question, of which the clergy boast, is clearly a written law. In
the context it is probable that the Deuteronomic law, promulgated in
Josiah's reign, is primarily intended, though it is not excluded that
other bodies of written law may also be in view. But we need not
conclude that Jeremiah is saying either that Deuteronomy is itself a
fraud, or that a genuine nucleus of laws has been falsified by later
additions (as the translations of RSV and other English versions
might lead one to suppose). If the translation of v. 8b adopted above
is correct, Jeremiah is not saying that the law is a lie, or that it has
been made into a lie (so RSV), but that it has *fathered* a lie, namely,
the conceit that possession of it gives all necessary wisdom and that a
mechanical and external compliance with it satisfies the divine
demands. It is just this conceit which has deafened Jeremiah's
hearers to the prophetic word and caused them to spurn it (v. 9b).

---

[32] The last bicolon of v. 8 is exceedingly cryptic, and its translation is disputed. The
one given here follows AB, p. 60 (cf. pp. 63 f. for further justification). But the reader
should consult the commentaries and EVV for other suggestions.

The law, and the reform made on the basis of it, has bolstered their complacency and contributed to their obduracy. It was out of their own complacency that the clergy was able to assure the people that all was now well between them and God, and that their future would be one of peace. But to Jeremiah this was a bald-faced lie (6:14; cf. 8:11)!

> Jer. 6:14   They treat my people's fracture
>   Superficially, and cry,
>   "It is well! It is well!"
>   But it is not well!

All his life Jeremiah collided with prophets who promised peace to an unrepentant and obdurate people. For them he had nothing but contempt. They are windbags and liars whose word did not come from Yahweh, but sprang from their own wishful thinking. They are false prophets, never commissioned by Yahweh at all, for, if they were true prophets, they would not lull the people into a false sense of security, but would warn of Yahweh's wrath and seek to turn the people to penitence. This collision of the prophet with the prophets surfaces throughout the Jeremiah book, but nowhere more clearly than in 23:9–40. For example, vs. 16–22:[33]

> Jer. 23:16   This is what Yahweh of Hosts has said:
>   "Do not listen to the words of the prophets!
>   They do but delude you.
>   It's a self-induced vision they utter,
>   Not one from the mouth of Yahweh—
>   17   Saying to scorners of Yahweh's word,
>   'All will go well with you';
>   And to all those who follow their own
>   stubborn wills,
>   'Misfortune will not overtake you.' "

Then, after declaring (vs. 18–20) that Yahweh's word *for that moment* was one of judgment and wrath, not of peace, and that any who had really stood in his council would know this and speak accordingly, he concludes:

> Jer. 23:21   "I sent not these prophets,
>   Yet—they ran!
>   I spoke not to them,
>   Yet—they prophesied!
>   22   But if they had stood in my council,
>   They'd proclaim my words to my people,

---

[33] On problems of text, translation, and interpretation, see again AB, pp. 148 f., 152.

> From their wicked ways they'd turn them,
> From their evil deeds."

The prophet's duty is to warn, to admonish, to correct, and to summon the people to penitence and conformity to Yahweh's will. To fail to do this is to encourage them in their obduracy (14:11–16; 23:13–15, 23–32; etc.). If the Josianic reform failed to produce the radical and heartfelt repentance that Jeremiah had wanted, it would appear that this was to no small degree the fault of the spiritual leaders, who for the most part seem to have been satisfied with the situation as it was.

2. As we have said, we do not know how soon Jeremiah reached this pessimistic evaluation of the situation. But it is certain that when Jehoiakim took the throne his alienation became complete. It will be recalled that Josiah met his death in 609 when he sought to halt an Egyptian force that was marching northward toward the Euphrates to assist the Assyrians in a last attempt to retake Harran from the victorious Babylonians. Though this attempt ended in failure, Egypt was able for a time to retain control of all of Palestine and Syria. Though the people in Jerusalem immediately acclaimed Josiah's son, Jehoahaz, as king in his place, within three months the pharaoh had summoned him to his headquarters in central Syria, deposed him, and exiled him to Egypt; he then placed another of Josiah's sons, Jehoiakim, on the throne as his vassal (II Kings 23:31–35). Under Jehoiakim the reform was allowed to lapse. While there is no evidence that non-Yahwistic cults were officially fostered, as they had been in Manasseh's reign, it appears that pagan practices crept back and public morality deteriorated. Violations of covenant law seem to have been common (cf. 7:1–15, etc.).

What made matters worse was the character of Jehoiakim himself. The Bible says no good word of the man. Apparently without deep religious convictions or regard for the rights of his subjects, he was a petty tyrant, unfit to rule, whose policies ultimately brought his country to disaster. Prophets who dared to oppose him met persecution and, in one case of which we know (26:20–23), death. Early in his reign he showed his true colors when, apparently finding his father's palace not good enough for his majesty, he built a larger and finer one and, possibly because his treasury was depleted by Egyptian taxation (II Kings 23:33, 35), leaving him strapped for funds, he impressed forced labor to do it. This brought from Jeremiah one of the most scathing utterances that ever escaped his lips (22:13–19).

> Jer. 22:13 Ah, the man who builds his house
> with unfairness,

His upper rooms with wrong,
Who works his neighbor for nothing,
Nor pays him any wage.

Then, after describing the luxurious appointments which Jehoiakim
had provided for his new house (v. 14), Jeremiah wheels on him (v.
15a). Do you think that surrounding yourself with more luxuries
than your predecessors enjoyed marks you as a king? Are these the
true qualities of royalty? No! If you really want to know what a king
is like—so Jeremiah says in effect to this spoiled young man (vs.
15b–16)—I suggest that you take a look at your father's portrait.
There was a king! And what, in Jeremiah's opinion, made Josiah the
model of what a king should be? He "ate and drank" (i.e., he was no
ascetic, but lived as befitted his station), and yet "did justice and
righteousness," especially to the poor and helpless who could not
defend themselves. In a word, he lived like a king, but he also
behaved like one. And this, says Jeremiah, was to exhibit the most
supreme of all virtues: the knowledge of Yahweh ("Is not this what it
is to know me?—Yahweh's word," v. 16b). Jeremiah could not have
paid a higher compliment to Josiah: he was what a king is supposed to
be! But when he turned from Josiah to his successor, this Jehoiakim,
he fairly gagged (v. 17): a man interested only in himself and personal
gain, and who would stop at nothing to get what he wanted. He
concludes by promising Jehoiakim that he would one day be given a
dishonorable burial, with no one in the least sorry to see him go.

Jer. 22:18   They'll not lament him,
              "Ah, my brother! Ah, sister!"
              They'll not lament him,
              "Ah, lord! Ah, his majesty!"
      19   They'll give him a donkey's funeral,
              Hauled out and dumped
              Outside Jerusalem's gates.

Need we be surprised that relationships between Jehoiakim and
Jeremiah remained somewhat less than cordial?

Under Jehoiakim, Jeremiah found the situation intolerable. The
abandonment of the ideals of the reform was to him no less than a
conspiracy against the Divine King, a breach of his covenant which
had invited his wrath (11:9–13).[34] He came increasingly to the

---

[34] The prose unit, 11:1–17, is in its present form of exilic date, as vs. 7 f. indicate; but
these verses seem to be an expansion (LXX omits them save for the last two Hebrew
words). Otherwise, the passage seems to relate mainly to Jehoiakim's reign as the
reform was allowed to lapse and, though it does not preserve Jeremiah's exact words,

conviction that his people were completely depraved and incorrigible. If one were to search the streets of Jerusalem, one would not find a single man who acted with integrity, or with awareness of, or concern for, the will of Yahweh (5:1–9; cf. 9:2–9 [MT, 9:1–8]). It is quite useless to expect such a people to repent: they do not know how to do right (4:22)—indeed, have lost the ability to do so:

> Jer. 13:23   Can the Cushite change his skin,
> Or the leopard his spots?
> Then you might also do good,
> Who are trained to do ill.

In a word, they are totally depraved! True, one might ask if Jeremiah's evaluation of his people was not *too* pessimistic. There *were* good men in Jerusalem, and we meet some of them in the pages of his book. But that—rightly or wrongly—Jeremiah reached such an evaluation seems certain. He became convinced that God had been alienated from his people and had turned against them in anger (12:7–13). They are condemned by the terms of the covenant to a judgment that would be fearful, certain, and complete—so fearful as to unhinge the fixed order of creation and to plunge it once more into primeval chaos (4:23–26).[35]

> Jer. 4:23   I saw the earth—lo, chaos primeval! [36]
> The heavens—their light was gone.
> 24   I saw the mountains—and lo, they were quaking,
> And all the hills rocked to and fro.
> 25   I looked—and see, no human was there,
> And the birds of the sky had all flown.
> 26   I looked—and see, the tilled land was desert,
> Its cities all lying in ruins—
> Before Yahweh,
> Before his hot anger.

---

may be assumed to reflect his sentiments accurately enough. The prose sayings of the book constitute its major critical problem; it cannot be debated here. I have expressed my views with regard to it elsewhere: cf. AB, pp. lxvii–lxxiii; "The Date of the Prose Sermons of Jeremiah" (JBL, 70 [1951], pp. 15–35); "The Prophetic Reminiscence: Its Place and Function in the Book of Jeremiah" (*Biblical Essays: Proceedings of the Ninth Meeting of Die Ou-Testamentiese Werkgemeenskap in Suid Afrika* [Potchefstroom: Pro Rege Pers-Beperk, 1966], pp. 11–30).

[35] None of the passages cited here can be dated with precision. But all reflect Jeremiah's feelings as his disillusionment with his people deepened.

[36] The words (Heb., *tōhū wābōhū*) are those used in Gen. 1:2 to describe the formless void that existed before creation. Indeed, in this poem one might say that the story of Gen., ch. 1, has been reversed: men, beasts, and growing things are gone, the dry land itself totters, the command, "Let there be light" (Gen. 1:3), has been revoked, and primeval chaos has returned. It is as if the earth had been "uncreated."

3. Jeremiah's pessimistic view of his country and its future brought him into head-on collision with what was apparently the vast majority of his fellow citizens, leaders and people alike. It was inevitable that it should have. They believed (or, perhaps better, they would not allow themselves to believe otherwise) that God had unconditionally committed himself through his promises to the defense of the nation; no punishment that he might send upon it could, therefore, ever be total. Jeremiah, on the contrary, had no place in his thinking for unconditional promises. The notion that God had guaranteed the continuance of the dynasty, or the existence of the Temple and its cult, or the defense of the city in which the Temple stood, was simply incompatible with his profoundest theological convictions. The existence of dynasty, of Temple, and of nation was alike subject to the stipulations of Yahweh's covenant.

On one occasion at least, Jeremiah even seems explicitly to place the promises to the Patriarchs under conditions. This is in 4:1 f.[37]

> Jer. 4:1   If you return, O Israel—Yahweh's word—
> To *me* return,
> If you put your vile things aside,
> Nor stray from my presence,
> 2   Then might you swear, "As Yahweh lives,"
> Truthfully, justly, and rightly;
> Then nations in him might bless themselves,
> And in him exult.

The pronoun "him" in the last bicolon seems unexpected and abrupt (one would expect "in you," or "in me"), but it is not to be emended as some scholars do. Its antecedent is Abraham. We seem to have here an allusion to, or even a citation of, the promise to Abraham as that is found in Gen. 18:18 and similar passages. As we read it in Genesis, the promise to Abraham carries no expressed conditions. But Jeremiah introduces one. He says that God will make good his promise to Abraham if—but only if—the people truly repent. Jeremiah knew of no unconditional promises. He declared that the dynasty could and would come to an end, the Temple could and would be destroyed, the nation could and would be ripped from its land if disobedience to the stipulations of Yahweh's covenant continued.

This does not mean that Jeremiah was opposed to the Davidic dynasty and would have liked to have seen it fall, still less that he was in principle hostile to the institution of monarchy as such. On the

---

[37] On the text and translation, cf. AB, pp. 21, 24.

contrary, he saw the monarchy as having a place in the divine economy. It had been ordained of God to establish justice and righteousness in the land, especially justice toward the weak who could not help themselves, as demanded by covenant law (e.g., Ex. 22:21–24) and, equally, by the royal ideal (e.g., Ps. 72). If it fulfilled this obligation, its survival was assured; but if not, God himself would bring it to an end (22:1–5). As we have said, Jeremiah saw in Josiah a king who fully lived up to his responsibilities (vs. 15 f.); but the other kings who reigned during his lifetime he found sadly disappointing if not positively depraved (Manasseh, Jehoiakim). He came to the conviction that at least the presently ruling Davidic line would lose its place on Judah's throne and would never in the future regain it (22:28–30; 36:29–31).

It is true that at one place Jeremiah seems to allow to the hope of an ideal Davidic king in the future (the "Messiah") at least a theoretical validity. This is in 23:5 f.[38]

> Jer. 23:5 See! The days are coming—Yahweh's word—
> When I will raise a true "Shoot" of David's line;
> As king he shall reign—and ably,
> And do justice and right in the land.
> 6 In his days shall Judah be saved,
> And Israel shall dwell in safety.
> And this is the name by which he'll be called,
> *"Yahweh-ṣidqēnū."*

The genuineness of this saying need not be questioned (though some have done so), but its interpretation has been much debated. The likeness of the future king's name to that of Judah's last ruler, Zedekiah, has been noticed by all and is scarcely accidental.[39] It is likely that the piece was uttered during that king's reign (possibly as dynastic hopes began to be attached to him by certain of his courtiers?).[40] It thus allows to the hope reposed in the Davidic dynasty a theoretical validity; but it does little more than that. By its

---

[38] On the critical problems and the translation of this much-debated passage, cf. AB, pp. 140, 143 f.

[39] The name *yhwh-ṣidqēnū* means "Yahweh is our righteousness" or, better, ". . . our vindication"; that of Zedekiah (*ṣidqīyāhū*) means "Yahweh is my vindication." At least an oblique allusion to Zedekiah must be assumed.

[40] Others believe that it was uttered prior to Zedekiah's accession and that because of it (but not by Jeremiah's intention) the king was given his throne name (his personal name was Mattaniah; II Kings 24:17). See the commentaries for discussion. Our interpretation follows generally that of W. Rudolph, *Jeremia* (HAT, 1947), pp. 125–127, and others.

play on Zedekiah's name it more than gently hints that these hopes will find their fulfillment not through him, but through a ruler of totally different stamp in the indefinite future. And aside from this passage, and its prose parallel in 33:14–16 (which LXX lacks), the hope of an ideal Davidic king plays no role in Jeremiah's thinking at all.[41]

But if Jeremiah's words betray no fundamental hostility to the institution of monarchy, it is equally wrong to suppose that he was in principle an enemy of the cult. It is difficult to believe that any of the prophets, however scathing their attacks upon the cult of their day may have been, were in principle so hostile to the cult as such that they would have abolished it, could they have had their way.[42] Nor was Jeremiah—whatever he may have thought of *these* priests and *this* cult. Not only was he himself of a priestly background; in his early career, as we have seen, he looked forward to the reunification of Israel and Judah in the worship of Yahweh on Mt. Zion (31:6), i.e., in the Temple. True, like all the prophets, he denied that God's demands could be met, and the covenant bond maintained, through sacrifice and cultic observance alone; and for this reason he declared that God was displeased with—nay rejected—the lavish cultus that an unrepentant people brought to him (e.g., 6:16–21). But this is far from a rejection of the cult as such. Not even such a passage as 7:21–26 can be driven so far. Here (v. 22) it might seem that Jeremiah is saying that God never instituted the sacrificial system at all, and that sacrifice had no place in Israel's religion in the earliest period. But the point lies in the balance between this verse and v. 23. The words, "Obey my voice, and I will be your God, and you shall be my people," are the formula of covenant. Jeremiah is not rejecting the cult as illegitimate in itself; he is saying that God's essential demands never had to do with ritual matters, but with obedience to the covenant stipulations.[43]

---

[41] As commentators generally agree, the clear allusion in 30:8 f. is a prose insert in a poetic context.

[42] It was at one time quite commonly held that the prophets were totally opposed to sacrifice and ritual observance and believed that such things had no rightful place in the worship that God required. But this view has rightly lost favor in more recent years. For an excellent summary discussion with balanced conclusions, cf. H. H. Rowley, "Ritual and the Hebrew Prophets" (1956; repr. in *From Moses to Qumran* [London: Lutterworth Press, 1963], pp. 111–138).

[43] For example, when Paul said (I Cor. 1:17), "Christ did not send me to baptize, but to preach the gospel," did he mean that baptism was illegitimate and ought not to be practiced? No, for he himself baptized (I Cor. 1:14–16). He meant that the essence of his mission was the proclamation of the gospel rather than baptizing converts—who

4. Yet it must be said that Jeremiah did flatly contradict the popular belief in Yahweh's eternal and unconditional choice of Mt. Zion—and in the strongest terms. This finds classical expression in the so-called "Temple sermon" (7:1–15), which (cf. 26:1) was delivered at the very beginning of Jehoiakim's reign (609/8).[44] Here Jeremiah denounces the belief that the physical presence of Yahweh's Temple guarantees protection. Said he (7:4), "Don't put your trust in that lie: Yahweh's temple, Yahweh's temple, Yahweh's temple is this." The "lie," of course, did not consist in their saying that the Temple was Yahweh's temple—which of course it was—but in their telling themselves that, because Yahweh has his dwelling there, the city is safe from all harm. On the contrary, Jeremiah says (vs. 5–7) that only if they make a total reform of their manner of living, only if they behave justly one toward another, cease to oppress the weak and the helpless, and refrain from worshiping other gods—only then will Yahweh continue to dwell in their midst and protect them.[45] He then goes on (vs. 8–11):

> (Jer. 7:8) Look! You are putting your trust in a worthless lie! (v. 9) What? Steal, murder, commit adultery, swear falsely, burn sacrifices to Baal, and follow other gods whom you have not known, (v. 10) and then come and stand before me in this house, which belongs to me,[46] and say, "We are safe!"—just so you can go right on doing all these abominations? (v. 11) A robber's hideout[47]—is that what this house which belongs to me has become in your opinion? . . .

---

might then boast that they were Paul's disciples. The balance of the clauses has the same force in Jer. 7:22 f.

[44] That the biographical account of ch. 26 relates to the occasion of the delivery of the discourse of 7:1–15 can hardly be doubted. The expression (26:1) "in the beginning of the reign of Jehoiakim" (so most EVV) does not refer vaguely to the early part of that king's reign, but is a technical term denoting his "accession year"—i.e., the period that elapsed between the king's actual assumption of power and the next New Year (in the spring), from which his first regnal year was counted. The "Temple sermon" was thus delivered between ca. September of 609 and April of 608.

[45] In vs. 3 and 7, MT (and most EVV) reads, "then I will let you dwell in this place"—i.e., I will allow you to remain in your land. With various commentators (and cf. JB) and with some manuscript evidence, I have preferred to read, "I will dwell with you in this place"—i.e., in the Temple. This involves no change in the consonantal text, but only in the vowel pointing (cf. AB, p. 55). In Deuteronomic usage (and the prose of Jeremiah is stylistically very similar to that of Deuteronomy) the "place" that Yahweh chooses is regularly the Temple (e.g., I Kings 8:29 f., 35; Deut. 12:11; 14:23)—as it is in this passage in vs. 12 and 14.

[46] Lit., "over which my name has been called." The expression has a legal background and signifies to claim legal title to the possession of a thing or a person. Cf. also in vs. 11, 14, etc.

[47] Lit., "cave" (where robbers hide).

In other words, Jeremiah's hearers are criminals. They are like bandits who commit all sorts of outrages and then flee to the Temple for safety, thinking through participation in its cult to escape the consequences of what they have done, just as robbers lie low in some cave until pursuit dies down, and then go out to rob and kill again. It is to be noted that in v. 9 ("steal, murder . . .") Jeremiah has ticked off at least half of the offenses prohibited in the Decalogue. They cannot commit such offenses and then expect to find protection in the Temple; Yahweh will not stay with them in the Temple if they continue to behave in this way. In a word, Jeremiah has made Yahweh's election of Mt. Zion and his promise to dwell there forever flatly subject to the conditions of the Mosaic covenant! He challenged his hearers (v. 12), who could not believe that God would destroy the house where he had his earthly habitation, and where men sang his praises, to travel to Shiloh, where once stood the shrine of the old tribal league, and see what had happened to it.[48] He can do it; he has done it—and he is going to do it again! Because of their crimes, and their stubborn refusal to hear, God will destroy his Temple and will deport his people far from their land, just as he once deported the people of northern Israel.

From the biographical account in ch. 26 we learn that Jeremiah was very nearly lynched for saying this. It is not surprising. He had flatly contradicted a central tenet of the official theology—and in the roughest language—and he had done so in the name of God. Since in the view of his hearers what he had said was simply untrue, he was guilty of prophesying falsely; and for this the Deuteronomic law itself demands the death penalty (Deut. 18:20). That this was the real point at issue is clear from Jeremiah's own defense of himself (26:12–15). He neither denied that he had spoken as charged (he obviously had), nor protested that he did not mean to contradict his hearers' beliefs as sharply as it might have seemed (he obviously did); his only defense was that Yahweh had indeed told him to speak as he had. His life was saved because certain of the nobles believed him and took his side on the grounds that a prophet ought not to suffer reprisals for speaking Yahweh's word. Prominent among these was Ahikam ben Shaphan (v. 24), whose father had been Josiah's secretary of state and a leading protagonist of the reform (cf. II Kings 22:8–13).

---

[48] Though the Bible does not tell of it, and though archaeological evidence is lacking, Shiloh was apparently destroyed by the Philistines after their victory described in I Sam., ch. 4; cf. Ps. 78:60–64.

It was a collision in theology. Both Jeremiah and his opponents were moved by strong theological convictions. Two fundamental factors in Israel's faith, two ways of viewing the nation's election and position under God, the one stressing God's sure and immutable promises which nothing could cancel, the other stressing his righteous commandments which no one might disregard with impunity, both ancient and always held in delicate balance, had now been so articulated as to issue in two diametrically opposite views of the nation's future. On the one hand, there was the memory of God's unconditional promise to the patriarchs of land, posterity and blessing, which had been taken up and projected into the future through God's eternal covenant with David and his choice of Mt. Zion as his everlasting abode, and which now had hardened into the national dogma which the people clutched to their hearts: *this* nation and *this* dynasty will always endure, for so God has promised! On the other hand, there was the covenant made in the wilderness, based in the prevenient grace of God and issuing in binding stipulations to which the nation was obliged to conform, lately reactivated and made the basis of Josiah's reform and now taken up by the greatest prophet of his day: this nation *can* be destroyed, this nation *will* be destroyed, because it has broken covenant with Yahweh.

III

Caught in this theological collision, Jeremiah's life became a history of persecution. The gates of Gethsemane swung open before him, never to close again as long as he lived.

1. We lack the information to re-create the details of Jeremiah's life and to set in order the many occasions upon which he suffered abuse. But his book lets us see glimpses. On one occasion, standing outside the gates of Jerusalem before a party of witnesses, he smashed a clay bottle and declared that just so would Jerusalem be smashed, like one breaking a potter's vessel so that it could never be mended again. When he had the temerity to return to the Temple and repeat the gist of his prophecy there, he was seized by a Temple officer, beaten, and clapped in the stocks overnight (19:1 to 20:6).[49]

---

[49] The section consists of a prose account of a symbolic action (19:1–13) in the style of a reminiscence (it begins, "Thus said Yahweh *to me*" [so with LXX]), to which has been attached the biographical account of 19:14 to 20:6. The account of 19:1–13 has been much expanded and probably consisted originally only of v. 1, a part of v. 2, and vs. 10 and 11a; cf. the commentaries for discussion.

For a time he was forbidden to enter the Temple at all (36:5). In the year 605 (ch. 36) he dictated a scroll containing a selection or digest of his prophecies to his friend Baruch, and sent Baruch to read it publicly in the Temple in the hope that this would have the effect of bringing his people to their senses; when the scroll came to King Jehoiakim's attention, the king burned it and sought to have Jeremiah and Baruch arrested, undoubtedly with the intention of executing them. It is interesting that, of the three nobles who tried to stop the king from destroying the scroll (v. 25), two—Gemariah ben Shaphan and Elnathan ben Achbor—were either certainly or probably sons of men who had been protagonists of Josiah's reform.[50] And, aside from such well-documented instances as these, we have abundant evidence that Jeremiah was generally hated and cursed, ostracized and jeered at; plots were made to kill him, in one of which at least members of his own family were implicated (11:18 to 12:6).

Only a saint or a man of steel could have endured such treatment with equanimity. And such Jeremiah was not. This we see from those laments and complaints which we—none too aptly—call his "confessions," and which are to be found scattered throughout his book.[51] No other prophetic book offers us anything quite like these passages. One is tempted to dwell upon them at length, for they are exceedingly fascinating and moving. Indeed, they constitute one of the most moving chapters in all the history of religion, for here the prophet lays bare before us his inmost feelings and lets us see something of his struggle and agony.[52] He hated the prophetic office and the misery that it had brought him, and he longed to quit it (9:2 [MT, 9:1]; 20:7-9). He cursed his enemies in positively classical fashion and called upon God to show them no mercy (11:20; 12:3; 17:18; 18:19-23). In his anguish he even addressed God in language that bordered on blasphemy, declaring (20:7) that God had "seduced"

[50] Gemariah was certainly the son of Josiah's secretary of state, as vs. 10 and 12 make clear. About Elnathan we cannot be certain; but his father's name, Achbor, is not a common one, and an Achbor ben Micaiah is listed among protagonists of the reform in II Kings 22:12.

[51] See especially 11:18 to 12:6; 15:10-21; 17:14-18; 18:18-23; 20:7-13, 14-18.

[52] Though these passages follow the form of the Psalms of Lament and employ many conventional locutions, they are not to be regarded as liturgical pieces, but are highly personal expressions of the prophet's own feelings: cf. J. Bright, "Jeremiah's Complaints—Liturgy or Expressions of Personal Distress?" (J. I. Durham and J. R. Porter, eds., *Proclamation and Presence: Old Testament Essays in Honour of Gwynne Henton Davies* [London: SCM Press; Richmond: John Knox Press, 1970], pp. 189-214); J. M. Berridge, *Prophet, People, and the Word of Yahweh* (Zurich: EVZ-Verlag, 1970).

him[53] in forcing him into the prophetic office and then leaving him to
bear the consequences. At the end of his spiritual resources, he
accused God of having failed him; he whom he had once called "the
fountain of living water" (2:13) was to him in his hour of need no
better than a dry brook (15:18).[54] And in moments of extreme
depression he cursed the day of his birth and cried out for the peace of
death (20:14–18).

Jer. 20:14	Cursed be the day
	On which I was born!
	The day my mother bore me,
	Let it be unblessed!
15	Cursed be the man
	Who brought news to my father,
	"It's a boy! You've got a son!"
	(Ah, how glad it made him!)
16	Let him be, that man, like the cities
	Which Yahweh overthrew without pity!
	Let him hear an outcry in the morning,
	The battle shout at noon,
17	Because he killed me not in the womb;
	So had been my mother my grave,
	And pregnant forever her womb.
18	Ah, why did I come from the womb
	To see but trouble and grief,
	And end my days in shame?

Sensitive souls have not infrequently been shocked by Jeremiah's
"confessions." They regret that the prophet allowed himself to speak
in this way, and they wish that such words had never been preserved.
But we ought to be grateful. The prophet was neither a saint nor a
hero, nor one who was a stranger to doubt, weakness, and despair. He
was a man—a weak mortal, a human being very like ourselves. But it
was this man who—in his weakness and in spite of his weakness—was
nevertheless God's prophet, commissioned to speak his judging and
saving word to his people. It would seem that then—as now, and
always—it pleases God to entrust the treasure of his word to the
"earthen vessels" of our humanity (II Cor. 4:7). And there is evidence
that Jeremiah knew—or came to know—that such talk was unworthy
of his calling, for after one of his more violent outbursts (15:10–18),

[53] The word (RSV, "deceived") can be so translated, and it probably has that force
here (as in Ex. 22:16 [H. v. 15], etc.); cf. AB, p. 132.

[54] The last bicolon of 15:18 is not to be read as a rhetorical question (so RSV), but as
an emphatic accusation (and so LXX): "you are indeed a dry brook . . ."

we are told (vs. 19–21) that he received an answering word from
Yahweh telling him that he would have to stop his complaining and
repent if he wished to continue in the prophetic office, from which he
could not, and would not, retreat.[55] Above all, we must remember
that these words, for all their bitterness and despair, were not the
words of a quitter! Jeremiah may have wanted to leave the prophetic
office, and it is doubtful that he ever achieved serenity of mind in the
midst of the struggle. But he did not quit. The word was like a fire
burning in his bones (20:9) and he could not hold it in. So he went on,
warning of the judgment to come, pleading with his people to repent,
praying for them, interceding with God for them and, in the end,
weeping over the ruin that had come upon them (e.g., 8:18 to 9:1 [MT,
8:18–23]).

2. It was not long before events brought to Jeremiah's words at
least a partial vindication. Jehoiakim's policy did indeed bring his
country to disaster. As we have said, Jehoiakim began his reign as a
vassal of the Egyptian pharaoh, and so he remained for several
years,[56] during which time the Egyptians and the Babylonians faced
one another along the Euphrates River, sparring for position. But in
605, Nebuchadnezzar, the Babylonian crown prince, crossed the river
at Carchemish, fell upon the Egyptian army, and sent it in headlong
rout (cf. 46:2–12). Pursuing them, he dealt them another and yet
more decisive blow near Hamath in north-central Syria. Egyptian
power in Asia was broken. Although the Babylonian advance was
delayed when the death of King Nabopolassar forced Nebuchadnezzar to hurry back to Babylon to assume the throne, it was shortly
resumed. By the end of 604 the Babylonian army was in the
Philistine plain, where it completed the siege and reduction of
Ashkelon. This was no doubt the occasion for the great fast that was
held in Jerusalem in December of that year (36:9), in the course of
which Jeremiah's scroll was read in the Temple. Jehoiakim faced a
fearful decision, for the Babylonian army was at his very frontier. If
he stuck with Egypt, what would happen to him if the Babylonians
should win (as they seemed likely to do)? But if Egypt should win,
and he had not been loyal, what then? At any rate, a decision was
made. Within a very short while (not later than early in 603)

---

[55] See my remarks on this passage in *Interpretation* 28 (1974), pp. 59–74.
[56] On the details of Judah's history from this point to the fall of Jerusalem, cf.
J. Bright, *A History of Israel* (Philadelphia: The Westminster Press; London: SCM
Press, 2d ed., 1972), pp. 323–331.

Jehoiakim switched his allegiance and became a vassal of Nebuchadnezzar (II Kings 24:1).

But three years later Jehoiakim rebelled. Scholars have always wondered how he could have been so foolish. The so-called Babylonian Chronicle probably supplies the answer.[57] Late in 601 a pitched battle between the Babylonians and Egyptians took place in which both sides suffered heavily. But it was not a Babylonian victory, for Nebuchadnezzar was forced to return to Babylon and refit his army. It was probably this that led Jehoiakim to believe that his chance had come. But it was a fatal mistake. Though Nebuchadnezzar was unable to take action at once, he sent contingents of his troops, as well as troops recruited from various vassal states, to harry the land and keep it off balance until he could bring full force to bear (cf. 35:11; II Kings 24:2). Late in 598 his main army marched, and by early in 597 it stood before Jerusalem.

In the meantime, Jehoiakim had died, to be succeeded by an eighteen-year-old son, Jehoiachin (in Jeremiah called Jeconiah, or Coniah). It is possible that Jehoiakim was assassinated, for, as one who had violated his vassal's oath, he was *persona non grata* with Nebuchadnezzar and would have been shown no consideration whatever. Perhaps men reasoned that his son, a young boy who was quite innocent of what had happened, would fare better. In any event, in March of 597 the city was surrendered. Nebuchadnezzar, no doubt mollified by this prompt capitulation, contented himself with looting the Temple and the royal treasury, and taking the boy-king, the queen mother, high civil and military officials, and numerous others, to exile in Babylon (II Kings 24:10–17). But he left the Kingdom of Judah in existence, placing Zedekiah, the boy-king's uncle and another of Josiah's sons, on the throne as his vassal.

3. But did this have the effect of vindicating Jeremiah in the eyes of the people? It seems not. Indeed, one may wonder (for we cannot do more than that) if, in the minds of many, it may not even have had the opposite effect. Jeremiah, it will be recalled, had predicted total destruction; and it had not been total. He had said that the city would be smashed like a clay pot (19:1–13); it had been surrendered but, so far as we know, it had suffered little physical damage. He had said that the Temple would be left a ruin heap (7:13–15); it had been

---

[57] Cf. D. J. Wiseman, ed., *Chronicles of Chaldean Kings (625–556 B.C.) in the British Museum* (London: The British Museum, 1956), pp. 23–35, 46–48, 67–73, on the period in question.

looted of most of its treasures, but it still stood intact. He had said that the people would be carried into exile, and a number of them had been; but the majority—a sizable "remnant"—still remained. And a ruler of David's line still sat on the throne.

One wonders if many did not reason within themselves: But this is quite in line with what we have always been taught! We have suffered a calamity, yes. But ought we not to interpret this as a chastisement from God, a sign of his displeasure with our king, Jehoiakim, who, as many of us were aware, was anything but an admirable man? But the nation still stands! The Temple is still here in our midst, and a prince of David's house is still our ruler. Yahweh may indeed discipline us, and he has disciplined us, perhaps more severely than ever before; but he has not revoked his eternal covenant with David. So let us not fear! Whatever the future may bring, this nation will always survive, secure in the promises of God. No, we do not know that men so reasoned. But they may well have done so. At least it is certain, as later events would show, that the disaster of 597 had taught the nation's leaders nothing.

So the tension was not resolved, but rather heightened. It would have to go on till the last tragic act of the drama had been played to the end. It would have to seek resolution beyond the tragedy, for only there could a resolution possibly be found.

6

Theology in Crisis:
The Last Days of the Kingdom
of Judah, and Beyond

We began this study with a question that arises out of the life and experience of Jeremiah. We observed—what is all too obvious—that Jeremiah was in lifelong conflict with the majority of his fellow countrymen, and that this was primarily because his view of the nation's future differed radically from theirs. But it was equally clear that this was no mere difference of opinion arising from differing assessments of the political situation; it was a collision in theology. Jeremiah continually warned that God was going to destroy the nation for its persistent violation of his covenant stipulations. His opponents were convinced that such a thing could never happen: God would be untrue precisely to his covenant promises if he allowed it. And we had to ask how it could be that members of the same religious community, worshipers of the same God, could have understood the nature of their relationship to that God, and their future under him, in two such mutually exclusive ways.

1. In the preceding chapter the answer to that question began to become clear. Two ways of understanding God's covenant with his people had come to stand in irreconcilable tension with each other. Both of these were ancient, and we have traced their history through centuries of time. Both gave expression to essential features in Israel's structure of belief. The one stressed God's election of Israel, his purposes for her and his sure promises to her, which nothing could cancel; the other stressed the righteous commandments which he had laid before his people, and which they were obligated to obey if the covenant bond was to be maintained. Both of these emphases were essential, indispensable to Israel's structure of belief. But the balance

between them was delicate, and always had been. And now, under the
pressure of circumstances, one might say, the balance had been upset,
and there issued two diametrically opposing views of the nation's
future.

In the theology that was officially affirmed in the Jerusalem
Temple—so we have said often enough—the nation's future was
assured by God's unconditional promises to David and his equally
unconditional election of Mt. Zion as his eternal abode. At least, so it
seems to have been generally understood in Jeremiah's day. Of
course, the situation was dangerous, and no one could be sure of what
the future might hold. The nation lay at the mercy of foreign
overlords, and wrong political choices might at any moment bring
down upon it their wrath. The immediate future was chancy, murky,
uncertain. But of the *ultimate* future one could always feel confident.
The dynasty would always endure, and the nation would always
survive; Yahweh, whose temple-palace was on Mt. Zion, and who was
both powerful and faithful to his promises, would see to that! People
nurtured in this theology could not believe—would not let themselves
believe—otherwise. To do so would be a sign of want of trust in God.

But in that other understanding of God's covenant with his people
which we have observed, and which we see classically expressed in the
book of Deuteronomy, the future of the nation was not assured at all.
Everything depended upon whether or not it was obedient to the
covenant stipulations. If it was obedient, it might rest assured of the
continuance of God's blessing and protection; but if it was not, it
might be equally sure that the covenant curses would be called down
upon it and that all the promised blessings would be taken away. The
future was thus an "either-or"; it was laid under the little word "if":
"If you obey the statutes and the ordinances which I set before
you. . . ."

Jeremiah, as we saw, was rooted in this latter theological tradition,
namely, that of the Mosaic covenant. The sure promises of God to
David, and his election of Mt. Zion, play no real role in his thinking,
save in a negative way. The belief that the physical presence of the
Temple guaranteed the nation's protection he rejected as a lie (7:4,
8).[1] The notion that the ruling dynasty could under no circumstances
be brought to an end he likewise rejected (22:1–5; etc.). He viewed
the nation's apostasy as a flagrant violation of Yahweh's covenant,
and he summoned it to a thoroughgoing and heartfelt repentance

---

[1] Scripture references in this chapter are to The Book of Jeremiah, unless otherwise
indicated.

before it was too late. When it became clear to him that Josiah's reform had not had the desired results and that no real change in the nation's character and conduct had been effected, his message became increasingly a stern warning that God would destroy both Temple and dynasty, and bring the nation to an end.

2. Against the background of this theological tension, the tragedy of Jeremiah's life becomes as understandable as it was inevitable. In dangerous times such as was the turning of the seventh to the sixth century B.C. in Judah, such talk as his was simply not to be tolerated. It was not only bad for the national morale; it was outright heresy! It earned for Jeremiah the enmity not only of the nation's leaders but—so it appears—of the bulk of the populace as well. This expressed itself, as we saw, not only in hatred, jeers, and ostracism, but also in physical abuse, and even in various attempts on his life. The marvel is that he survived at all. We know of at least one prophet who spoke as Jeremiah did who did not survive: Uriah ben Shemaiah of Kiryat-yearim whom King Jehoiakim executed (26:20–23).

Such abuse is all the more shocking in view of the ancient tradition in Israel that the prophet's person was inviolable: a prophet might not be harmed for speaking Yahweh's word, however unwelcome that word might be. One can think of numerous occasions when prophets addressed their kings with scathing censure and, though their words could not have been pleasing, nevertheless came off scot-free. Samuel's rejection of Saul (I Sam. 15:10–33), or Nathan's rebuke of David in the affair of Bathsheba (II Sam. 12:1–15), or Elijah's confrontation with Ahab after the latter's crime against Naboth (I Kings 21:17–29), are examples that leap to mind. This tradition was still alive in Jeremiah's day, and it served to save his life on one occasion, as we have seen (ch. 26). But the time had clearly come when a prophet could no longer rely upon this to save him, especially from a king like Jehoiakim!

But this was not so much that the tradition of prophetic immunity was breaking down. Rather, it was that the official theology was so firmly entrenched in the minds of the people that to contradict it was to tell a lie—and to accuse God of lying. Prophets who did this would be put down as false prophets; and under Deuteronomic law to prophesy falsely in Yahweh's name was a capital crime (Deut. 18:20). In other words, Jeremiah was persecuted not merely because of the unpopularity of what he said, but because his fellow citizens thought him to be a false prophet, and so felt justified in persecuting him. A true prophet doesn't say such things! A true prophet says, "You shall not see the sword, nor shall you have famine, but I will give you assured peace in this place" (14:13). Jeremiah knew of no way to convince his people that his was indeed a word from Yahweh. This was a major problem with him throughout his entire life, and one to which he could find no satisfactory solution; it was the chief source of the tension in which he was forced to live.

I

Jeremiah's later years brought no lessening of the tension which his preaching provoked. Rather, the tension deepened.

1. The situation in Judah during the last years of the nation's existence is in many ways difficult to understand.[2] As we have said, Jeremiah's gloomy predictions found at least a partial fulfillment in the first deportation of 597. It will be recalled that Nebuchadnezzar had reacted to Jehoiakim's rebellion against his authority by invading the country as soon as he was in a position to do so. But before his army could arrive Jehoiakim, whether through death or assassination, had been removed from the scene and replaced by his eighteen-year-old son Jehoiachin (Jeconiah) who, within three months (in March 597), surrendered the city to the Babylonians. Nebuchadnezzar then seized the young king, the queen mother, certain of the nobility and the ranking clergy and military officers, plus the skilled artisans and others of the citizenry, and deported them to Babylon. Then, taking a considerable booty from the Temple and the royal treasury, he retired, leaving Zedekiah (Mattaniah), the boy-king's uncle and another of Josiah's sons, to rule as his vassal.

One would think that this would have spelled the end to any confidence in the inviolability of Jerusalem. True, the city had been surrendered, not taken by storm. Though outlying towns had no doubt suffered severely, so far as we know there had been no extensive destruction where Jerusalem itself was concerned; city and Temple still stood, and a Davidic ruler still sat on the throne. But the Temple had been looted of its treasures by a foreign army. And Zedekiah was not really a king, but rather a regent ruling by the sufferance of a foreign conqueror; the legitimate king was Jehoia-

---

[2] For the details of the history of this period, cf. J. Bright, *A History of Israel* (Philadelphia: The Westminster Press; London: SCM Press, 2d ed., 1972), pp. 327–331; also *Jeremiah* (AB, 1965), pp. xlix-liv.

chin, and he was a captive in a far country.[3] Moreover, Nebuchadnezzar had demonstrated both the overwhelming superiority of Babylonian arms and the fact that he was himself not a man to be trifled
with. One would think that the nation's leaders would have accepted
the inevitable and would have acted with extreme caution, at least
until such time as signs of the weakening of Babylonian power should
manifest themselves (which as long as Nebuchadnezzar ruled was
never the case).

But nothing of the kind! The ensuing years saw nothing but
unrest, plots, and sedition, till finally the nation brought the roof
down on its head. As early as 594 (the fourth year of Zedekiah; cf.
chs. 27 to 28),[4] possibly sparked by a revolt that had taken place in
Babylon in the preceding year involving elements of the army,[5] a plot
was being hatched in Jerusalem. The kings of Edom, Moab, Ammon,
Tyre, and Sidon had sent their envoys (27:3) to meet with Zedekiah,
undoubtedly to formulate plans; probably a promise of Egyptian help
was hoped for. At the same time, prophets in Jerusalem were
whipping up a popular frenzy by declaring in Yahweh's name that the
deported king, Jehoiachin, together with all the exiles, would soon
return in triumph to Jerusalem, bringing the looted Temple treasures
with them. At least one of them, Hananiah ben Azzur, went so far as
to declare with sublime confidence that this would take place within
two years' time (28:2–4):

> (Jer. 28:2) This is what Yahweh of Hosts, the God of Israel, has said: I
> have broken the yoke of the king of Babylon. (v. 3) Within two years'
> time I am going to bring back to this place all the movable objects
> belonging to Yahweh's house which Nebuchadnezzar, king of Babylon,
> took from this place and carried to Babylon. (v. 4) I am also going to
> bring back to this place Jeconiah ben Jehoiakim, king of Judah, and all the
> exiles of Judah who have gone to Babylon—Yahweh's word—; for I will
> break the yoke of the king of Babylon.

Similar unrest was being stirred up among the exiles in Babylon by
prophets there, who were telling the people that they would soon be

---

[3] Though the Bible calls Zedekiah "king," there is abundant evidence that Jehoiachin
was regarded as the legitimate ruler both by the Babylonians and by large numbers of
his own subjects; cf. Bright, *A History of Israel*, pp. 329 f., for a summary of the
evidence; also AB, p.L. Jehoiachin was treated as a hostage, and at first received as a
pensioner of the Babylonian court; imprisonment (cf. II Kings 25:27–30) came later.

[4] The date in 27:1 ("in the beginning of the reign of [i.e., in the accession year of]
Jehoiakim"; so MT) is erroneous and seems to be a mistaken recopying of 26:1, where it
is correct; LXX rightly lacks the verse. The correct date is in 28:1, following the
reading of LXX ("in the fourth year of Zedekiah," i.e., 594).

[5] Cf. D. J. Wiseman, ed., *Chronicles of Chaldean Kings (626–556 B.C.) in the British
Museum* (London: The British Museum, 1956), pp. 36 f., 48, 73 f.

going home (29:4–9). Certain of these prophets were apparently executed by Nebuchadnezzar for their seditious talk (vs. 20–23). This projected rebellion, to be sure, came to nothing. At least, the Bible says no more of it, and other sources are silent.[6] Whether this was because the plotters could not agree among themselves, or because a promise of Egyptian aid could not be secured, or simply because saner counsel prevailed, we have no way of saying. It appears (v. 3) that Zedekiah sent ambassadors to Babylon—perhaps felt it was wise to go himself (51:59)[7]—to assure Nebuchadnezzar of his loyalty. But, whatever the facts may have been, the respite was brief. Within scarcely five further years the final revolt had begun.

2. It is more than a little difficult to understand how the nation's leaders could have dared even to toy with so foolhardy a course. Patriotic fervor alone cannot explain it, nor can political naiveté, however great a part both may have played. It was a theological madness. It is true that the cream of the nations' leadership, including those men mentioned in ch. 36 as members of Jehoiakim's cabinet, at least some of whom, as we saw in the preceding chapter, had shown themselves to be sympathetic to Jeremiah and his views, had been carried away in the deportation of 597 (at least we hear of them no more). Those left to serve—and to dominate—Zedekiah may well have been politically inexperienced, and they certainly seem to have been chauvinists of the most reckless sort. Nor is it in any way surprising that many in Judah should have wished to continue the struggle for independence: that would only be natural, and what one would expect of a patriotic people. And ever since the days of Assyrian rule the standing policy of those who desired independence had been to wait for a favorable opportunity, form a coalition, and seek Egyptian aid—which aid Egypt was usually glad to promise, it being in line with her interests to do so. It would, therefore, not be in itself surprising if Judah's leaders had eventually committed themselves to such a policy. What is surprising is that they should have done so at this time, and apparently with every hope of success. One would think that, in the light of recent experience and the present realities, even the most chauvinistic of patriots would have known better. One can only put it down to a fanatical and theologically supported madness.

---

[6] The Babylonian Chronicle (see preceding note) breaks off with the year 594 and does not resume for more than thirty-five years (in 557).

[7] The Hebrew text of 51:59 states that Zedekiah went, apparently accompanied by a considerable entourage. The reading of LXX, however, suggests that a party was sent by Zedekiah; cf. AB, p. 210.

It appears that the calamity of 597 had not even dented the popular confidence in God's sure defense of Mt. Zion. This seems incredible, but so it must have been. It must have been that men were able to see the events of 597, not as a contradiction of the official theology, but as fully harmonious with it—perhaps even as a positive illustration of its truth—and so were able to explain those events in the light of that theology, just as Isaiah had explained the horrors of Sennacherib's invasion a century previously—though without a tithe of that great prophet's spiritual perception and depth. We are still here! God saw us through *this* crisis, just as he saw our fathers through *that* (and that was as bad as this). We have suffered a humiliation; perhaps we should understand it as a chastisement from God. But we are still here! The nation stands, the city stands, the Temple and the Davidic dynasty stand—and so it will always be! We cannot finally lose! God, who is both powerful and faithful to his promises, will see to that!

Indeed, it seems that we are dealing with nothing less than a perversion of certain features in Isaiah's message which that great prophet would have flatly repudiated, had he been present to do so. Isaiah, it will be recalled, had expected that the judgment Yahweh was sending upon his people would serve a pedagogical function; he had hoped that it would prove to be the needed discipline that would drive his people to sincere repentance and trust in Yahweh. To be sure, his hopes in this regard were repeatedly disappointed. But so far as his words let us see, he never expected God's judgment to bring the end of the nation; rather, he hoped that it would purify and produce a chastened remnant (e.g., Isa. 1:21–26). He also looked beyond the judgment to the time when God would make good his promises and, through an ideal scion of David's line, would establish his kingly rule on earth. But now? Why, the purifying judgment has fallen! We who are left are the true remnant of God's people! The future is bright with promise! Soon the great day!

That some in Jerusalem regarded themselves as the purified remnant, the rightful heirs to the promises, seems clear. Ezekiel, the priest-prophet who had been among those deported in 597, heard them from faraway Babylon and growled at them over the miles:

> (Ezek. 11:15) Son of man, your brethren, yes your brethren, your fellow exiles, the whole house of Israel, are those of whom those living in Jerusalem say, "They have gone far from Yahweh; it is to us that the land has been given for a possession."

They say—Good riddance of bad rubbish! The dross has been removed; we who are left are Yahweh's true people to whom the land is given. Or again:

> (Ezek. 33:24) Son of man, those living in these ruins in the land of Israel keep saying, "Abraham was only one man, yet he got possession of the land. We are many; to us is the land given for a possession."

We—they say—are the true seed of Abraham, the legitimate inheritors of the promises made to him.[8] And we have already seen that there were those in Jerusalem who were eagerly awaiting God's imminent intervention to reverse their humiliating situation, break the power of Babylon, and restore King Jehoiachin to his throne. Elevated by such a belief, the nation dared to hurl itself against the might of Babylon, confident that God would save it and give it the victory. It seems that Isaiah's word spoken when Sennacherib threatened the city ("I will defend this city to save it, for my own sake and my servant David's sake," Isa. 37:35) had been absolutized and turned into a dogma of undebatable validity for every situation that might arise through all the future. Down to the end, to the last desperate hour, men were still hoping for a repetition of God's miraculous deliverance of the city a hundred years earlier. King Zedekiah's request (21:1 f.), forwarded to Jeremiah through his envoys as the Babylonian siege of Jerusalem began, can hardly have any other meaning.

> (Jer. 21:2) Inquire, please, of Yahweh for us; for Nebuchadrezzar, king of Babylon, is attacking us. Perhaps Yahweh will perform for us one of his mighty acts and force him to withdraw from us.

He will do it again, won't he? Tell us that he will! He will save us now, as he always has in the past—surely he will! It is his nature to do so; it is his métier!

3. Jeremiah, as one might expect, opposed such talk resolutely. It's a pack of lies spoken in Yahweh's name! There has been no purge, there is no purified remnant, and the future is *not* bright with promise. In one place (6:27–30), speaking as God's appointed "assayer" (v. 27), whose duty it is to examine and evaluate his people's character, Jeremiah seizes upon Isaiah's metaphor of the judgment as a refining process (see, classically Isa. 1:24–26) and reverses it. The

---

[8] Cf. R. de Vaux, "Le 'reste d'Israël' d'après les prophetes" (1933; repr. *Bible et Orient* [Paris: Les Éditions du Cerf, 1967], pp. 25–39, esp. pp. 33–36). See also the commentaries, esp. W. Eichrodt, *Ezekiel* (Eng. tr., OTL, 1970), pp. 142–146, 460–464; W. Zimmerli, *Ezechiel* (BKAT, 13, 1969), pp. 247–249, 815–821.

people are hopelessly impure metal—slag in fact—and they cannot possibly be refined.[9]

Jer. 6:28   They are all the most stubborn of rebels,
                 Peddlers of slander,[10]
                 Corrupt to the very last man.
     29   The bellows blow fiercely.
                 But the lead comes whole from the fire.[11]
                 It's useless to go on refining,
                 The wicked are not removed.
     30   Refuse silver will men call them,
                 Because Yahweh's refused them.

In another place (ch. 24) Jeremiah tells how, in a vision, he saw two baskets of figs placed before the Temple of Yahweh, the one containing excellent figs, the other fruit so rotten as to be inedible. He then received the word that the good figs symbolized those who had been deported to Babylon: God would show them favor and provide for them a happy future. The rotten figs, on the other hand, represented Zedekiah and the others who had been left behind in Judah: God would treat them as one would treat rotten figs—throw them out! In other words, the deportation of 597 had not removed the refuse of the nation, but its very best fruit, leaving only worthless culls, unfit for use.

But though Jeremiah's sympathies lay with those who had been deported to Babylon, and though he firmly believed that God would one day restore them to their land (29:10–14), he certainly did not share the wild hopes of those who expected that they would soon be coming home in triumph. When, in 594 (ch. 27),[12] inspired by the wild promises of certain prophets, plans for a revolt against Babylon were being laid, Jeremiah appeared before the plotters with an ox yoke on his neck. He declared that Yahweh, who is Creator and Lord of all things, can in his sovereign wisdom give the earth to whomsoever he pleases (vs. 5 f.), and that he has now chosen to give it into the power of Nebuchadnezzar. This yoke, said he, is Nebuchadnezzar's yoke; Yahweh has put it on your necks—now wear it, or die (vs. 8–11)! In a

---

[9] The precise date of 6:27–30 cannot be determined. But its thought is similar to that of ch. 24 (see below), and it may well, like ch. 24, have been composed after the deportation of 597. At any rate, it reflects Jeremiah's exceedingly pessimistic evaluation of his people's character.

[10] MT adds "bronze and iron," which seems out of place. On the text, cf. AB, p. 49.

[11] The text is difficult and apparently corrupt; cf. the commentaries. But, however it is read, it means to say that the refining process has failed; the alloys are not removed.

[12] On the date of chs. 27 and 28, cf. note 4 above.

word, Jeremiah was assured that Nebuchadnezzar's authority had
been imposed upon the nation as a judgment from God; to rebel
against that authority was therefore to rebel against God's judgment
and to court inevitable disaster.

So it was that, apparently in the same year (ch. 29), Jeremiah
wrote a letter to the exiles in Babylon and, though he assured them of
God's mercy in the farther future, he bluntly told them to disregard
all talk of a speedy return and to settle down for a long stay. As for
king Jehoiachin, not only will he not soon return to Jerusalem,
bringing the looted Temple treasures and all the exiles with him; he
will never return at all! Neither he nor any of his descendants would
ever sit on Judah's throne again (22:28–30).

> Jer. 22:28　Is Coniah a castoff pot,
> 　　　　　　A utensil no one wants?
> 　　　　　　Why, then, is he hurled, cast out
> 　　　　　　To a land he does not know? [13]
> 　　　29　　O land, O land, O land,
> 　　　　　　Hear the word of Yahweh!
> 　　　30　　"Write down this man as childless,[14]
> 　　　　　　A man who'll not succeed in his lifetime,[15]
> 　　　　　　Nay, no offspring of his will succeed
> 　　　　　　In sitting on David's throne,
> 　　　　　　Or ruling in Judah again."

Of course we know that Jehoiachin (Coniah) was not childless.
According to the genealogy in I Chronicles, ch. 3 (cf. vs. 17 f.) he had
seven sons, and texts discovered in Babylon mention five of these as
being, like their father, pensioners of the Babylonian court a few
years after the deportation of 597;[16] at least the oldest of them had
undoubtedly been born when Jeremiah spoke. But Jeremiah does not
mean to say that Jehoiachin has no children, but that he is to be
entered as childless—in the census list or, perhaps better, in the
register of the Judahite royal house. Though not childless, he is to be
entered as childless, because—so Jeremiah means to say—he might as
well be! Neither he nor any descendant of his will ever reign as

---

[13] The translation of this verse follows the shorter text of LXX. MT has a somewhat
expanded text that obscures the meter; cf. AB, p. 139.

[14] MT begins the verse with "Thus Yahweh has said," which seems somewhat
superfluous after v. 29 and may be an expansion; LXX omits.

[15] LXX, which misunderstood "childless" in the preceding colon, seems not to have
read "who will not succeed in his days." The colon may not be original; cf. AB, p. 143.

[16] Cf. E. F. Weidner, *Mélanges syriens offerts à M. René Dussaud*, Vol. II (Paris: Paul
Geuthner, 1939), pp. 923–935; ANET, p. 308.

Judah's king again. With such words as these Jeremiah flatly contradicted the wild hopes that were being attached to the young exiled king and asserted the futility—nay, the wicked presumption—of rebellion against Babylon. The nation, said he, has no hope of survival save in submitting to Nebuchadnezzar's yoke, which has been laid upon it as the judgment of God.

4. Talk such as this earned for Jeremiah all sorts of enmity, especially from prophets who had been saying just the opposite. One of these, Hananiah ben Azzur, whose words we have already heard, met Jeremiah in the Temple, snatched the ox yoke that he was wearing from his neck, and broke it, thus symbolically announcing that the yoke of Babylon had been broken. Prophetic word was hurled in the teeth of prophetic word, and prophet called prophet a liar (ch. 28). How could the onlookers, who may sincerely have wanted to know what the will of Yahweh was, possibly tell which prophet was speaking the truth—or, indeed, if either was? How could Jeremiah prove that his word had indeed been given him by Yahweh? The incident shows his helplessness before the question. He simply could not prove it. All he could say was: Hananiah, I wish that I could believe you (v. 6),[17] but your pleasing prophecies (v. 8) do not sound to me like the words of the great prophets who preceded us (one supposes that Jeremiah was thinking of such men as Amos, Hosea, Isaiah, and Micah), for they never offered God's peace to a rebellious and disobedient people; all we can do—so Jeremiah somewhat lamely concludes (v. 9)—is to wait and see whose word comes to pass. An unsatisfactory answer indeed! History alone can vindicate the word—and its verdict will come too late to be of help to those who must make immediate decisions on the basis of it. But it was the only answer that Jeremiah could give.

But Jeremiah knew within himself that the prophets who opposed him were not speaking Yahweh's word. He had always stood in tension with them, and was by now completely alienated from them. He was convinced that their optimistic promises of divine protection were lies. God is simply not going to protect a people who stubbornly disobey his will, and prophets who promise such protection merely prove that they never stood in his council at all. They are frauds! If they were true prophets, they would warn the people of God's displeasure and would seek to turn them from their evil ways, instead

---

[17] There is no reason whatever to find sarcasm in Jeremiah's words in v. 6, as most commentators agree. As a patriot, he sincerely wished that Hananiah were right, and that the future would bring the deliverance of his people, not their ruin.

of lulling them to sleep with their fatuous words. Jeremiah's alienation from the prophets, and the reasons for it, finds its clearest expression in the section 23:9–40, most sharply perhaps in a passage that was alluded to in the preceding chapter (23:16–22).[18]

Jer. 23:16   This is what Yahweh of Hosts has said:[19]
            "Do not listen to the words of the prophets!
            They do but delude you.
            It's a self-induced vision they utter,
            Not one from the mouth of Yahweh—
    17   Saying to scorners of Yahweh's word,
            'All will go well with you';
            And to all those who follow
                their own stubborn wills,
            'Misfortune will not overtake you.' "

    18   But who has stood in Yahweh's council
            And seen—and heard his word?
            Who has carefully marked his word?
    19   Look! The storm of Yahweh[20] is unleashed,
            A whirlwind blast;
            It will burst on the head of the wicked.
    20   The wrath of Yahweh will not turn back
            Till he's finished, accomplished
            His inmost intents.
            When that day has passed
            You will see this clearly and well.

    21   "I sent not these prophets,
            Yet—they ran!
            I spoke not to them,
            Yet—they prophesied!
    22   But if they had stood in my council,
            They'd proclaim my word to my people,
            From their wicked way they'd turn them,
            From their evil deeds."

It has often been suspected—and with much reason—that Jeremiah's opponents thought of themselves as Isaiah's disciples.[21] But

---

[18] Ch. 23:9–40 is a collection of sayings that have been brought together because of their common theme. These sayings might have been uttered at almost any time in Jeremiah's career, but one suspects that the bulk of them reflect his feelings as his tension with the prophets became acute. On the structure and interpretation of 23:16–22, see the commentaries. My own views will be found in AB, pp. 148–155.

[19] The translation of vs. 16 f. follows the shorter text of LXX. MT has a somewhat expanded text that obscures the meter; cf. AB, p. 148.

[20] MT adds "wrath"; a (correct) gloss or a variant reading.

[21] Cf. G. von Rad, *Old Testament Theology*, Vol. II (Eng. tr., Edinburgh and London:

Jeremiah was actually closer to Isaiah in this than they were.[22] Isaiah had viewed Assyria as the instrument of God's judgment, and he opposed rebellion against Assyria in reliance upon military power and foreign alliances. He urged the nation to trust Yahweh and wait for him to give the signal, for he would in his own good time intervene to break Assyria and save his people (e.g., Isa. 10:5–19; 14:24–27; 18:1–6; 31:4–9; etc.). Jeremiah did not unconditionally announce the doom of the nation any more than Isaiah had. In a way quite similar to Isaiah, he saw Babylon as the instrument of God's judgment. Submit, said he, and save yourselves! To rebel against Babylon is to rebel against God's judgment and to make disaster inevitable. But, though he did not expect it to be soon, Jeremiah—again in a way parallel to that of Isaiah—looked for God's eventual judgment on Babylon. Indeed, we are told (51:59–64) that he caused a symbolical doom-oracle to be uttered against Babylon in the very year in which he wore the ox yoke (594). And down to the last desperate hour he declared that the nation could even then save itself if it would submit to the judgment that was laid upon it in obedience and trust.

II

But Jeremiah's warnings, as they always seemed fated to do, fell on deaf ears. Though the projected rebellion of 594 came to nothing, within five further years the fatal step had been taken and the nation's doom sealed.

1. The events can be quickly summarized. We do not know how, or just when, the revolt began. The Bible is silent on the point, and the Babylonian Chronicle, which breaks off after 594 and does not resume until 557, tells us nothing concerning these fateful years. Presumably, fierce patriotism could no longer be restrained and, at least by 589, tribute to Babylon had been withheld. The revolt does not seem to have had widespread support. Although Egyptian aid had been promised (and it later materialized), few of Judah's neighbors seem to have joined in; so far as we know, only Ammon and Tyre did. Other neighboring states were apparently either lukewarm or cold to the idea, with Edom even coming in finally on the Babylonian side. The

Oliver & Boyd; New York: Harper & Row, 1965), p. 210; W. L. Holladay, *Jeremiah: Spokesman Out of Time* (Philadelphia: United Church Press, 1974), p. 79. W. Zimmerli asks if Hananiah may not have been influenced by such passages as Isa. 14:25; 9:4 [MT v. 3]; cf. *Studien zur altestamentlichen Theologie und Prophetie: Gesammelte Aufsätze II* (Munich: Chr. Kaiser Verlag, 1974), p. 95.

[22] Cf. Zimmerli, *op. cit.*, pp. 102 f.

revolt was foredoomed from the start. Judging by his frequent consultations with Jeremiah (21:1 f.; 37:3, 16–21; 38:14–27), Zedekiah himself had little stomach for it, but was pushed into it by his chauvinistic nobles, whom he had not the courage to resist (cf. 38:5).

The Babylonians reacted swiftly. Apparently by late in 589 their army had arrived in the land, for by January of 588 Jerusalem was under siege (52:4). The Babylonian strategy was simple and logical. Driving such of Judah's troops as they could not destroy in the open field back upon their fortified strong points, they proceeded to reduce these one by one, meanwhile holding Jerusalem under ever tighter blockade. This operation continued into 588, until finally only two such strong points still held out: Lachish and Azekah (34:7).[23] Meanwhile the situation in Jerusalem grew more and more desperate. Temporary relief came when, probably in the summer of 588, the approach of an Egyptian relief force compelled the Babylonians to lift the siege of the city and move to meet it (37:5). But the reprieve was brief; the Egyptians were quickly disposed of, the Babylonian army returned, and the siege was resumed.

The city held out with heroic stubbornness for approximately another full year (until July of 587, 52:6 f.),[24] when, just as its food supply was exhausted, the Babylonian battering rams made a breach in the walls and their troops poured in. Zedekiah, when he saw that all was lost, fled in the night (vs. 7–11), slipping through the Babylonian lines, apparently with the hope of reaching sanctuary in Ammon, where resistance still continued. But he was caught near Jericho and hauled before Nebuchadnezzar at his headquarters at Riblah in central Syria (Nebuchadnezzar had not personally been before Jerusalem during its last siege). Nebuchadnezzar showed him no mercy (after all, he was a rebel who had violated his vassal's oath, and he could expect none). Having forced him to witness the execution of his own sons and others of Judah's nobility, he had him blinded and shipped in chains to Babylon, where he died. A month later (52:12–16) Nebuzaradan, the general in command of the royal

---

[23] The fall of Azekah may be illustrated by one of the Lachish Ostraca, a group of letters written on pieces of broken pottery found in the ruins of Lachish and dating for the most part to the year before the fall of Jerusalem. In this letter (No. IV), the officer in charge of an observation post writes to the garrison commander in Lachish that the fire signals of Azekah can no longer be seen; cf. ANET, pp. 321 f.

[24] Some scholars argue that Jerusalem fell in 586; cf. Bright, *A History of Israel*, p. 329, for references. But the arguments that this took place in 587 seem to me fully convincing; cf. especially E. Kutsch, "Das Jahr der Katastrophe: 587 v. Chr." (*Biblica*, 55 [1974], pp. 520–545); earlier, *idem*, ZAW, 71 (1959), pp. 270–274.

bodyguard, arrived at Jerusalem and, acting on orders, burned the city to the ground and leveled its walls. A further deportation of the people to Babylon was then carried out. The Davidic dynasty was ended, never to be restored again.

2. All this, of course, came as no surprise to Jeremiah, for it was just what he had predicted. All through Jerusalem's last siege his message had borne but a single burden: the city is doomed! As the siege began and Zedekiah turned to him for encouragement (21:1 f.), he warned the king (vs. 3–7) that there would be no intervening miracles but that Yahweh, far from coming to the rescue of the city, was himself fighting—nay, waging holy war—against it on the Babylonian side. When the siege was temporarily lifted because of the Egyptian advance and people were telling themselves that the hoped-for miracle had happened (He has saved us! We knew he would!), Jeremiah dampened their joy by telling them that the Babylonians would soon return (37:3–10); nay, said he, even if they had been so soundly beaten that their army consisted only of wounded men, these casualties would scramble from their bunks and take the city. It hasn't a chance! Nothing can save it! Consistently, throughout the siege, he again and again begged Zedekiah to surrender (34:1–7; 38:17–23). He even went so far as to advise people, in Yahweh's name, to desert if they wished to save their lives (21:8–10).

> (Jer. 21:8) . . . This is what Yahweh has said: Look! I offer you a choice between the way of life and the way of death. (v. 9) Whoever stays in this city will die by the sword, by starvation and disease. But whoever goes out and surrenders to the Chaldeans [the Babylonians] who are blockading you will live; he will at least escape with his life. (v. 10) For I regard this city with hostility, not with favor—Yahweh's word; it will be handed over to the king of Babylon, who will put it to the torch.

Dangerous advice to give in wartime! But it was welcome advice to many, for not a few heeded it, and desertion apparently became a problem (cf. 38:19; 39:9).

There is no reason to question Jeremiah's sincerity in speaking as he did, or that he did so out of a genuine concern for the best interests of his fellow citizens. But it was not the sort of talk for which those in authority were likely to thank him. On the contrary, they viewed it—and understandably—as nothing less than high treason; Jeremiah suffered dearly for it, very nearly losing his life (chs. 37 to 38).[25]

---

[25] Whether the narrative of chs. 37 and 38 is a single continuous account, or

When, while the siege was lifted, he attempted to leave the city to go to his home in the land of Benjamin on a matter of family business (very probably having to do with the transfer of real property of which we read in ch. 32), he was arrested at the city gate by the officer of the guard on suspicion of desertion (understandably, since he had advised others to desert). In spite of his protestations of innocence, he was hauled before a panel of nobles, charged with treason, beaten, and placed in a waterless cistern with deep mud at the bottom, and left to die there. He undoubtedly would have died had not a negro palace servant, one Ebed-melek, had the courage to intercede with the king (who apparently had washed his hands of the whole matter and did not know what had been done with Jeremiah) in his behalf and gain for him more lenient confinement in the court of the guard, where he remained until the city fell. After the city had fallen he was released by the Babylonians (38:28b to 39:14; 40:1-6), whose commanding generals themselves believed him to have favored their cause.[26]

But even though it is not surprising that those who controlled the affairs of the nation thought him to be such, Jeremiah was not a traitor, and certainly not one who was moved by pro-Babylonian sentiments. His only thought was to save what was left of his country from ruin. He urged Zedekiah to surrender because he knew that was the only chance the king had of saving his own life and preventing the city from being destroyed. He did not desire a Babylonian victory, and to predict it was something that brought him no pleasure at all. Nor should we forget that when, after the fall of the city, the Babylonian general offered him privileged treatment if he would come with him to Babylon, Jeremiah without hesitation refused (40:1-6). A strange traitor, this, who would accept no reward for his treason, indeed pointedly spurned it! On the other hand, to suppose that Jeremiah spoke as he did because of pacifistic leanings, or out of personal cowardice, would be, if possible, to do him even greater injustice. Of course he was not a pacifist. Not only was pacifism in the modern sense (i.e., the refusal in principle to

---

represents the weaving together of two parallel accounts of Jeremiah's sufferings, is not of material concern here. But the latter seems to me likely. As the story now reads, everything seems to happen to Jeremiah twice (and we clearly have two accounts in 38:28b to 39:14; 40:1-6). For further discussion of the point, cf. AB, pp. 232-234.

[26] We have two accounts of this, one in 38:28b; 39:3, 14, and the other in 39:11 f.; 40:1-6. While these are not necessarily contradictory, they are not entirely harmonious; cf. AB, pp. 240-246 on this section.

participate in war under any circumstances) unknown in the ancient Orient; Jeremiah, far from being in principle opposed to war on religious grounds, was convinced that Yahweh was actively engaged in the struggle—but on the Babylonian side (21:3–7)! And as for thinking him a coward—well, it is hard to imagine how anyone who endured so much so bravely could possibly be called a coward! And one has only to remember that, though Jeremiah advised all and sundry to desert, one person who did not take Jeremiah's advice—was Jeremiah! Had he been a coward intent only on saving his own life, he would simply have said nothing and slipped out to the Babylonians at the first opportunity. No, Jeremiah was just as patriotic, and just as brave, as were his country's leaders. It was simply that he knew that they were leading the nation to its destruction.

But Jeremiah did not arrive at this conclusion merely by weighing the military and political odds. Any sane person might have realized that Judah by itself stood no chance against the Babylonian army, and that Egyptian help would in all likelihood prove as worthless as it had so often in the past. One can readily believe that Jeremiah was realistic enough to have reached a similar assessment of the situation. But Jeremiah's attitude is not to be explained merely in terms of political realism. His political position was in fact the logical outgrowth of his lifelong *theological* position. He believed that the nation had by its stubborn disobedience broken covenant with Yahweh and fallen under his judgment. And now it has rebelled against Nebuchadnezzar's yoke, the very judgment that God had laid upon it; it has rebelled against the judgment of God and its doom is sealed.[27] The confidence of divine protection that propelled the nation's leaders into their suicidal course Jeremiah knew to be fatuous. Since God now fights against his own people, resistance is futile; the nation is doomed. God will tear his people from their land, bring the Davidic dynasty to an end, and leave his Temple in ruins. The only small chance of saving anything from the wreckage lay therefore in prompt surrender, i.e., in submission to God's judgment.

III

Events proved Jeremiah right. The national confidence was every bit the lie he said it was; it led the nation to no future save

---

[27] See especially our remarks on Jeremiah's reasons for opposing the projected revolt in 594 as expressed in ch. 27; cf. above, pp. 179 f.

destruction. It was Jeremiah (together with Ezekiel and others like-minded)[28] who pointed the way to the future.

1. He did this, not least, in that he refused all false confidence and announced the disaster both as certain and as Yahweh's just judgment upon the nation for its violation of covenant. The official theology was bankrupt in the face of the disaster. This was just what it had said could never happen: Yahweh would not allow it! But it *had* happened! The city—the impregnable city—had been taken, the Temple—Yahweh's chosen dwelling place—had been laid in ruins, and the eternal dynasty had been ended. How could such a thing be? The official theology, at least as it was generally understood in Jeremiah's day, had no answer to give whatever.

This meant that the way was laid open for a spiritual crisis of the first magnitude. For many, it must have been sheer disillusionment: Yahweh's very status and character as God was thrown into question. Some, half paganized in their thinking as they were, must have reasoned that the fall of Jerusalem was ample proof that Marduk, god of Babylon, was a mightier god than Yahweh, who seemed to have been unable to defend his city and his temple-palace as he had promised to do. These would have been tempted to abandon their ancestral faith altogether, or at least to begin to propitiate the gods of Babylon alongside of (in preference to?) Yahweh. If we may judge by the sweeping polemic against the worship of idol gods found in Isaiah, chs. 40 to 48, which was uttered a little more than a generation later, the temptation to do this was very real. (Prophets were not given to tilting with windmills, or demolishing straw men!)[29] Others of the people, feeling that they had done nothing to deserve the calamity that had befallen them, were moved to question the justice

---

[28] Aside from Jeremiah and Ezekiel, one thinks in this connection especially of those writers who gave us the so-called Deuteronomic historical corpus (Joshua through II Kings, plus the narrative framework of Deuteronomy). This work was apparently first composed before the fall of Jerusalem (perhaps in Josiah's reign) and was later re-edited and brought down to date in the exile; cf. above, Ch. 4, note 44. Its authors, both of the original and the exilic editions, were concerned to make the point that the nation's well-being—indeed, its very existence—depended upon its faithfulness to Yahweh's covenant stipulations, and that its fall had been occasioned by its persistent disobedience to his will.

[29] Notice, too, how (according to Jer. 44:15–19) among those Jews who had taken refuge in Egypt there were those who felt it wise to propitiate the Queen of Heaven, since—so they reasoned—troubles had come upon them ever since (apparently with Josiah's reform) they had ceased to do so. See the commentaries; e.g., W. Rudolph, *Jeremia* (HAT, 1947), p. 225; A. Weiser, *Das Buch des Propheten Jeremia* (ATD, 1955), p. 380.

of God. There was a popular saying that seems to have enjoyed a wide currency at the time (31:29; Ezek. 18:2):

> The fathers have eaten sour grapes,
> But it's the children's teeth that rasp.

This was their complaint: We are being punished for sins that were committed before we were born—and that is not fair (cf. Lam. 5:7; Ezek. 18:25)! And still others, accepting the tragedy as Yahweh's just judgment, were trapped in hopeless despair. They felt borne down by a burden of guilt, both inherited and personal, from which they could never get free, and they feared that Yahweh had finished with them, cast them off forever, canceled their destiny as his people. Ezekiel in faraway Babylon heard their despairing lament: "Our bones are dried up, our hope is lost; we are clean cut off" (Ezek. 37:11). Or again: "Our inexcusable misdeeds[30] bear down on us, and we waste away because of them. How can we live?" (Ezek. 33:10). Such people hardly had the will to survive.

The foundations of faith had been shaken. Israel's very survival as a definable community was at stake. And, humanly speaking, one can say that she could not possibly have survived if she could not have found some explanation of the tragedy in terms of her faith, specifically in terms of Yahweh's sovereign power, justice, and faithfulness to his promises. One shudders to think of the outcome had the only voices of religion in her midst been those of priest and professional prophet proclaiming the inviolability of Zion and the eternity of the Davidic line. That was just not so! If her religion could have said no more, Israel would surely have been sucked down into the maelstrom of history and would have disappeared like the other little nations destroyed before the might of Assyria and Babylon.

But it was just that desperately needed explanation that Jeremiah (together with Ezekiel and the Deuteronomistic writers) gave. Precisely in that his message was one of judgment—of stern and uncompromising judgment—it was a saving message. It gave the tragedy explanation—and in advance—precisely in terms of the covenant that had made Israel a people in the first place: the tragedy came as Yahweh's righteous judgment on the nation for its violation of the covenant stipulations. Through the message that he proclaimed, Jeremiah drew the tragedy within the framework of faith

---

[30] Lit., "our iniquities (our crimes, our rebellions) and our sins."

and thus prevented it from destroying faith. Those who received his word would know that the death of the nation was neither the death of God nor the unfairness of God: it was God's own doing—and quite just.

2. But—one is moved to ask—does not such a word simply slam the door to the future? If the bond between God and people has been broken and voided, what hope can there be, theologically speaking, for the future at all? Is this not simply to say that God has finished with Israel? It might seem so; and we can hardly doubt that there were many sincere souls who felt so. But that was never Jeremiah's position.

Jeremiah's message had never been one that excluded hope. Since the day of his call to the prophetic office he seems to have been assured that his message, though primarily one of warning and judgment, was also to serve a constructive purpose. He had felt God's hand on his lips and had heard God's voice as he gave him his commission (1:9 f.):

> Jer. 1:9   There! I have put my words in your mouth.
>   10   See! I have made you an overseer this day
>   Over nations and kingdoms,
>   To uproot and tear down,
>   To destroy and to raze,
>   To build and to plant.

And we recall that in his youth, as Josiah extended his control—and his reform—into the territory of the long-defunct North Israelite nation, Jeremiah had entertained a lively hope for the restoration of northern Israel in the mercy of God (3:6–13; 31:2–6, 15–22).[31] Moreover, the judgment of which he continually warned had, in principle, always been a conditional one: sincere repentance could avert it. As he said when he interpreted the symbolism of the potter at work at his wheel (18:1–12), the character of the "clay" (Israel) will determine what the "potter" (God) will do with it. And even though Jeremiah reached the point when he no longer expected his people to repent—indeed (e.g., 13:23) thought them incapable of it—there is not the slightest evidence that he abandoned the belief that if true repentance should be shown, God would mercifully pardon.

Even when the judgment began to fall on the nation, Jeremiah did not expect it to signal the total end of his people's existence. On the eve of the deportation of 597, he assured groups such as the

---

[31] On the date of these passages, see above, Ch. 5, p. 150, and note 20.

Rechabites, whose loyalty to their principles had been outstanding, that they would survive the catastrophe, and would always live before their God and stand in his service (ch. 35; cf. vs. 18 f.). Nor did he, when the first deportation had taken place, abandon all hope for those unfortunate souls who had been carried away to exile in Babylon. Far from agreeing that they had deservedly been cast off by Yahweh because of their sins, he declared that they were precisely the ones to whom Yahweh would, in his own good time, show especial favor (ch. 24). In 594, as unrest began to flare, he wrote, as we have seen, a letter to the exiles in Babylon (ch. 29) and, though he dashed all hope of a speedy return, he assured them that God had a future for them and would one day bring them back to their land; meanwhile they could find their God (without temple and without sacrificial cult!) there in the land of their exile, if they sought him with all their hearts.

> (Jer. 29:11) Surely *I* know the plans that I have for you—Yahweh's word—plans for your welfare, not for your hurt, to give you the future you hope for. (v. 12) When you call on me, and come and pray to me, I will hear you. (v. 13) When you seek me, you will find me. Yes, when you seek me wholeheartedly, (v. 14) I will be found by you—Yahweh's word. I will reverse your fortunes and will gather you out of all the nations and places to which I have driven you—Yahweh's word—and will restore you to the place from which I have deported you.[32]

But did Jeremiah then abandon hope as the Babylonian army finally closed in on Jerusalem and it became evident that the nation was doomed? He did not! True, he lost all hope of the nation's survival; but he had a farther hope, a hope for the more distant future. This is made unmistakably clear by an autobiographical account which has been transmitted to us in ch. 32 (vs. 6–15), and which must derive from Jeremiah's own reminiscences. Here Jeremiah tells us how during Jerusalem's last siege, while he himself was confined in the court of the guard, at God's command he purchased from his cousin Hanamel a piece of real estate. (And remember that real estate must have been literally worthless at the time.) The sale was consummated with full legal formality, the money weighed out and the documents signed before witnesses, who also affixed their signatures, and the deed in two copies then handed over to Baruch, who filed it away for future reference. The whole transaction was

---

[32] On the shorter, and perhaps more original, text of LXX, see the commentaries; e.g., AB, p. 205.

intended as symbolical, and its meaning was explained through a word from Yahweh that had been given to Jeremiah:

> (Jer. 32:15) This is what Yahweh of Hosts, the God of Israel has said: Houses and fields and vineyards shall once again be bought in this land.

Normal economic activity will one day resume! Israel has a future beyond the disaster that is even now falling—and here in her own land!

It is true—at least if we may judge by the prayer that he is reported to have uttered after completing the above transaction (32:16–25)[33]—that Jeremiah himself scarcely dared to believe this. Rather, he complained to God that he had been made to do a foolish thing. The hope that he offered did not spring from any optimism on his part (of which he seems to have had none), but from the compulsion of the Word; and he offered it, one might say, almost in spite of himself. He was a man, so it would seem, who had lost all hope, but who was constrained by his theology to act in hope nevertheless! It was no doubt this conviction that his people had a future in their own land—a conviction, as we have said, that was born not of optimism, but of the compulsion of the Word—that caused Jeremiah later to refuse the opportunity that he was given to accompany his country's conquerors to Babylon with the promise of privileged treatment there (40:1–6) and, still later (ch. 42), to resist with all his might the decision of his fellow countrymen to seek sanctuary in Egypt (he was taken there, loudly protesting, against his will).

The truth is that Jeremiah believed in the sure and unconditional purposes of God for his people just as firmly as (more firmly than?) his opponents did. He dashed their fool's hope that God, because he had established his temple-palace on Mt. Zion and given his covenant promises to David, would never allow the nation to be destroyed. That, said he, is a lie (7:1–15, etc.)! God will judge the nation and destroy it. But he never surrendered the conviction—or, better, the conviction would not let him go—that beyond the judgment God would once again come to his people in mercy; he would never finally cast them off. We see this beautifully expressed, for example, in 31:35–37.[34]

---

[33] The prayer in its original form was probably quite brief, perhaps consisting only of vs. 16–17a, 24 f. It seems to have been greatly expanded in the course of transmission by the addition of a series of conventional liturgical expressions; see the commentaries.

[34] On the critical problems of chs. 30 and 31 generally, see the commentaries. With many others, I see no compelling reason to deny 31:35–37 to Jeremiah. It may be, as

Jer. 31:35 This is what Yahweh has said—
Who provides the sun to illumine the day,
The moon and the stars to illumine the night,
Who lashes the sea so its billows resound—
Yahweh of Hosts is his name.

36 "If this fixed order should vanish
From before me—Yahweh's word—
Then Israel's descendants might also cease
From being a nation forever before me."

37 This is what Yahweh has said:
"If the heavens above can be measured,
Or earth's foundations below be explored,
Then might *I* reject all of Israel's seed
For all that they have done—Yahweh's word."

As clearly as does the church's ancient hymn, the passage says: "I'll never, no, never, no, never forsake. . . ." The future is dark indeed; but it is God's future.

3. In view of what has been said, there can really be no doubt that Jeremiah did entertain a hope for the farther future beyond the destruction of the nation—the destruction of which he had incessantly warned, and which he lived to witness. This leaves us only with the question: What form would that hope for the farther future take?

Certainly it would not take the form of a promise of the restoration of the state and the state religion along the old lines, or of the coming of a "messianic" deliverer of the house of David. This whole complex of ideas really plays no positive role in Jeremiah's thinking at all. Indeed, except for the rather oblique allusion in 23:5 f.,[35] and its prose parallel in 33:14–16—which, together with vs. 17–26, is lacking in the Septuagint and probably represents a later addition to Jeremiah's words—the hope reposed in the Davidic line is not even mentioned. (The clear allusion to it in 30:8 f. is a prose insertion in a poetic context and, as perhaps most commentators believe,[36] probably not original with Jeremiah.) It is true that the poem in 30:18–21 tells of the felicity of the restored city, and of its future ruler. But, although there is no positive reason to question the Jeremianic origin of this piece, some scholars believe that it was

_____

some think (e.g., Rudolph, HAT, p. 172; Weiser, ATD, pp. 296 f.), that these words were first directed to northern Israel in Jeremiah's youth (as were 31:2–6, 15–22, etc.). But, even if so, they would later have been understood as applying to Judah also. On the text and translation of the passage, cf. AB, p. 277.

[35] On this passage, see above, Ch. 5, pp. 161 f.

[36] But cf., e.g., Weiser, ATD, p. 277.

uttered, not of Jerusalem after its destruction, but, like other poems in chs. 30 and 31 (e.g., 31:2–6, 15–22), was spoken by Jeremiah in his youth of northern Israel.[37] In any event, the future ruler, as he is depicted here, is more of a sacral mediator than a king;[38] indeed, the word "king" is avoided, and the name of David is not invoked.

No, the eschatological future in Jeremiah's preaching took the only form that, in view of his theology, it *could* take: the promise of a new covenant. The passage that gives this thought classic expression is, of course, 31:31–34, one of the best known and justly most admired passages in the whole of the Jeremiah book. Though it is couched in the characteristic style of the prose of the book, and thus shares in the problem that this material occasions, there is little reason to doubt that it accurately represents the mind of the prophet, if not his exact words.[39] It is hope expressed as Jeremiah *would* express it; it accords perfectly with the prophet's theology as we know it, and it deals with problems which that theology had raised. Since, in Jeremiah's view, Israel's life with her God had been a covenantal one, and since the nation had suffered destruction as a consequence of its breach of covenant, what future could there be except in terms of a new covenant? Of course the question immediately arises: But is such a thing possible? Israel is in no position to patch up the covenant which she has through her own fault so grievously broken; and it does not lie within the vassal's power to institute covenant in any case. To that Jeremiah replies: God will see to it! He initiated covenant in the first place, and he has not broken it; he can therefore restore it, and he will in his grace do so. But then a further objection arises: What conceivable good would that do? To live in covenant requires obedience to the covenant stipulations, and Israel has repeatedly

---

[37] So, e.g., Rudolph, Weiser, *opera cit.;* also P. Volz, *Der Prophet Jeremia* (KAT, 1922), p. 287. I myself am inclined to believe that the prophet has Jerusalem after 587 in view. Would Jeremiah, who apparently longed at least for the cultic reunification of Israel and Judah (cf. 3:14; 31:6), have also looked forward to a restored northern-Israelite state with its own ruler?

[38] Cf., e.g., H.-J. Kraus, *Worship in Israel* (Eng. tr., Oxford: Basil Blackwell; Richmond: John Knox Press, 1966), pp. 199 f., who sees in this ruler a royal mediator, like Josiah, who would renew the covenant between Yahweh and Israel.

[39] As we have said before, the prose sayings of Jeremiah constitute the major critical problem of the book, with not a few scholars regarding this material as the work of exilic and post-exilic Deuteronomists. Some scholars have rendered a similar judgment upon 31:31–34; most recently E. W. Nicholson, *Preaching to the Exiles: A Study of the Prose Tradition of the Book of Jeremiah* (Oxford: Basil Blackwell, 1970), cf. pp. 82 ff., 138. For reasons developed elsewhere I am unable to agree; cf. above, Ch. 5, note 34 for references.

shown her complete inability to meet that condition. Is there any reason to believe that she would do better in the future? Would she not break any covenant her God might make with her? To that also Jeremiah has an answer: God will see to that too! Forgiving past sins and erasing them from his memory, he will write his covenant law, not on tables of stone (cf. Ex. 24:12; 34:1) or in a book (cf. Ex. 24:7; II Kings 22:8, 11), but on the hearts (i.e., the minds and wills) of his people, thus giving them both the desire and the ability to obey it and live as his people.

And this is an unconditional promise! When it will come to pass Jeremiah does not know. It will be "after those days," in the indefinite future, the eschatological future. But it will surely be (31:31–34):

> (Jer. 31:31) Look! The days are coming—Yahweh's word—when I will make a new covenant with the house of Israel and the house of Judah:[40] (v. 32) not like the covenant that I made with their fathers when I took them by the hand to bring them out of the land of Egypt, which covenant of mine *they* broke, though *I* was their Lord—[41] Yahweh's word. (v. 33) But this is the covenant that I will make with the house of Israel after those days—Yahweh's word: I will put my law within them, and on their hearts will write it; I will be their God, and they shall be my people. (v. 34) And no longer need each man teach his neighbor, and each his brother, saying, "Know Yahweh!" For they shall all know me, from the least of them to the greatest—Yahweh's word; for I will forgive their iniquity, and their sin I will remember no more.

One sees at once that, though this is called a "new" covenant, neither in its form nor in its content does it differ from the old. Like the old, it is given through divine initiative, solely on the basis of the divine grace, and it presupposes that the recipients will live in obedience to its stipulations, which are in no way changed. The difference is that now, since the stipulations are inscribed on their minds and wills, the

---

[40] The words "and the house of Judah" are not repeated in v. 33 and may be an expansion. Some commentators believe that the prophecy was originally spoken of northern Israel and that it was later readjusted to apply to Judah as well. But it is equally probable that "the house of Israel" was intended to refer to the whole people, north and south alike.

[41] Or, "though I was their husband" (so RSV). The figure of Yahweh as the husband, Israel as the wife, had been current in prophetic speech since Hosea and is employed elsewhere by Jeremiah (cf. ch. 3). The meaning, however, is much the same, since in ancient Israel the legal relationship of husband and wife was not one of parity; the husband was the wife's *ba'al* (lord). For other suggested translations of the line, cf. NEB, JB, etc.

people are enabled to conform to them, and truly to be God's people. It is a new covenant in that it is made anew, renewed; but it is the people who are made new.

So it is that God, who has condemned his people by the terms of his covenant, will come to them again in the wilderness of exile and will make with them a new and eternal covenant. The awful chasm between the demands of covenant by which the nation was judged, and the sure promises of God which faith could not surrender, is bridged from the side of the divine grace.

But what, then, is the conclusion? Jeremiah was right, and his opponents were wrong—that is clear. Does this mean that the theology of the Mosaic covenant, in which Jeremiah's preaching was based, was the correct theology, while the theology of God's eternal covenant promises to David and his sure defense of Mt. Zion, which so misled his opponents, was a wrong theology? Certainly in the form in which it was so widely held in Jeremiah's day, the latter must be marked down as decidedly wrong. But to dismiss outright as erroneous those convictions to which it sought to give expression would be far too hasty a judgment. Actually, both patterns of covenant, as we have tried to make clear, gave expression to essential features in the structure of Israel's normative faith. Both had been there from the beginning, and both were necessary. Though the balance between them was delicate and easily upset, and the possibility of tension very real, neither could well be dispensed with. The Mosaic covenant reminded Israel of God's grace to her which had saved her and made her his people, and of her obligation to live in obedience to his commandments if she wished to continue in his favor and receive his blessing. The promises to Abraham and to David assured her that, in the final analysis, her future rested ultimately not in what she was—or had, or had not, done—but in the sure, immutable purposes of God which nothing could cancel. Without the one, Israel could not have been God's people; without the other, she might well have lived—to despair.

Both patterns, therefore, lived on until "the fullness of time." Later prophets and writers affirmed the essential validity of both types of covenant, as Jeremiah himself in fact did.[42] And in the

---

[42] The point has been well discussed by D. N. Freedman, "Divine Commitment and Human Obligation" (*Interpretation*, 18 [1964], pp. 419–431). As for Jeremiah, though he totally rejected the perverted confidence of the official theology of his day, he never surrendered the belief that God's sure purposes would go on beyond the nation's destruction, as we have just seen.

centuries that followed, Israelites generally, while giving ever more earnest attention to the observance of God's law down to the minutest detail, clung steadfastly to the confidence that, in God's good time, his purposes on earth would be accomplished and all the promises made to the fathers, and through the prophets, fulfilled. The certain expectation of the coming of the Messiah-Redeemer lived on in Jewish hearts, as every reader knows. Though repeatedly disappointed and befooled, it was never surrendered, but rather intensified with the passing years. In the New Testament both patterns of covenant are taken up, brought together in Christ, and announced as fulfilled. Jesus is the hoped-for Messiah, the fulfillment of the sure promises to David. He is also, as it were, the new Moses, who has reinterpreted the law, and who has made with his followers the new covenant promised by Jeremiah when, on the night in which he was betrayed, he took a goblet of wine, and said: "This cup is the new covenant in my blood" (I Cor. 11:25).[43]

The church, therefore, like Israel, lives under both patterns of covenant. We have received from Christ sure, unqualified promises to which no conditions are attached. For example (Matt. 16:18): "On this rock I will build my church, and the gates [i.e., the powers] of Hell [Hades] shall not prevail against it." Or this (Luke 12:32): "Fear not, little flock, for it is your Father's good pleasure to give you the kingdom." Or this (Phil. 2:9–11): "Therefore God has highly exalted him . . . that at the name of Jesus every knee should bow, in heaven, on earth, and under the earth, and every tongue confess that Jesus Christ is Lord, to the glory of God the Father." Or this (Rev. 22:5): "And they [i.e., Christ's true servants] shall reign for ever and ever." These promises we are called to receive in faith, and to live in absolute trust that the outcome of God's purpose in history does *not* depend on us—our good works, our merit, our zeal; it rests in his promise and his faithfulness alone. But we have also received grace. And the reception of grace involves us in binding obligation; it lays upon us stipulations—hard, impossible stipulations: "If you love me, you will keep my commandments" (John 14:15); "You must be perfect, as your heavenly Father is perfect" (Matt. 5:48); "Not every one who says to me, 'Lord, Lord,' shall enter the kingdom of heaven,

---

[43] The original form of the words of institution has given rise to a considerable literature and cannot be debated here; see the commentaries. In the parallel accounts (Mark 14:22–25; Matt. 26:26–29) the word "new" is attested only in certain manuscripts, and many believe this to be an assimilation to the Pauline form. In any event, the Pauline form seems to be the oldest, and, in it, an allusion to 31:31–34 seems clearly intended.

but he who does the will of my Father who is in heaven" (Matt. 7:21); and much more in the same vein. As we have received the grace of God in Christ, we are obligated to obey his commandments; if we refuse to do so, we cannot be his people or receive his promises.

Both of these patterns of covenant, therefore, are essential to our faith; we can do without neither. To accept the promises while ignoring the commandments would be to sink into complacency, to become a church with no sense of grace, a travesty of a church, a church that is so much lukewarm water to be spat from the mouth of God (Rev. 3:16). Such a church can know nothing of the promises to which it so complacently clings. But to shoulder the burden of Christ's commands without the promises—that would be despair, or a self-righteous legalism, an arid works-righteousness that, turning the commandments of Christ into trivialities, conceals from us our inability to keep them and live in covenant with him. So, like Israel of old, we have ever to live in tension. It is the tension between grace and obligation: the unconditional grace of Christ which is proferred to us, his unconditional promises in which we are invited to trust, and the obligation to obey him as the church's sovereign Lord.

Index of
Names and Subjects

Index to
Scripture References